almanac

association for welsh writing
in english

PARTHIAN

almanac

a yearbook

of

welsh writing

in english

critical
essays

edited by Katie Gramich

association for welsh writing
in english

almanac – a yearbook of welsh writing in english: critical essays is
supported by the Association for Welsh Writing in English

and is published by
Parthian
The Old Surgery
Napier Street
Cardigan
SA43 1ED
www.parthianbooks.co.uk

First published in 2009
© Contributors and the *almanac*

ISBN 978-1-90576275-0

The publisher acknowledges the financial
support of the Welsh Books Council.
Cover image: Giorgio de Chirico *Mystery and melancholy of a Street*
© DACS, London, 2007
Cover design: theundercard.co.uk
Pictures between pages 81-108 from *The Man Who Made Penguins –
The Life of William Emrys Williams*, by Sander Meredeen, available
from Darien-Jones Publishing
Printed and bound by Dinefwr Press, Llandybïe, Wales

British Library Cataloguing in Publication Data

A cataloguing record for this book is available from the British Library.

almanac
a yearbook of welsh writing in english: critical essays

vol 13 | 2008–9

Editor: Dr Katie Gramich, Cardiff University
Associate Editors:
Professor Jane Aaron, University of Glamorgan
Professor M. Wynn Thomas, Swansea University
Professor Tony Brown, University of Wales, Bangor

Contents:

Information on contributors

'Yeats Said That':

R.S. Thomas and W.B. Yeats

Damian Walford Davies
Aberystwyth University

Celebrated as Wales's most eminent literary figure of the second half of the twentieth century and as one of the most challenging religious poets in the English language, R.S. Thomas also fulfilled the role of a salutary cultural irritant whose strictures on national identity and on the 'fissiparous tendencies'[1] of his nation elicited powerful responses across the cultural and political spectrum. Adept at highlighting what Robert Minhninick called the 'breathtaking cartography of the difference between us',[2] he became a cultural icon. So many of the debates within Wales about cultural identity and national allegiance became, in some form, debates with R.S. Thomas. For Thomas himself, forging a cultural and spiritual identity – or identities, since the poetry became increasingly concerned with shifting, plural selves – consistently involved measuring himself against a revered precursor: W.B. Yeats.[3]

My aim here is to consider a series of negotiations with Yeats in Thomas's poetry and prose that constitute a protracted dialogue over fifty years. Yeats emerges as an explicit and implied interlocutor and auditor, a hallowed antagonist, a second self and double, invoked at critical junctures in the career. 'We talk about Zeus and Leda and Yeats/as if they were real people', wrote the American poet, William Meredith,[4] and Yeats in Thomas's work assumes the power of a constructed, mythical 'resource'. Yeats's frequent summoning of shades has a parallel in the way in which Thomas calls on Yeats through both direct invocation and more embedded allusion. It is a relation that involves Thomas in Yeatsian counterpointings, contradictions and dialectic; the antinomies that so fascinated the Irish poet form the very ground of the engagement. The dynamics of the relationship shift as Thomas establishes fellowship with Yeats only to insist on difference; proximity in one poem becomes distance in the next, and Yeats serves as an exemplar in relation to whom Thomas both grounds and deconstructs himself. 'We make out of the quarrel with others, rhetoric, but of the quarrel with ourselves, poetry',[5] Yeats famously declared; Thomas makes out of a 'quarrel' with Yeats both rhetoric and poetry. That famous Yeatsian dictum offered Thomas an ambiguous purchase on an acute, career-long 'dismantling'[6] of the self. He quoted it often, most obviously in that challenging 'spiritual autobiography',[7] *The Echoes Return Slow* (1988), in which elliptical prose passages are played off against facing poems:

> Casualty of the quarrel with strong men, bandaging himself with Yeats' sentence about the quarrel within, he limped on through an absence of sympathy. His poetry was bitter.[8]

One is tempted here to see Yeats himself as one of those 'strong men', suggesting a Bloomian anxiety of poetic influence. At the same time, given the meditation on wartime action and inaction in which they figure, the statement can be read as a subtle calibration of Thomas's position vis-à-vis Yeats's enunciations on war and violence. And again, in the context of Thomas's retirement, as he weighs up public and private selves: 'A man who had refrained from quarrelling with his parishioners for fear of rhetoric, over what poetry could he be said to preside from his quarrel with himself?' (*ERS*, 112).[9] Yeats also plays a part in Thomas's continued wrestling with the implications of technological 'advancement' and applied science in the great metaphysical poetry, offering the Welshman a series of images that focus the tensions of a belief located 'somewhere between faith and doubt' (*F*, 32). And since Yeats's career is so closely bound up with the death of Romantic Ireland and the coming into being of its contemporary terrible beauty, the dialogue necessarily reveals wider historical and political comparisons and disjunctions between Thomas's Wales and Yeats's Ireland.

Though stylistically divergent – Yeats's mature lyrical orotundity contrasting with the astringent austerity and anti-lyricism cultivated by Thomas – the two poets share fascinating common ground. The suggestive alignments between these two 'national' voices throw into relief the contested nature of that very term. Justin Wintle has observed that 'Yeats provides Thomas with an example of a poetry that is successful in terms of an off-centre cultural nationalism'[10] proceeding from what Marjorie Howes has identified as Yeats's 'complicated personal relation'[11] to several competing cultural and political groups and causes: middle-class Irish Protestantism, the Catholic Irish peasantry, the Anglo-Irish aristocracy, Irish revolutionary nationalism, and Irish cultural nationalism. 'Yeats's Anglo-Irish nationality', Howes argues,

> was a contradictory one whose very foundations contained the corrupting seeds of its demise, and whose most valuable strengths and reassuring continuities were also the sources of its debilitating weaknesses and fragmentations.[12]

Thomas's cultural identity was hardly without its tensions: his Anglicanism set him apart from the religious orthodoxy of a nonconformist nation; his Welsh nationalism and Anglophobia disguised a Yeatsian sympathy for the custom, ceremony and (in Yeats's phrase from 'The Municipal Gallery Re-visited') 'approved patterns'[13] of aristocratic privilege that he could not readily discover in his rural Welsh parishes (though one might say he eventually found his Lady Gregory in the Keating sisters, who in 1978 gave Thomas the tenancy of Sarn-y-Plas near the levelled lawns and gravelled ways of the Plas-yn-Rhiw estate, a kind of Coole Park above Hell's Mouth, close to his last parish).[14] Moreover, Thomas's decision to learn Welsh in his thirties helped repair a cultural 'lack' and alienation that nevertheless remained a source of deep regret for the rest of his life. A recent comment by Geoffrey Hill offers further categories within which the cultural critic may juggle comparisons: 'I have come to think that whereas Thomas saw himself as an existential nationalist he was in fact closer to being a politicized aesthete, as were Yeats, Eliot and Pound'.[15]

Such conflicted and unstable cultural identities no doubt increased Thomas's sense of himself as in some way 'Yeatsian'. Both poets are hyphenated – Yeats as 'Anglo-Irish', Thomas as 'Anglo-Welsh' – and while Yeats may have been less distressed balancing on that cultural fulcrum,[16] Thomas deplored it, remarking that 'hyphenisation is betrayal'[17] and employing a discourse of physical wounding to figure the psychic pain of subsisting 'in a no-man's-land between two cultures': 'Who is wounded, and am I not wounded? For I bear in my body the marks of this battle'.[18] In a 1967 review of Daniel Hoffman's book on Yeats, Muir and Graves, *Barbarous Knowledge*, and of Donald T. Torchiana's *W.B. Yeats and Georgian Ireland*, Thomas explicitly raised this issue of division, identifying a link with the Irish poet: 'like so many another hyphenated writer Yeats was drawn to two backgrounds'; 'Yeats experienced the ambivalences which bedevil most hyphenated writers'[19] – ambivalences identifiable as the consequences of a (post-)colonial condition.

Both poets could valorise older versions of Irishness and Welshness, presenting them as more 'authentic' and 'organic', fully aware of the ahistorical essentialism involved in such cultural constructions.[20] At the same time, both were fascinated by the violent forces shaping history and modern identities – for Yeats, it was revolution, for Thomas, 'the would[-]be absolutism of the machine'[21] – and both became furiously contemporary, 'major prophets and pioneers of our human future'.[22] (In one of Thomas's late poems, Yeats is found 'quarrell[ing] upon the floor/for the cheerless scraps/from history's table' in the company of George Orwell (*R*, 64)). A constant remaking in relation to modernity – in terms of both subject matter and poetic style – characterises both careers.[23] This goes hand-in-hand with a willingness to reposition and revise oneself, to court – indeed, make a virtue of – inconsistency. Howes describes Yeats as a 'dialectician and self-critic'[24] – terms profoundly relevant to Thomas's exploration of relational selves across his oeuvre. In *The Echoes Return Slow*, Thomas talks of 'Salving his conscience in the face of the Gospel's commandment to judge not with the necessity for the writer of poetry to be his own critic' (*ERS*, 60). The title of his autobiography, *Neb*, published in Welsh in 1985, signifying both 'no one' and 'someone', is a pun-paradox that suited Thomas's compulsion constantly to ironise himself. Both poets relished dramatic forms, anti-selves and what Yeats in 'The Circus Animals' Desertion' called 'counter-truth[s]' (*The Poems*, 394). Thomas pushed Yeats's love of dialectic into the realms of the postmodern. At the same time, both bodies of poetry involve themselves in deepening iterations, echoes and returns, Thomas's oeuvre being a great self-reflexive meditation on the *fear* of repeating oneself (and of repeating others, including Yeats).

A number of critics have drawn attention to the 'cumulative effect' of the work of both poets – the way in which the poems set up 'mutually enriching' echoes with others. Both are poets of repeated emblems. Justin Wintle refers to the 'astonishing capacity' of Thomas's poems 'to gather meaning and momentum from their companions':

> It was a trick learned from other poets, most notably W.B. Yeats, and like Yeats, Thomas is adept at creating tranches of metaphor and image that endure not only from one page to another, but across volumes.[25]

Thus, as A.E. Dyson notes, 'the best comment' on Thomas's counterpointing of positions and selves 'is often... an interplay of echoes... Clearly, any single poem is not the last word'.[26] Both poets set up 'an antiphonal music//in infinite counterpoint', as Thomas puts it in a late poem ('Sonata in X'; *MHT*, 82). Like Yeats, then, Thomas 'thought it all out twenty years ago' ('The Tower'; *The Poems*, 242).

If in the 1920s Yeats was the 'sixty-year-old smiling public man' ('Among School Children'; *The Poems*, 261), visiting schools and delivering speeches to the Irish Senate on coins and copyright, then Thomas in the 1970s in the parish of Aberdaron on the Llŷn peninsula, nearing the end of his career as a priest in the Church in Wales, was – if the clichéd image of him is to be believed – the sixty-year-old scowling private man, hardly a 'comfortable kind of old scarecrow' ('Among School Children'; *The Poems*, 262). But it is Yeats who offers Thomas the personal and cultural lenses through which his move to remote Aberdaron – a kind of Aran – is filtered: 'Go to that lean parish; let them tread/on your dreams' (*LS*, 50); 'Had he like John Synge come "towards nightfall upon a race passionate and simple like his heart"?'; 'Yeats said he had found nothing half so good as his long sought solitude. But this one, had he ever been anything but solitary?' (*ERS*, 68, 118) – lines that invoke Yeats's 'He Wishes for the Cloths of Heaven', 'In Memory of Major Robert Gregory' and 'The Apparitions', respectively (*The Poems*, 90, 182, 391). Yeats's cultivation of a hieratic personality and public image has its parallel in Thomas's own 'cold and passionate' personality and (since he could also be the playboy of the west of Wales) in his knowing performance, especially for the English media, of a persona 'high and solitary and most stern' ('No Second Troy'; *The Poems*, 140). There was certainly no Steinach operation for Thomas, and yet he was seen to have achieved a kind of rejuvenation of both flesh and spirit in old age. Certainly, by the late 1970s, Thomas had become the 'arch poet', and remained so until his death at 87, the power of the late work evoking further comparisons with Yeats.

Thomas often constructs himself as no one in relation to Yeats. If, as Eliot said, Yeats's 'history' was 'the history of [his] own time',[27] his place the troubled centre of the 'living stream' of 'Easter 1916', then Thomas, as he himself frequently emphasised, lived life 'a little aside from the main road'.[28] And yet, such admissions of belated insignificance, such erasures of self, are characteristically counterbalanced by the dynamics of Thomas's appropriation and revision of Yeats, through which Thomas emerges as a forceful, if often fractured and mirror-haunted, personality. In a 1983 letter to his friend, the poet Raymond Garlick, Thomas referred to 'Sailing to Byzantium' as one of the 'yardsticks' he had fallen short of; 'And when one falls short of those', he said, 'one knows one hasn't been chosen'.[29] Deploying a formula that would gyre back in startling contexts in the later work, he stated in a 1964 essay: 'I am not W.B. Yeats, and am without his talent', calling himself 'inferior' while at the same time emphasising that 'the whole organization of [Yeats's] personality' was 'different'.[30] In the same essay, referring to a line from Yeats's 'Two Songs from a Play' (*The Poems*, 259), he asserted that he would have been glad 'to have hit on a word like "resinous" as an adjective qualifying the human heart' – neglecting to mention that he had made good use of Yeats's adjective a few years earlier in the poem 'On Hearing a Welshman Speak' (*PFS*, 16) to describe the interior of a church. Thomas's insistence on difference from Yeats is often mediated through Yeatsian paradigms, which have the effect of strengthening the contiguities between the two poets. Thus in 1990, Thomas remarked:

> Some people think I was being falsely modest or that I was joking when I entitled the incomplete autobiography *Neb*... Some people aim to be personalities. There is quite a bit about it in Yeats's *A Vision*. I don't think that a really creative being should try to wear a persona. Keats's negative capability is relevant... It is Keats's feeling that possesses me, too, when I visit a municipal art gallery and look at the rows of 'personalities' who become mayors and chairmen and prime ministers and heaven knows what. I feel entirely insignificant.[31]

Yeats's account in *A Vision* of the 'struggle to find personality' and to 'lose it', his system of lives lived in and out of 'phase',[32] are offered as a contrast to Thomas's 'insignificance', and yet Thomas's unceasing exploration of the instabilities of his own identity testifies to a conception of self that is in many ways Yeatsian:

> As, on a dull
> day, the sun shines
> in its own sky, I knew

> somewhere beyond the eye's
> range [god] maintained
> his fullness; that it was I
> getting in my own
> way was subject to phases.
>
> ('Planetary'; *R*, 19)

And the example used to assert difference in the prose passage quoted above – that of the municipal art gallery – is
taken directly from Yeats's 'The Municipal Gallery Re-visited' – a poem that manages to aggrandise the self in the
very process of celebrating others.

Yeats goes in deep. 'I have already confessed that I am
a romantic', Thomas told John Barnie in 1990,

> rather like the early Yeats... I have walked westward from
> Galway into the dark, into the peat smoke... I have known
> the silence of the countryside before many machines
> destroyed it and have enjoyed a darkness in which one
> could see the wealth of the stars... All changing or
> changed.[33]

Prompted by his explicit mention of Yeats, Thomas sum-
mons the refrain from 'Easter 1916' – 'All changed,
changed utterly:/A terrible beauty is born' (*The Poems*, 228)
– as he laments the changes wrought by his inveterate
antagonist, the Machine, which, from the groundbreaking
volume *H'm* (1972), is invested with mythopoeic terror.
MacDonagh and MacBride become rural silence broken by
fighter planes and cars; Connolly and Pearse become stars
occluded by light pollution. The echo serves both to link
Thomas with Yeats and to set the two poets indisputably
apart: Thomas, and Thomas's Wales, never experienced the
terrible beauty brought to birth by contemporary revolutionary crisis. That fact is implicit in echoes of 'Easter
1916' and of Yeats's other political poems throughout
Thomas's career: at the end of the poem 'A Land', for example – 'It is at such times that they sing, not music/so much
as the sound of a nation/rending itself, fierce with all the
promise/of a beauty that might have been theirs' (*WA*, 43)

– and in such Thomasian constructions as 'The terrible poetry of his kind' (*T*, 9) and 'There is/a sacrament there more beauty than terror' (*F*, 37). For Thomas, Yeats's 'terrible beauty' will be that of the new science and of the 'radioactive God' (*Fr*, 26). Thomas's echoes of Yeats transpose political crisis into new existential and metaphysical contexts.

One should note the 'Irishness' of R.S. Thomas's early career as an 'Anglo-Welsh' writer. Thomas emphasised that it was Seumas O'Sullivan who 'first responded' to his poems, publishing them in *The Dublin Magazine*,[34] and Patrick Crotty reminds us that Thomas 'contributed twenty-one poems' to the magazine between 1939 and the mid-1950s.[35] Thomas met O'Sullivan first in Wales, then in Dublin in the company of Austin Clarke – a poet whose use of 'vernacular prosodic techniques', as Jason Walford Davies has noted, served early on as a significant cultural model for Thomas, who admired the 'skilful counter-pointing' through which 'the atmosphere of old Irish verse' was 'brought into English' in Clarke's poems. Thomas remarked that it was Clarke who showed him that 'We have no need to migrate to London to have the strings of our tongue unloosed'[36] – something that Hugh MacDiarmid also confirmed for Thomas at this time by offering the Welshman a model of how poetry could inscribe and drive a separatist national and cultural identity.[37] As Crotty has also shown, Patrick Kavanagh was another important influence on Thomas's early work.[38] These Celtic affiliations were often invoked by Thomas at the outset of his career in the wider context of 'Anglo-Welsh' cultural debates.

Tony Bianchi's suggestive piece of literary history, 'R.S. Thomas and his Readers', documents the struggle of an aspiring 'Anglo-Welsh' cultural intelligentsia to constitute itself in the 1940s and 1950s as a 'clerisy' alongside an established Welsh-language 'grouping' initially perceived as more 'authentic', and to institute, alongside a 'new literature', a new 'corporate readership' for itself. Bianchi argues that R.S. Thomas's early poems on Welsh subjects played a key role in this process, 'interpellat[ing] his English-speaking readership within the discourse of cultural nationalism'.[39] (It is important, however, to note Thomas's early distaste for what he called 'that foolish epithet, "Anglo-Welsh" ' – for him, the marker of a compromised culture; if the movement had any validity for him, it was only as 'a phase in the re-cymrification of Wales', a 'halfway house on the road back to Welsh'.[40]) For Saunders Lewis in that intransigent 1937 enunciation, *Is there an Anglo-Welsh Literature?*, the figure of Yeats and the perceived authentic separateness of 'Anglo-Irish' literature served to define the very non-being of a comparable 'Anglo-Welsh' phenomenon. Bianchi reminds us that during the 1940s and 1950s, the Irish model, and the cultural representativeness of Yeats, continued to be points of reference for a nascent 'Anglo-Welsh' movement seeking its own cultural location:

> The Irish literary renaissance was an early model for these aspirations: H. Idris Bell, in 1922, toyed with the notion of a new 'Anglo-Welsh movement' headed by a Welsh Yeats, an idea which R.S. Thomas himself took up in 1946. In the same year the nationalist historian A.W. Wade-Evans looked to an 'Anglo-Welsh literary movement... on the Anglo-Irish model' for 'the resurrection of Wales'.[41]

However, although the (Anglo-)Irish parallel, and the example of Yeats, were rhetorically useful and inspiring in broad cultural terms, they were also recognised as ultimately 'misleading', given the raft of cultural and political differences between Wales and Ireland.[42] Affiliation is tempered by an acknowledgement of dissimilarity, and Wales emerges in the cultural debates of the mid-1940s, conducted in such magazines as Keidrych Rhys's *Wales* (that 'sounding board for ideas of national and cultural identity'[43] that published seminal essays on Welsh and Scottish writing by Thomas), as a kind of Ireland *manqué*. The image of Ireland personified as a young girl or old woman made a deep and lasting impression on Thomas, and he repeatedly returns to the image in his prose, singling out Yeats's 'Red Hanrahan's Song about Ireland' and *Cathleen ni Houlihan*, whose ending, he said, gave him a 'thrilling of the flesh'.[44] It was an inspirational image he sought to translate into a Welsh cultural and political (and indeed personal) context. But again, the Irish parallel becomes a marker of difference; in the pamphlet *Cymru or Wales?* (1992), Thomas remarked: 'when we think of Wales we see too often that caricature of the map of an old woman plodding along with England on her back. No poetry there'.[45] Therefore as Thomas sought to locate himself culturally and politically as a Welshman and poet from the 1940s on, various Irish and Scottish paradigms provided him with cultural coordinates that both sharpened his perspective on his nation's predicament and increased his desire for 'an enlargement of national consciousness'.[46] The pattern of broad cultural alignment and differentiation outlined above also marks Thomas's negotiations with Yeats himself.

Thomas invoked Yeats early regarding the fraught question of audience. It was in the pages of *Wales* in 1946, as a response to a cultural questionnaire issued by Keidrych Rhys to Welsh writers, that Idris Bell's call for a 'Welsh Yeats' was answered – if characteristically ambiguously – by R.S. Thomas. *'Do you consider yourself an Anglo-Welsh writer?'* was the first question. 'No! A Welsh writer', Thomas replied; *'For whom do you write?'* The answer: 'Yeats' words come to mind: "All day I'd looked in the face/What I had hoped 'twould be/To write for my own race/And the reality" '; *'What is your opinion of the relationship between Literature and Society?'* 'Yeats' gyres, Jacob and the angel, Paul's flesh and spirit, there come to mind a hundred images which seek to express two mutually dependent entities, each striving to be free, yet each reacting upon the other.'[47] At this moment in 1946, when the 'Anglo-Welsh' movement was seeking to constitute itself and fashion an appropriate audience, Thomas invokes the contrast drawn in Yeats's 'The Fisherman' between the poet's ideal audience – one that 'does not exist' (*The Poems*, 198) – and 'the reality' of a glib and philistine public. Thomas's summoning of Yeats is an articulation of his own conflicted cultural position at this time. For Thomas, 'To write for [his] own race' in 1946 would have meant writing in Welsh for a Welsh-speaking audience – something he was to achieve only in prose. An ideal 'Anglo-Welsh' audience was a problematic concept in that such a constituency was still in the process of becoming, and its sensibilities and cultural allegiances would be fatally hyphenated. The 'reality', therefore, brought home Thomas's own cultural displacement and division. (Interestingly, Thomas's decision to quote Yeats in the *Wales* questionnaire compelled Oliver Edwards to write in to remind readers of the correct syntactical construction of Yeats's (often misconstrued) lines – a choice example of not trusting one's Anglo-Welsh audience.[48])

Thomas's own poem 'The Fisherman', published in his 1968 collection, *Not That He Brought Flowers*, marks a return to the issues raised in the 1946 questionnaire, once again in the context of a dialogue with Yeats:

> A simple man,
> He liked the crease on the water
> His cast made, but had no pity
> For the broken backbone
> Of water or fish
> ...
> I could have told of the living water
> That springs pure.
> He would have smiled then,
> Dancing his speckled fly in the shallows,
> Not understanding.
>
> (*NTHBF*, 19)

The inflection of Yeats's poem is clear: this fisherman – a portrait of Thomas's father, who was, like Yeats, a dab hand with rod and fly – personifies the lack of an 'ideal' audience, one that would instinctively understand 'the living water that springs pure' not only in Christian but also in cultural–political terms, as the defining birthright of the Welsh language, which Thomas was denied by his parents. And in the light of the poem 'Resort' in the same collection, this fisherman becomes a type of the unknowing English tourist – another emblem there – who 'look[s] at the water with dull eyes/Resentfully, not understanding/A syllable. Did they expect the sea, too, to be bi-lingual?' (*NTHBF*, 23).

Thomas's first volume, *The Stones of the Field*, published in 1946, contains an engagement with Yeats that testifies to Thomas's need creatively to conjure the Irish poet in a particularly direct way at the beginning of his career. In 'Memories of Yeats whilst Travelling to Holyhead', Thomas envisages a meeting with Yeats on the train to his home town – Yeats's staging-post back to Dublin. This fictional crossing of paths, this Welsh–Irish main line *entente*, raises issues of likeness and dissimilarity that were to be further explored during the course of a long writing life:

> How often he went on this journey, think of it, think of it:
> The metrical train, the monosyllabic sea,
> The listening hilltops, aloof and resentful of strangers.
> Who would have refrained from addressing him here, not discerning
> The embryonic poem still coiled in the ivory skull?
> Boredom or closeness of age might have prompted, his learning
> Concealed by his tweed and the azure, ecstatic tie;
> But who would have sensed the disdain of his slow reply
> Of polite acquiescence in their talk of the beautiful?
> Who could have guessed the futility even of praising
> Mountain and marsh and the delicate, flickering tree
> To one long impervious and cold to the outward scene,
> Heedless of nature's baubles, lost in the amazing
> And labyrinth paths of his own impenetrable mind?
>
> But something in the hair's fine silver, the breadth of brow,
> Had kept me dumb, too shy of his scornful anger
> To presume to pierce the dark, inscrutable glasses,
> His first defence against a material world.
> Yet along with him in the indifferent compartment, hurled
> Between the waves' white audience, the earth's dim screen,
> In mutual silence closer than lover knit
> I had known reality dwindle, the dream begin.
> (*SF*, 22)

Published in the same year as the *Wales* questionnaire, the poem is another statement about ideal audiences and auditors. The railway carriage is a space apart in which Thomas and Yeats constitute – almost erotically – each other's ideal audience. Readers will also notice the way in which this sketch of Yeats was to prove an uncanny proleptic delineation of Thomas himself post- (say) 1978: substitute 'scarlet tie' for 'azure tie', and the late Thomas is wholly present. The selves conjured here are fluid and shifting, and Thomas's Yeats becomes a suggestive prototype. The line 'The embryonic poem still coiled in the ivory skull' anticipates the description of the Welsh peasant-farmer in 'The Welsh Hill Country': 'Contributing grimly to the accepted pattern, The embryo music dead in his throat' (*AL*, 7). Moreover, aspects of this Yeats seem to condition the representation of the peasant-figure of the early poem, 'Enigma' – clearly a type of the Iago Prytherch persona with whom Thomas was to conduct a profound (self-)interrogation in the poetry of the early Manafon period:

> The earth is beautiful, and he is blind
> To it all...
> ... could he speak, would not the glib tongue boast
> A lore denied our neoteric sense,
> Being handed down from the age of innocence?
> Or would the cracked lips, parted at last, disclose
> The embryonic thought that never grows?
> (*AL*, 31)

The poem brutally cymrifies Yeats, dramatically returning a dapper Anglo-Irish poet to the soil and to the rag and bone shop of a Welsh peasant heart. Further, the inscrutable Yeats, with whom Thomas experiences a quasi-religious moment 'in mutual silence' on the train in 'Memories of Yeats whilst Travelling to Holyhead', is a forerunner of the *deus absconditus*, whose silence was to energise the great metaphysical poetry of Thomas's later years: 'The relation between us was/silence' (*NTF*, 83). In various forms, then, Thomas grew into the imagined Yeats of this early poem.[49]

In the early verse, Thomas gets close to Yeats by choosing subjects with Yeatsian connections in poems such as 'On a Portrait of Joseph Hone by Augustus John' (*SF*, 35) and by offering both a wealth of local echoes and 'set-piece' versions of Yeats. Thus 'The Unborn Daughter' is clearly a miniature 'A Prayer for my Daughter':

> On her unclothed with flesh or beauty
> In the womb's darkness, I bestow
> The formal influence of the will
> The wayward influence of the heart...
>   (*AL*, 21)

'Poetry for Supper' – 'Man, you must sweat/And rhyme your guts taut, if you'd build/Your verse a ladder' (*PFS*, 34) – conflates Yeats's 'Adam's Curse' ('A line will take us hours maybe;/Yet if it does not seem a moment's thought/Our stitching and unstitching has been nought'; *The Poems*, 106) and 'The Circus Animals' Desertion' ('I must lie down where all the ladders start/In the foul rag and bone shop of the heart'; *The Poems*, 395). Such poems can be viewed as poetic rites of passage, exercises set by the master for Thomas to fulfil. Certain later poems can be seen as constituting a more subtle mapping of personal experience onto Yeatsian exemplars. The poem 'Sarn Rhiw', for example – Thomas's meditation on 'the foundations of a house' ('The Tower'; *The Poems*, 241), on stoniness, artistry, architecture and inheritance – might be read as a Welsh version of Yeats's 'The Tower' and of sections I ('Ancestral Houses'), II ('My House') and IV ('My Descendants') of 'Meditations in Time of Civil War':

> Thousands of years later
> I inhabit a house
> whose stone is the language
> of its builders...
>
> ... boneless presences
> flit through my room.

Will they inherit me
one day?

(*EA*, 26)

Thomas's poetry of the middle and late periods – Yeatsian categories, those – develop more reticular and candid engagements. The word 'Yeats' itself becomes part of Thomas's poetic vocabulary, a lexis that during the 1970s began to co-opt the language of sub-atomic physics as the poet extended his negotiations with 'the god of the gaps' into the realm of what one critic has called 'theo-sci' (an apt hyphenisation). The word 'Yeats' becomes a trigger for highly charged mythopoeic and symbolic modes of representation. Contemplating the inexorable end of the Christian era in 'The Moon in Lleyn', as 'The last quarter of the moon/of Jesus gives way/to the dark', Thomas, on his knees in Aberdaron, admits that 'it is easy to believe/Yeats was right' – the gyres have revolved, and the Christian dispensation is to be succeeded by a Yeatsian 'antithetical' age. And yet, by the end of the poem, it is Yeats's concept of history in such works as A Vision ('that strange book', as Thomas called it) and 'The Phases of the Moon' that offers Thomas consolation (even though he could later reject cyclical views of history as an imprisoning 'labyrinth'[51]):

> But a voice sounds
> in my ear: Why so fast,
> mortal?...
> ... Even as this moon
> making its way through the earth's
> cumbersome shadow, prayer, too,
> has its phases.

(*LS*, 30–1)

Thomas had been fascinated by Yeatsian portrayals of violent historical annunciation before his metaphysical poetry become saturated in the discourse of modern science, as poems such as 'Parent' – 'Her haired breast heaving against

his,/... And the warm day indifferent,/Not foreseeing the
loading/Of that huge womb' (BT, 28) – and 'Swifts' – 'Sometimes they meet/In the high air; what is engendered/At contact?', both echoing 'Leda and the Swan' – attest.[52]
Yeatsian imagery became increasingly valuable for
Thomas as a mode of figuring the monstrous tyrannies of a
technological age. From the pivotal volume *H'm* onwards,
Yeats's 'The Second Coming' and the famous first section of
'Fragments' ('Locke sank into a swoon; The Garden died;
/God took the spinning-jenny/Out of his side'; *The Poems*,
260) are constantly reworked and updated to figure the
birth of the modern age. God's side is forever being
breached by the horrific Caesarean births of insolent technological fiends and rough mechanical beasts (their hour
come round at last): 'So they left the fields to assist/at the
delivery of the machine//from time's side' (*MHT*, 39);
'once men looked/in a manger, failing to see the beast for
the god' (*C*, 32). There are personal physical and psychic
wounds inscribed in these Yeatsian figurings: Thomas himself was delivered by Caesarean section, and the poetry
dramatises a disturbingly resentful relationship with his
breached mother.[53] In Thomas's 'AD 2000', 'The gyres
revolve' and 'man comes to the confrontation/with his terror', begotten by the 'contemporary mind' that eclipses the
'Janus-faced' god (*EA*, 25). Yeats in 'A Dialogue of Self and
Soul' may have been content to 'live it all again' (*The Poems*,
286) – a statement on which Thomas meditates more than
once in his autobiographical prose: 'I have thought many
times that I am not like Yeats, willing to live it all again. And
yet the voice at my side whispers: of course you're willing';
'Yeats said that he would be willing to live it all again.
Would I? An answer to the contrary seems abhorrent' (*Autobiographies*, 119, 124). Yet faced with the machine and the
global capitalism that feeds it, Thomas can articulate the
contrary position even more forcefully:

> The bone's song will be:

'Let me sleep. I am not
Yeats. I cannot face
over again the coming
of the machine.'
                        ('Then'; *NTF*, 21)

– a dramatic modification of his 1964 admission 'I am not
W.B. Yeats, and am without his talent'. In the volume
Counterpoint (1990), the angels

are prostrate
'beaten into the clay'
as Yeats thundered. Only
Satan beams down,
poisoning with fertilisers
the place where the child
lay, harrowing the ground
for the drumming of the machine-
gun tears of the rich that are
seed of the next war.
                        (*C*, 29)

In Yeats's 'The Curse of Cromwell' it is 'The lovers and the
dancers' who are 'beaten into the clay' (*The Poems*, 351),
and in 'Under Ben Bulben', the Irish 'lords and ladies gay'
are similarly 'beaten into the clay Through seven heroic
centuries' (*The Poems*, 375). Thomas transforms Yeats's
folk-poet persona of 'The Curse of Cromwell' into a modern Jeremiah confronting the implications of a now global
imperialism. 'A Dialogue of Self and Soul' is conflated with
'All Souls' Night' in 'Hallowe'en', in which Thomas, faced
with the machine howling at the centre of the 'mind's
labyrinth' – a recapitulation of his earlier portrait of Yeats
('And labyrinth paths of his own impenetrable mind') –
quarrels both with Yeats's wish to re-live his life and with
his summoning of dead friends and foes ('I call MacGregor
Mathers from his grave'; *The Poems*, 281):

Outside a surfeit of planes.
Inside the hunger of the departed

to come back. 'Ah, erstwhile humans,
would you make your mistakes
over again? In life, as in love,
the second time round is
no better.'
...
'Stay where you are,' I implore.
'This is no world for escaped beings
to make their way back into.'

(*NTF*, 63)

Positioning himself 'beside the gene-pool' (*MHT*, 83) in
the later poetry, Thomas boldly modernises the anachro-
nism of Yeats by revising the occult poet, the Yeats of the
gyres, of cyclical history and the phases of the moon, while
at the same time locally appropriating such systems. In
'The Cones', for example, by

Following his star,
we will find in the manger
as the millennium dies neither
the child reborn nor the execrable
monster, but only the curled-up
doll...

(*LP*, 183)

– 'his', there, identifiable as both Christ and Yeats. Yeats's
gyres become inbuilt structures of the metaphysical quest
for the absent god: 'we climbed,/not to look down, but to
feel your glance/resting on us at the next angle/of the gyre'
(*EA*,3); 'As though/coming round on a new/gyre, we approached God/from the far side, an extinct concept' (*MHT*,
48). That last poem, 'Eschatology', also transposes the arti-
fice of the golden bird of 'Sailing to Byzantium' into the
unlovely mechanistic products of scientists in their 'space-
stations' – 'clockwork birds/and fabricated lilies'. At the
same time, the poetry acknowledges the outdatedness of
such Yeatsian imagery: whereas the owls in section IV of
'Meditations in Time of Civil War' move in Yeatsian circles

– 'The Primum Mobile that fashioned us/Has made the very owls in circles move' (*The Poems*, 249) – Thomas's barn owl with its 'acetylene/eyes' (an image of divine terror) takes the beeline of the modern age, like an invasive medical probe:

> The owl calls.
> It is not Yeats'
> owl; it moves
> not in circles
>
> but direct through
> the ear to the heart,
> refrigerating it . . .
>   ('Barn Owl'; *NTF*, 72)

The spiralling double cones of Yeats's gyres are superannuated in Thomas's late poetry by DNA's 'twin helix' (hardly, to quote Yeats, 'An image out of Spenser and the common tongue'), in which 'the dancing chromosomes/pass one another back to back to a tune from the abyss' (*ERS*, 109). Thus as Thomas knew, the geneticists, as well as Yeats, may ask: 'How can we know the dancer from the dance?' ('Among School Children'; *The Poems*, 263). In Thomas's 'Pavane', Yeats's birds of 'The Second Coming' and 'Sailing to Byzantium' have 'Grown hoarse' (*H'm*, 14), and the 'Artificer of the years' invoked in the poem is at once a confused god, suffering from a form of historical and metaphysical dementia, and Yeats himself who, despite his historical far-sightedness, cannot cope with the traumas of the modern era.

Such modernisations often result in a kind of parody of the Irish poet. A late, unpublished manuscript poem constitutes another version of sections II and IV of 'Meditations in Time of Civil War' and 'The Tower':

> Do not come
> as Childe Harold to an unlighted
> tower. Company is needed
> to outstare the furies. Yeats

> alone was prey to the desolation
> of the night owl. I am
> no Habakkuk. I take the lift
> to my tower. Why should I toil
> on yesterday's staircase?[54]

In a poem from *Counterpoint*, Yeats 'in his tower' can appear as one of the 'shining sentinels/at hand' on an evening of great peace, 'the moon come to its fifteenth phase' (*C*, 57); in the above poem, however, Yeats's 'winding stair' is yesterday's news, an obsolescent means of attaining the vantage point from which Thomas eventually looks out over a diminished present. 'Yesterday's staircase' might be taken here as a reference to Yeats's poetry itself – a body of lore that, despite its modernity, shows its age in the face of the 'silicon angels', 'mineral poetry', 'transmitted prayers', 'computed darkness' 'irradiated kiss' and 'asbestos countenance' of Thomas's 'biochemical'[55] god.

Yeats can, however, still offer the poet a means of articulating brief moments of tenderness and sympathy amid fury and terror, as in Thomas's recollection of his parishioners' lives, in which he quotes directly from the first section ('Ancestral Houses') of 'Meditations in Time of Civil War': 'They were not to be judged by him. Is there a judgement? They were part of "life's own self-delight" from which had sprung "the abounding, glittering jet"' (*ERS*, 94). Yet Yeats can be exposed, exploded, the sheer magnificence of his voice rejected by the priest-poet moving towards an acknowledgement that the most appropriate mode of understanding god is silence:

> Yeats said that. Young
> I delighted in it:
> there was time enough.
>
> Fingers burned, heart
> seared, a bad taste
> in the mouth, I read him

again, but without trust
any more. What counsel
has the pen's rhetoric

to impart? Break mirrors, stare
ghosts in the face, try
walking without crutches

at the grave's edge? Now
in the small hours
of belief the one eloquence

to master is that
of the bowed head, the bent
knee, waiting, as at the end

of a hard winter
for one flower to open
on the mind's tree of thorns.
                    ('Waiting'; *BHN*, 83)

Note the presence here of another Hibernian ghost – the Beckettian figure on crutches at the grave's edge. If Yeats showed Thomas how to quarrel fruitfully with himself (and with Yeats), he nevertheless proves inadequate here as co-respondent in the quarrel with god.

Clearly, then, Yeats, who for Thomas had said both everything and nothing, did not always 'Suffice the ageing man as once the growing boy' ('Meditations in Time of Civil War'; *The Poems*, 252):

                    Young
I pronounced you. Older
I still do, but seldomer
now, leaning far out
over an immense depth, letting
your name go and waiting,
somewhere between faith and doubt,
for the echoes of its arrival.
                    ('Waiting'; *F*, 32)

These lines, addressed to Thomas's god, serve also as a comment on W.B. Yeats, who – from that early attempt to conjure him in a Welsh train carriage to the late poems of fury and acceptance – serves as a suggestive double of the *deus absconditus*, that 'great absence that is like a presence, (*F*, 48): a spirit to believe in, and doubt.

NOTES
I am grateful to the two external readers for their valuable suggestions. Thanks are due to Gwydion Thomas, Kunjana Thomas and Rhodri Thomas for permission to quote from the work of R.S. Thomas.

1   R.S. Thomas, *Cymru or Wales?* (Llandysul: Gomer, 1992) 23.
2   See Robert Minhinnick, 'Living with R.S. Thomas', *Poetry Wales*, 29, 1 (July 1993): 11–14.
3   Neal Alexander has recently compared Thomas and Yeats as encountered in their prose autobiographies. Alexander considers 'both writers' complex, sometimes agonised strategies for self-presentation' and the way in which multiple selves are performed 'dialectically' in their autobiographical writings; see 'Dialogues of Self and Soul: The Autobiographies of W.B. Yeats and R.S. Thomas', *almanac: A Yearbook of Welsh Writing in English*, 12 (2007–8): 1–31.
4   William Meredith, 'Poem', in *Effort at Speech: New and Selected Poems* (TriQuarterly Books/Northwestern University Press, 1997) 158.
5   W.B. Yeats, *Mythologies* (London: Macmillan, 1977) 331.
6   See John Pikoulis, '"The Curious Stars": R.S. Thomas and the Scientific Revolution', Damian Walford Davies, ed., *Echoes to the Amen: Essays After R.S. Thomas* (Cardiff: University of Wales Press, 2003) 94.
7   M. Wynn Thomas, ' "Time's Changeling": Autobiography in *The Echoes Return Slow*', *Echoes to the Amen* 184.
8   R.S. Thomas, *The Echoes Return Slow* (London: Macmillan, 1988) 22. Hereafter, references to Thomas's poetry are given in the body of the text, abbreviated as follows: *The Echoes Return Slow* (*ERS*); *The Stones of the Field* (Carmarthen: Druid Press, 1946; *SF*); *An Acre of Land* (Newtown: Montgomery-shire Printing Co., 1952; *AL*); *Poetry for Supper* (London: Hart-Davis, 1958; *PFS*); *Tares* (London: Hart-Davis, 1961;

T); *The Bread of Truth* (London: Hart-Davis, 1963; *BT*); *Not That He Brought Flowers* (London: Hart-Davis, 1968; *NTHBF*); *H'm* (London: Macmillan, 1972; *H'm*); *Laboratories of the Spirit* (London: Macmillan, 1975; *LS*); *Frequencies* (London: Macmillan, 1978; *F*); *Between Here and Now* (London: Macmillan, 1981; *BHN*); *Later Poems, 1972–1982* (London: Macmillan, 1983; *LP*); *Experimenting with an Amen* (London: Macmillan, 1986; *EA*); *Welsh Airs* (Bridgend: Poetry Wales Press, 1987; *WA*); *Counterpoint* (Newcastle upon Tyne: Bloodaxe Books, 1990; *C*); *Frieze* (Schondorf am Ammersee: Babel, 1992; *Fr*); *Mass for Hard Times* (Newcastle upon Tyne: Bloodaxe Books, 1992; *MHT*); *No Truce with the Furies* (Newcastle upon Tyne: Bloodaxe Books, 1995; *NTF*); *Residues* (Tarset: Bloodaxe Books, 2002; *R*).

9   See David Lloyd, 'Through the Looking Glass: R.S. Thomas's *The Echoes Return Slow* as Poetic Autobiography', *Twentieth-Century Literature*, 42, 4 (Winter 1996): 451.

10 Justin Wintle, *Furious Interiors: Wales, R.S. Thomas and God* (London: Harper Collins, 1996) 251–2.

11 Marjorie Elizabeth Howes, *Yeats's Nations: Gender, Class, and Irishness* (Cambridge: Cambridge University Press, 1996) 4–5.

12 Ibid. 103.

13 W.B. Yeats, *The Poems*, ed. Daniel Albright (London: J.M. Dent, 1990) 367. All quotations from Yeats's poetry are taken from this edition, hereafter *The Poems* in the body of the text.

14 The poet's son, Gwydion Thomas, notes: 'in moving [in the mid-1990s] to be near [his second wife] in Titley, Herefordshire, [Thomas] was able to indulge his hankering to be an English country gentleman. He used to appear regularly in tweed jackets and cavalry twills like a retired Colonel'; see '"Quietly as Snow": Gwydion Thomas interviewed by Walford Davies', *New Welsh Review*, 64 (Summer 2004): 30.

15 Geoffrey Hill, 'R.S. Thomas's Welsh Pastoral', *Echoes to the Amen* 51–2. See also 54.

16 See Alexander, 'Dialogues of Self and Soul' 25: 'Thomas, like Yeats, attests to an unbridgeable sense of self-division, but one that is viewed more as a curse than as a source of creative tension'.

17 Thomas, *Cymru or Wales?* 30.

18 R.S. Thomas, *Autobiographies*, ed. and trans. Jason Walford Davies (London: J.M. Dent, 1997) 22. Hereafter, *Autobio-*

graphies.

19 *Critical Quarterly*, 9, 4 (Winter 1967): 380, 381.
20 See Damian Walford Davies, ' "Double-entry Poetics": R.S. Thomas – Punster', *Echoes to the Amen* 151–2.
21 Unpublished MS poem, 'That year also I saw God...'; archive of the R.S. Thomas Study Centre, Bangor University.
22 A.E. Dyson, *Yeats, Eliot and R.S. Thomas: Riding the Echo* (London: Macmillan, 1981) xvi.
23 For a reading of Thomas as 'anti-modern', see Grahame Davies, *Sefyll yn y Bwlch: R.S. Thomas, Saunders Lewis, T.S. Eliot, a Simone Weil* (Caerdydd: Gwasg Prifysgol Cymru, 1999) 13–14, 135–90, 191–4. My own sense is that Thomas – troublingly *avant la lettre* – was always already (post-)post-modern.
24 Howes, *Yeats's Nations* 12.
25 Wintle, *Furious Interiors* 83 and 300.
26 See Dyson, *Yeats, Eliot and R.S. Thomas* 302, 306, 313–14, 320. See also Lloyd, 'Through the Looking Glass' 439.
27 T.S. Eliot, 'Yeats', *On Poetry and Poets* (London: Faber and Faber, 1957) 262.
28 'R.S. Thomas writes...', *Poetry Book Society Bulletin*, 59 (1968): no pagination.
29 Quoted in Jason Walford Davies, *Gororau'r Iaith: R.S. Thomas a'r Traddodiad Llenyddol Cymraeg* (Caerdydd: Gwasg Prifysgol Cymru, 2003) 12.
30 Thomas, 'Words and the Poet', Sandra Anstey, ed., *R.S. Thomas: Selected Prose* (Bridgend: Seren, 3rd ed., 1995) 63.
31 'Probings: An Interview with R.S. Thomas', William V. Davis, ed., *Miraculous Simplicity: Essays on R.S. Thomas* (Fayetteville: University of Arkansas Press, 1993) 29.
32 W.B. Yeats, *A Vision* (1925; London: Macmillan, 1962) 83.
33 'Probings: An Interview with R.S. Thomas' 35.
34 Ibid. 30. See also *Autobiographies* 45 and 47.
35 Patrick Crotty, 'Lean Parishes: Patrick Kavanagh's *The Great Hunger* and R.S. Thomas's *The Minister*', Katie Gramich and Andrew Hiscock, eds., *Dangerous Diversity: The Changing Faces of Wales* (Cardiff: University of Wales Press, 1998) 133.
36 See Walford Davies, *Gororau'r Iaith* 144–8.
37 See R.S. Thomas's 1946 essay, 'Some Contemporary Scottish Writing', *Selected Prose* 24–35, and Fflur Dafydd, ' "This is I; there is Nothing Else": R.S. Thomas and Hugh MacDiarmid', *Welsh Writing in English: A Yearbook of Critical*

Essays, 11 (2006–7): 102–21.
38 See the article cited in note 35. See also Tony Brown, *R.S. Thomas* (Cardiff: University of Wales Press, 2006) 18–22.
39 Tony Bianchi, 'R.S. Thomas and his Readers', Sandra Anstey, ed., *Critical Writings on R.S. Thomas* (Bridgend: Seren, 1992) 170.
40 *Selected Prose* 26, 28; 'Probings: An Interview with R.S. Thomas' 26.
41 Bianchi, 'R.S. Thomas and his Readers' 159–60.
42 See H. Idris Bell, 'Correspondence', *The Welsh Outlook* (August 1922): 196.
43 Dafydd, 'This is I; there is Nothing Else' 117.
44 See Walford Davies, *Gororau'r Iaith* 149–51.
45 Thomas, *Cymru or Wales?* 9.
46 *Selected Prose* 33.
47 'Replies to "Wales" Questionnaire, 1946', *Wales*, 6, 3 (Autumn 1946): 22.
48 See *Wales*, 7, 25 (Spring 1947): 222–3.
49 Cf. M. Wynn Thomas's reading of 'Memories of Yeats whilst Travelling to Holyhead' as 'the occasion for what may be termed [Thomas's] own summary of the growth of a national poet's mind'; 'For Wales, See Landscape: Early R.S. Thomas and the English Topographical Tradition', *Welsh Writing in English: A Yearbook of Critical Essays*, 10 (2005): 23–5.
50 See Pikoulis, 'The Curious Stars' 76–111.
51 See R.S. Thomas, 'Time's Disc Jockey: Meditations on Some Lines in *The Anathemata*', Belinda Humfrey and Anne Price-Owen, eds., *David Jones: Diversity in Unity* (Cardiff: University of Wales Press, 2000) 157, 159.
52 The Yeatsian resonance of 'engendered' is noted by Pikoulis, 'The Curious Stars' 83.
53 See Katie Gramich, 'Mirror Games: Self and (M)other in the Poetry of R.S. Thomas', *Echoes to the Amen* 132–48.
54 'Giving up the struggle...'; archive of the R.S. Thomas Study Centre, Bangor University.
55 See Pikoulis, 'The Curious Stars' 92.

'He was thinking in Welsh now, though he spoke in English':

Negotiating identity in the language of Hilda Vaughan's novels.

Lucy Thomas
Cardiff University

Hilda Vaughan's novels, set largely in the Radnorshire countryside, attracted a worldwide readership. Reviews suggest that her books were being read as far and wide as Ireland, America, Sri Lanka, India, South Africa, Australia, New Zealand, Canada and Egypt.[1] Rural Wales, its languages, customs and people, was being interpreted by multiple audiences with varied frames of reference. This lends further complexity to the depiction of language, which, often, is already ideologically loaded for the Welsh author writing in English. Vaughan had an extremely tentative grasp of the Welsh language. Born in Builth Wells into the anglicised upper-middle class, Vaughan moved to London in the 1920s where she lived with her English husband, the novelist and dramatic critic for *The Times*, Charles Morgan. Much of her writing, however, sensitively depicts the complicated linguistic topography of her neighbouring county, which was subject to the influences of England to the east and Ceredigion to the west. The effect of this cultural encounter was described by Benjamin Heath Malkin in 1804:

> in the south-east part of the county, about Clyrow, Paine's Castle, and other places in that neighbourhood... the Welsh language is still understood, and all are able to speak it, though they decidedly affect the English. About Presteign [sic], no natives understand Welsh, but it is partially known to all or most in the places five or six miles to the westward.[2]

Though Radnorshire was anglicised earlier and more thoroughly than many other parts of Wales, it is a situation that can be related in varying degrees to the country as a whole.[3] In this extract, language is localised and no longer reliable as a marker of national identity. Instead of distinguishing the Welsh from the English, language could, and often still does, form a dividing and divisive line between the Welsh themselves. The association between language and boundaries is pertinent to Vaughan's work as she was, of course, a border writer, but also as her hometown was on a linguistic fault-line during Vaughan's youth, where the receding Welsh language could still be heard.[4] Indeed, Vaughan recounts the 'dramatic' Welsh 'in which our maids conduct their private quarrels' in her autobiographical essay 'A Country Childhood'.[5] Monica Heller has remarked that code-switching, the use of multiple languages or modes of expression, is 'a boundary levelling or a boundary maintaining strategy.'[6] The use of a language can include those who are familiar with it while excluding those who are not, simultaneously constructing similarity and difference. This can be seen in Vaughan's novels as the author employs code-switching, and language in a broader sense, as a conciliatory or distancing device in order to repeatedly negotiate and renegotiate issues of identity.

I

In *The Dragon Has Two Tongues*, Glyn Jones laments the language-based 'split' in Welsh culture. He writes that: 'The division, even in some instances the hostility, between Welsh and Anglo-Welsh writers, has always been to me regrettable and distressing...'[7] Homi K. Bhabha describes such a rift in postcolonial countries in *The Location of Culture*:

> The problem is not simply the 'selfhood' of the Nation as opposed to the otherness of other nations. We are confronted with the Nation split within itself, articulating the heterogeneity of its population. The barred Nation *It / Self*, alienated from its eternal self-generation, becomes a liminal

signifying space, the heterogeneous histories of contending peoples, antagonist authorities and tense locations of cultural difference.[8]

Hilda Vaughan's novels acknowledge the antagonism generated as such boundaries and divisions are created according to language. When John Bevan travels west (and thus towards the Welsh-language heartlands) to the market town, Aberyscir, in *The Battle to the Weak*(1925) he is greeted by the,

> high pitched voices of a Welsh crowd, engaged in congenial pursuit of bartering, [who] made a deafening clamour. John Bevan, coming from an anglicized border country, could not speak his own language, and despised his fellow countrymen who were able to do so as much as they despised him.[9]

Here, the linguistic differences mark the border between counties but in *The Candle and the Light*(1954) language divides the community within a town. Vaughan's novel is reminiscent of Bhabha's description, as the outbreak of the Boer War highlights community divisions that are rooted in language, politics and class:

> The professional class, to a man, and most of the wealthier trades-folk, were anglicized, members of the Church of England and Tories, like the neighbouring landed gentry. But the town's poorer classes and the farming community of the district spoke Welsh, were Nonconformist, Liberal and opposed to the war.[10]

Vaughan's matter-of-fact, omniscient view of the divisions is significant in both texts. She refrains from taking sides or passing judgement and merely comments on the existence of opposing groups.

The latter quotation also draws attention to the idea that language is one marker of a prescribed set of ideological beliefs that creates a 'type' of Welsh identity. The language used by a character, it seems, goes hand in hand with a corresponding religion, politics and class position. For example, *The Invader*(1928) is set in a 'remote agricultural district where folk were divided into small mutually hostile groups according to their race, class and religion'.[11] The parson is baffled by the Squire's failure to fit into these categories: he 'did not understand why one who spoke good English and despised Dissenters never attended his parish Church' (pp.15-16). The Squire's language, it seems, should be an indicator of other attributes expected of an 'Anglicised' person, just as the Welsh identity of other characters is expected to conform to an established mould.[12] If the Welsh language is part of a Welsh identity, along with Nonconformity, radicalism and membership of the lower class we are left to wonder where this positions the English-speaking Welsh characters of Vaughan's novels. It begs the question of whether the English-speaking Welsh can indeed have access to a Welsh identity.

An answer to this question can be found in the examination of Nonconformity, which is often closely identified with the Welsh language. The link between Nonconformity and Welsh can also be seen in *The Candle and the Light* as embodied in the character of Amos Rhys. His Welshness is constantly emphasised and it is no coincidence that he is called 'The Minor Prophet'. The text's intertwining of language with religion can be seen in the following passage:

> Whenever the Minor Prophet grew excited he shed his veneer of English accent, rolled his *r*'s, broadened his vowels and stressed his syllables in the lilting chant he used for his mother tongue. He was thinking in Welsh now, though he spoke in English, and was carried away by the *hwyl* that had gained him local fame as a chapel preacher. (p.23)

It is as if his Welshness audibly grows with the progress of the description. The shift in tense gives the effect of a metamorphosis taking place immediately before us. He begins with a 'veneer of English accent' before his voice becomes increasingly Welsh, the words 'mother tongue' alert us to his true identity, he translates his speech from his Welsh-language thoughts and ends up at the pinnacle of Welsh language and identity, the 'hwyl' of a Methodist preacher. Vaughan, however, complicates this prescribed identity with her association of religiosity with English-speaking as well as Welsh-speaking Wales; with the Anglican Church in Wales as well as Nonconformity. In *The Battle to the Weak* characters of various denominations pepper their speech with biblical language and quotations. Esther, an English-speaking church-goer, describes a period of suffering as, 'like the lean kine in the dream of Pharoh as did swallow up the fat kine' (p.196). Elias Lloyd, an English-speaking Methodist threatens John Bevan in biblical-style curses. He rages:

> Do thou requite mine enemies for this... Let them be as the dust before the wind, and the angel of the Lord scatterin' them. Let their way be dark and slippery, and let the angel of the Lord persecute them. (pp.21-2)

Vaughan alters the perception of religious fervour as a common feature of the Welsh-speaking populace only. She broadens the identity to encompass all Welsh people, regardless of their language. This is evident in *Her Father's House*(1930) as Uncle Mark's voice contains 'the lugubrious sing-song which Nell had learnt to connect with acts of worship'.[13] Here it is the Welsh accent and not the language that is linked with religion.

Instead of a boundary that divides the Welsh, Vaughan shows that the predilection for biblical language is a feature that differentiates the Welsh from the English. She essentially moves the boundary elsewhere. This is illustrated in *The Battle to the Weak* as the invalided Gladys lies in bed reading the Bible:

> She seized upon any modern story-books that Esther was able to bring her, and spelled her way through them laboriously. But she never enjoyed them as she enjoyed the simpler stories of the Testaments... To her it was just a book full of adventures, battles and love-making, of the journeys, the business and pleasures of a pastoral people who were nearer to her than more sophisticated heroes and heroines whose psychological intricacies bewildered her. Not only were the

characters in the Bible more comprehensible, but their stories
were told with a simplicity that left her to fill in the details
to her own satisfaction. She did not want to stumble with difficulty through descriptions of dress and appearance. The
word 'comely,' or the brief phrase 'good to look upon,' were
sufficient to set her mind at work... (p.172)

Although Gladys is a monoglot English-speaker her relationship with the texts that she reads is specifically Welsh. It is
significant, here, that the English novel is established as
alien and unsuitable for the Welsh. The morality of the two
nations, and even the way their minds work are depicted as
fundamentally different. Vaughan constructs a Welsh identity that responds to the stories of the Bible, though interestingly not so much its religious messages. Even the language
of the Bible is presented as more relevant to a Welsh person
of either language. Vaughan blurs the boundaries that are
'tense locations of cultural difference' in Bhabha's model of
a split nation.

This linguistic and cultural blurring goes further. If we
examine the English words spoken by the Welsh characters,
particularly those belonging to the working class, it is clear
that Welsh syntax and direct translations of Welsh phrases
and expressions are being used. For example, in *Iron and
Gold*(1948) Owain's mother asks: 'Whatever's on you?'
p.(94), to mean 'what is the matter with you?', a direct
translation of the Welsh 'Beth sydd arnat ti?'[14] When Glythin
declares to Owain 'Catch you this if you can' (p.66), the syntax may appear odd to an English speaker as it is a translation of 'Dal di hwn os fedri di'. Similarly, in *The Battle to the
Weak* Esther says to Rhys, 'Go you on' (p.54). The emphatic
here is used as it would be in the Welsh language ('Cer di
'mlaen'). Such a borrowing from the Welsh would seem to
adhere to Bill Ashcroft's description of a postcolonial text
that uses 'devices of otherness' such as 'syntactic fusion, in
which the english prose is structured according to the syntactic principles of a first language; neologisms, new lexical
forms in English which are informed by the semantic and
morphological exigencies of a mother tongue'.[15] Vaughan,

however, is not solely using a device of postcolonial literature
but is also often faithfully transcribing the dialect of Radnorshire. Despite the rapid decay of the Welsh language in
the county, W.H. Howse, writing in 1949, identified the fact
that 'the Welsh influence has persisted in many of the expressions still in use, and in the construction of certain phrases
which form the common language of the county'.[16] Vaughan's characters often use terms from Howse's glossaries such
as 'allus' for 'always' (for example, Annie Bevan says she 'do
allus seem to be sayin' the wrong thing' in *The Battle to the
Weak*, pp.22-3); 'liefer' for 'rather' (Dame Hafod says 'I'd
liefer not talk of it' in *Harvest Home*)(1936);[17] and the use
of 'en' for a person or object (for example in *The Invader* a
group of workers declare 'as we are all friends of Daniel
Evans, we have promised to shift his furniture for 'en',
p.117). Radnorshire dialect is a form of anglicised Welsh, a
hybridised language that traverses the borders of England
and Wales, incorporating the language of both countries. It
is significant that it crosses over into the old kingdom of
Mercia, literally crossing the dyke built by the Mercian
king Offa.[18] It is a dialect that replicates the devices used by
postcolonial literature to portray the language of the
colonised culture.

In fact, Vaughan's use of the Radnorshire dialect contains
so many translations of Welsh words, phraseology and
grammar that when the plot moves to other parts of Wales
and different historical periods it is difficult to discern what
language the characters are actually speaking in many of her
novels. While *Harvest Home*'s setting in eighteenth-century
Ceredigion suggests that its characters must be speaking in
Welsh, Vaughan never specifically states that this is the
case. *Iron and Gold* is also set in the distant past and so
would conceivably contain Welsh-speaking characters but
Vaughan does not tell us and the clues from the text are con-
flicting. Owain's mother refers to the 'sour old English-
speaking clergy' (p.83) which suggests that she and her son
are different from them and are therefore Welsh-speaking.
Owain sings a song, however, in which it is suggested that

Welsh is no longer spoken in the district. As he sang he 'repeated these words until they were defaced as a coin by long usage and their meaning quite forgot' (p.96). Similarly, in *The Invader* it is stated that Davey, the shepherd, shouts to his dogs in Welsh (p.71). While the characters, therefore, can speak Welsh, it is never stated whether they do so for the remainder of the novel, and perhaps due to the specific mention of its use here, it is unlikely. The language being spoken is frequently withheld as a marker of identity in Vaughan's work. It is the characters' Welsh identity and not their language that becomes important, leaving the linguistic boundaries as markers of difference wide open.

Where Vaughan's boundary levelling between the Welsh-speaking and English-speaking Welsh characters becomes slightly more problematic, however, is in their relationship with place names and the land. Roy Palmer has identified the fact that in anglicised Radnorshire, the last bastion of Welsh is its place names:

> As with farms so with fields and other features of the land-scape such as woods and valleys, Welsh names remain widespread. Over and over again words recur such as *bryn* (hillside), *cae* (field), *coed* (wood), *cwm* (dingle), *dol* [sic] (meadow), *ffin* [sic] (boundary), *ffrwd* (stream), *llwyn* (tree, grove), *nant* (stream, valley), *rhos* (moor, bog), *rhyd* (ford), *tir* (land), and *twyn* (hillside).[19]

This is certainly the case in Vaughan's novels, whose settings, on the whole, have thoroughly Welsh names such as Aberyscir in *The Battle to the Weak* and *The Invader* and Cwmbach in *A Thing of Nought*, which is significant given the importance placed upon naming by postcolonial theory. In *The Battle to the Weak*, the warring Bevans and Lloyds live on farms named, respectively, Pengarreg and Henallt. Their Welsh names denote their topographical features (the head or end of the rock and old hill). Yet the farms are situated near the village Lewisbridge, whose name has been anglicised, presumably from Pontlewis. Howse comments that while many places in Radnorshire retain their original

Welsh names, 'It is true that many of the Welsh names have come "unstuck" in their spelling, as might be expected when their meanings have been forgotten... There is a mixture of two languages in a few names'.[20] The erosion and anglicisation of place names can be seen in Vaughan's work. In *A Thing of Nought* Megan is seldom allowed to visit the neighbouring town of Pont Noyadd; 'noyadd' seemingly a corruption of 'newydd' (new) or, less convincingly, 'neuadd' (hall).[21] In *Harvest Home* a farm is called The Plas, the hybridised form of Y Plas and names are misrecorded, such as Dinas Llas to which an extra 'l' has been added, presumably because this 'sounds' Welsh (Dinas Las means Blue Fort). Howse's words also remind us that while the inhabitants of Pengarreg and Henallt live in their Welsh-named farms, they may not be able to understand the meaning of those names. Hooson-Owen recounts a Welsh visitor to the district in the early 1900s who said of its inhabitants:

> [N]i ddeallent yr un o enwau eu sir... Arhosodd tri gwr [sic] oedd yn canlyn ceffyl a throl i ymgomio a mi. Yr enw ar y drol oedd Blaenglynolwen, yr un gair hir. Ni wyddent ar wyneb daear beth oedd 'blaen' na 'glyn' a phan awgrymais y gallai mai ffrydlif oedd Olwen fel Claerwen cofiasant fod rhyw nant fach yn rhedeg heibio'r lle... Mae'n rhaid mai tuedd i suo eu meddwl i gysgu wna...'r [p]lant, codi'n bobl ieuainc, a thyfu'n henafgwyr [sic] heb wybod ystyron y cartrefi y maent yn byw ynndynt [sic].[22]

> (They do not understand any of the names of their county. Three men that were following a horse and cart stopped to converse with me. The name on the cart was Blaenglynolwen, the one long word. They had no idea what on earth 'blaen' or 'glyn' was and when I suggested that Olwen could be a stream like Claerwen they remembered that there was a small stream flowing past the place... There must be a tendency to soothe their minds to sleep amongst the children, to become young people, and grow into old men without knowing the meaning of the names of the homes in which they live.)

The Kenyan writer, Ngugi wa Thiong'o describes language as 'a collective memory-bank of a given people' and that taking it away is 'like uprooting a community from history'.[23] This recalls a scene in *Iron and Gold* in which Owain reaps, while:

> Generations, whose blood throbbed through his veins, had toiled with these same movements to this rugged tune and had repeated these words until they were defaced as a coin by long usage, their meaning quite forgot. Knowing no more than a bird does what it was he sang, he heard his chant rise and fall and gave it no heed. (p.96)

Owain's innocent, 'birdlike' ignorance is reminiscent of the Radnorshire children whose minds are asleep to their Welsh culture. Here, he is linked to the land and his ancestors in his toil and its accompanying song but he is simultaneously severed from them, and what they have meant in the past, in his ignorance of the meaning of his song's words. The divide between the English-speaking Welsh and their land caused by language is not fully explored by Vaughan but is hinted at as an unsettling rift in the unified Welsh identity that she attempts to construct for them.

While the Radnorshire Welsh have lost their language and its potent link with their homeland, all is not lost. This is seen if we take another look at John Bevan as he visits the market-town, Aberyscir. Here, as previously noted, he encounters the Welsh language that alienates him from his fellow-countrymen. The passage continues, however,

> [b]ut he could shout as loud and gesticulate as freely in a bargain as the best of them; and when he had struck his man's extended hand with a dramatic gesture of finality signifying that the deal was made, he led away the cow he had bought, satisfied that he had done a creditable morning's work. (p.14)

What emerges from this passage is not merely the division between the Welsh-speaking and the English-speaking Welsh but also their ability to communicate in their shared values and similar traits. They do not share a language but hey do share a characteristic way of communicating. This can be seen in both *The Soldier and the Gentle-woman*(1932) and *The Invader* as English incomers struggle to understand and be understood in their new locale. In the latter text Miss Webster's mode of address quickly alienates the rest of the community. When she first meets the Jones family she demands ' "Is there a man here who can help with my car?"... without any of those preliminary remarks on weather and condition of agriculture which the custom of Wales demands' (p.95). Her deficiency in the Welsh way of language causes offence. Nor can the Welsh understand English modes of address. Daniel misreads Miss Webster's kind offer of more time to move out as 'he detected patronage and offence even in these well-meant words' (p.88). The Welsh and English ways of communicating are established as different and incompatible. This is a cause of paranoia for Dick in *The Soldier and the Gentle-woman*. He is a subject of interest to the small community who attempt to communicate with him:

> To be followed, smiled at and saluted by strangers had made him shy, but until Jones had exchanged winks with the crowd there had been compensations in flattery. You couldn't tell what thought was moving behind those dark, keen eyes. You couldn't be sure why the man winked. (pp.11-12)

He cannot understand the motive behind their communicative signals and is alienated. It is significant that the Welsh cannot communicate with the English even when they are speaking the same language, although as John Bevan's experience at the market suggests, a lack of common language does not deter successful intercourse between the Welsh.

While there are differences between the Welsh, they are united in their greater difference from the English in Vaughan's novels. The idea of a specifically Welsh character independent of language can be seen in an edition of *Cymru* from 1892:

> Y mae iaith Maesyfed yn Seisnig, ond y mae'r bobl mor
> Gymreig eu cymeriad a phobl Meirionnydd – yr un yn eu
> hofergoelion a'u traddodiadau,... Nid oes fymryn o waha-
> niaeth rhwng pobl Maesyfed a phobl Maldwyn...[24]

> (The language of Radnorshire is English, but the people are
> as Welsh in character as the people of Meirionnydd – the
> same in their superstitions and their traditions,... There
> isn't a bit of difference between the people of Radnorshire
> and the people of Maldwyn...)

Vaughan uses this idea and extends it, creating the notion of
a Welsh 'voice' rather than a Welsh language. It is expressed
at its superficial level in a conversation between Valentine
Gould and Grace Felin in *The Candle and the Light*:

> 'You *are* Welsh, aren't you?'
> 'Of course.'
> 'And proud of it,' he laughed. 'How was I to know?' I did
> all the same. Your voice is softer, more flexible, than an
> Englishwoman's. (p.12)

More than an accent, the 'Welsh voice' is a signifier of
identity that unites rather than divides the Welsh. The idea
that the voice betrays a true identity linked with national
identity at times of heightened emotion recurs in Vaughan's
novels. It can be seen in Amos Rhys' loss of his 'veneer' of
English accent when he is impassioned as well as in Nest's
return of her sing-song when she is excited in *The Curtain
Rises*(1953)[25] and Rhys 'dropping back into the idiom of
his own people' (p.285) when he confronts his love for
Esther in *The Battle to the Weak*. The latter quotation is
reminiscent of a 1926 review by Dr J. Gwenogvryn in the
Western Mail which states that 'Hilda Vaughan... has perfect mastery of the Welsh idiom in English guise.'[26] This
'Welsh idiom', rather than language, approaches the idea of
a specifically Welsh way of communicating, of the Welsh
voice that unites the Welsh and levels the boundaries that
the two languages construct. Vaughan's Welsh voice is
accessible to all the Welsh as a unifying identity that,

unlike the politics of language, maintains its border of difference from the English. While Vaughan does not join Glyn Jones in voicing consternation over inter-Welsh linguistic divisions, her novels go a little way in attempting to heal the breach that they create.

II

Vaughan's attempt to use language as an equaliser becomes problematic, however. Language is not simply a means of constructing an identity but is, of course, a marker of the status of that identity as well. John Bevan's might is verbally flaunted in *The Battle to the Weak*. We first encounter him as master of all he surveys. Before he leaves on his journey to market he takes stock of his possessions: '*My* farm', '*My* stock', '*My* house' and even '*my* missus' (p.7). As he rides away his voice displays his status:

> He threw up his head and began to sing his favourite hymn – 'Jerusalem the golden, with milk and honey blest.' The words echoed from the far side of the narrow dingle down which he had begun to ride, and died away long after they had been uttered. He enjoyed making so much noise when he alone could be heard. The sound of his singing seemed to fill the universe. (p.10)

In the same way that he owns his farm and its contents his voice lays claim to ownership over his whole surroundings. The listing of his wife along with his other possessions in this context alludes to the patriarchal power implicit in his use of language. His words 'fill the universe,' rendering him God-like and prefiguring his tyrannical power that is displayed later in the novel. It is significant that his mastery over language is linked with his ownership of the land in this passage. It hints at the seizing of land and control of language that are part of the process of colonisation. Similarly, the battle for supremacy and land between Miss Webster and Daniel Evans in *The Invader* is partly played out in language. The English Miss Webster has inherited a farm in Wales and ejects the tenant, Daniel Evans. The novel depicts the battle of wits that rages, culminating in Daniel forcing Miss Webster to leave the district so that he can buy her farm. One exchange between them shows the relationship between language and power. Daniel tells Miss Webster,

> 'I am letting you cull fifty sheep.'
> 'Cull?' Miss Webster repeated the word to herself, not sure of its meaning but unwilling to confess her ignorance. Daniel was quick to detect it. 'I must be teaching you our terms here, I see, ma'am,' he remarked with condescension. (p.86)

Here, the colonised subject who has had the English language imposed upon him as the instrument of empire has achieved such mastery over it that he wrests the power associated with it from the grip of the coloniser.

The politics of language and its implications in the postcolonial context have an important bearing on Vaughan's work, particularly in her relationship with her audience. She was, of course, a Welsh writer who was writing in English for a large and diverse readership, as we saw in the introduction to this article. While her novels were being read by inhabitants of a country that had colonised Wales, they were also being read by inhabitants of countries that the Welsh had aided to colonise, rendering the portrayal of Welsh culture open to interpretations from different vantage points. The fact that Welsh readers, with their varying grasp of the Welsh language, were also reading the novels meant that what words, expressions, history, geography and cultural terms and points of reference to translate or to gloss was a difficult and ideologically loaded question. As Bill Ashcroft, Gareth Griffiths and Helen Tiffin point out in *The Empire Writes Back*:

> Ultimately, the choice of leaving words untranslated in postcolonial texts is a political act, because while translation is not inadmissible in itself, glossing gives the translated word and thus the 'receptor' culture, the higher status.[27]

Vaughan's novels are interspersed with Welsh words such as

'cariad', 'bach', 'cwm', 'diawl' and 'duwch' as well as the Welsh names of places and characters. While they generally go unglossed they are usually either familiar or rendered comprehensible by the context in which they appear. Their use constitutes what Gordon and Williams in 'Raids on the Articulate' categorise as 'extrinsic' use of a language. This is the least obtrusive of three levels of code-switching and defined as the use of italicised 'foreign' words 'merely to provide local colour'.[28] Vaughan does gloss some Welsh words, however, when she wants to ensure that the non-Welsh-speaking reader can understand. For example in *Iron and Gold* Owain tells his mother, and more importantly the audience, that he has named his fairy wife and will 'be calling her Glythin, which is meaning dewdrop' (p.47). Presumably his mother, who has the same background as Owain, would understand the meaning of Glythin, so this interjection is for the benefit of the audience alone. The act of glossing privileges the dominant-culture language, English, and the Welsh word here is misspelled (it should be Gwlithyn) so the Welsh language is doubly undermined. Interestingly, Gordon and Williams state that this level of code-switching 'is only ever used by people whose second language ability is extremely weak.'[29] This can conceivably be argued of Vaughan's grasp of Welsh, since preparatory notes for her novels contain detailed glossaries provided by a friend more familiar with the language.[30]

Not only did Vaughan use Welsh words but her novels, as we have seen, were also filled with Radnorshire dialect. Vaughan's use of dialect is extensive but she only uses the most accessible forms, avoiding the more obscure terms that would be incomprehensible and therefore alienating to an outside audience. One 1925 review published in *World Today* enthuses that Vaughan's 'transcription of the Welsh dialect is a very happy one and does not in the least hold up the easy flow of the narrative'.[31] Vaughan, it seems, was all too aware of the pressures from her multiple audiences. Kirsti Bohata writes that the 'lack of English-language publishers in Wales until the 1960s and 1970s forced Welsh authors writing in English to publish in England and therefore to fulfil the requirements of an English audience'.[32] This would have been made clear to the young author when she received a letter from W. Robertson Nicoll at *The British Weekly* rejecting a story. He informs her that:

> Many years ago I made great efforts to find a Welsh writer of idyll who would do for Wales what has been done for Scotland. I tried at least half a dozen. They found their severest critics among the Welsh themselves. Every idyll I published drew fierce criticism, and in truth the stories were not very good.[33]

While he urges her to go on to write a book, the letter also highlights the problems faced by a Welsh writer. The agenda of the publishers to find 'a Welsh writer of idyll', presumably that presented Wales in a palatable form to an English audience, is constrictive and as the correspondent points out, the Welsh themselves have to be pleased. Vaughan was aware that she could offend Welsh sensibilities in her writing and in a speech entitled 'Why authors are cads' she describes an encounter with one such unhappy reader:

> [S]he was a Welsh woman – a patriot – and had been deeply shocked, and personally grieved, by some of my fictitious characters, as though I had drawn the most brutal portraits of her own nearest and dearest! Holding my hand and petting it, she implored me in future to describe only what was brightest and best in our national character; in other words, to conform to her conception of what the Welsh ought to be, to make Welshmen in my story all brave, noble, generous and sincerely religious, and all the women all alike dutiful and chaste! Above all, she besought me to give to my stories an uplifting, moral tone, and an encouragingly happy ending! Being a Welshwoman, she was so eloquent and persuasive, and her earnest exhortations went on for so long, that I was almost reduced to tears of contrition, when the return of her family made my escape possible. I believe I was on the point of perjuring my soul and damning whatever artistic integrity I possess, by promising never again to

let my imagination take charge of me, but to write only at
her piously nationalistic dictation![34]

The Welsh press, however, was largely supportive of Vaughan. Post-Caradoc Evans they were painfully aware of how
their country's depiction would be viewed by their colonial
neighbours. A reviewer in *Cambrian Leader* in 1925
declared 'here is the strongest novel he has had in his hands,
dealing with Welsh life, for years. The progress of Hilda
Vaughan, as a competent and understanding interpreter of
Welsh life, will be of interest to her people.'[35] This view of
Vaughan as an interpreter of Wales to the English seems an
accurate portrayal of the positioning of the texts as Welsh-
based but with a clear awareness of the English audience.
This can be seen in a passage from *The Curtain Rises* in
which Nest interprets Wales to her English suitor, Julian:

> 'They're mostly chapel folk in Llangeld and Welsh speak-
> ing. I was learning to talk it a bit myself.'
> 'Oh,' Julian said with raised eyebrows. 'Then isn't it your
> native tongue?'
> 'No. I'm Welsh, o' course. But Radnorshire born. We were
> only coming down close to the Works when I was a lump
> of a girl. Father doesn't hold much with the hilly people.'
> 'The hilly people,' Julian repeated. 'Who are they? Fairies
> or something?'
> Nest's embarrassment vanished in laughter. 'No, no! The
> people o' the hills, o' course. Up where the pits are.
> They're a rough lot mostly – same as Cardies.'
> 'Cardies? Who on earth are they?'
> 'Why, from the county of Cardigan. You've heard it said,
> no doubt, as it's only breeding pigs or parsons.'
> He threw back his head and laughed. 'No, I've never
> heard that. I shall learn a lot from you. And the people of
> Radnorshire are the salt of the earth – between the hilly
> folk and the Cardies?'
> 'Oh, you're laughing at me,' Nest pouted. (p.61)

Nest gives a brief overview of the language and inter-Welsh
relations for the benefit, not just of the English Julian, but
for the English audience as well, in a sort of double English

glossing. It is interesting that Nest is concerned that her 'audience' is laughing at her at the end of the passage and that she is anxious about how she is being perceived. Nest, like Vaughan, glosses Wales itself for the English audience.

While her work is subject to the politics of language, Vaughan cleverly exploits the tension it creates in her novels. In *The Soldier and the Gentlewoman* Dick's encounter with unfamiliar language dramatises the politics of reading as outlined by Ashcroft above. Dick can be read as representing the English reader who is simultaneously encountering the Welsh words in the text. He informs Gwenllian that he has 'got the Williamses – the old lady and those two pretty daughters from the place with the unpronounceable name coming to tea' (p.88). More than a shared difficulty in pronunciation, however, the potential process of alienation that a foreign language text can create is played out as Dick meets his tenants:

> He failed to understand half they said, and was at times unsure whether they were addressing him in English, or in the Welsh language which they used amongst themselves. When the good news had reached him that he had inherited an estate at home, he had not bargained for its being inhabited by a lot of jabbering foreigners. He had thought of the principality as a remote part of England where the miners gave trouble but the fishing was good, and he had imagined tenant-farmers as red-faced fellows, honest but slow, quaint as rustic characters in a play. It was a shock to discover that most of his own tenants were bright-eyed folk, whose speech and dramatic gesture showed that they were quicker-witted than himself, and *he began to wonder whether the studied monotony of his own speech might not seem as comic to them as the chanting cadence of theirs was to him strange and irritating. Well, not comic perhaps. They would know of course that his way of speaking English was correct. But he was ill at ease among them* [my emphasis]. (pp.55-6)

The entire process of reading a postcolonial text is played out here. First Dick does not understand and feels 'unsure'. He then expresses resentment, questions the supremacy of his own language and is left feeling alienated. As we have seen, Vaughan seemed to be aware of her audience or rather audiences. She glossed or adapted her use of language accordingly, pandering to an English-speaking audience on a superficial level. Her portrayal of Dick's encounter with language, however, is a subtle way of alerting the English to linguistic and cultural differences. The text undermines the privileging of Standard English and suggests that while it is 'correct', that there might be more interesting linguistic alternatives.[36]

While Vaughan's use of the Welsh language subtly undermines the supremacy of Standard English, it is also used in a far less subtle way against the English by some of the characters. Amos Rhys in *The Candle and the Light* uses Welsh in his abuse of English incomers as he strides down the middle of the road:

> Strangers who drove through the town in motor-cars – their numbers had become a nuisance of late – swore at him. He enjoyed retorting in a blasphemous torrent of Welsh, enjoyed their stare of amazement when he shook his fist at the insolent 'foreigners'. (pp.191-2)

In a similar manner, Davey uses the Welsh language to aid him in duping the English Squire in *The Invader*. Daniel Evans plans covertly to sell off his best sheep before Miss Webster can take them from him. His shepherd is caught doing this by the Squire. However, Davey tells Daniel,

> I touched my hat and spoke like butter just. 'Them's not ewes, sir,' I was telling him, and shouting to the dogs in Welsh to take 'em on quick out o' his sight. 'You were mistook, sir,' I said, 'them was wethers!' (p.71)

Such a use of Welsh is double edged, as well as, perhaps, double-audienced. While Welsh is used to secure a sort of victory over the English, its use also confirms anti-Welsh stereotypes of the language being used only to insult the English or for underhand purposes. Some Welsh readers might enjoy the joke, while their English counterparts might have their prejudices confirmed. It is also interesting that the text does not give Amos Rhys authority in the first quotation as it places the word 'foreigners' in inverted commas, suggesting that the narrator would not consider the English as such.

In a similar way, mimicry serves an ambivalent purpose in the novels. In *The Soldier and the Gentlewoman* Gwenllian tells Dick that her father 'was a gifted mimic, like so many Welshmen' (p.64). This evokes Homi Bhabha's idea that mimicry of the coloniser is a trope often employed by a colonised culture and 'results in the *splitting* of colonial discourse,' rendering its authority ambivalent and open to subversion.[37] It is indeed seen to be used in this manner in the novel as the insolent Jones 'mimicked Dick's drawl' (p.14), undermining his authority as his social superior, and his colonial superior (the text goes on to describe Jones as a 'squatting' 'native', p.14). It is characteristic of this whole exchange between them, 'making him [Dick] uncomfortable' (p.17). In *The Invader*, however, it is Monica, an English incomer who mimics the Welsh. Monica is accepted by the community, as Mary Anne's father says, 'You'd almost say she was one o' us, she's that pleasant' (p.113). However, Monica isn't quite one of them and when she visits the Jones family she is honoured with an enormous and rather comical feast. As she and Doctor Langdon, another of the Jones's esteemed English guests, leave they talk about the hospitality they have received. The doctor tells Monica:

> 'Mercifully, not many of my patients can afford to be as extravagant as Mrs. Jones. But if they like you, as I can see they do, you'll find they'll all set before you the handsomest feast they can provide. Will you risk seeing more of them?
> 'Yes,' she said, 'but won't they "see me terrible strange"?' (pp.135-6)

Monica's mimicry of her Welsh hosts is affectionate; 'she had been happy in their company' (p.136). Her social and colonial position of superiority, however, adds a hint of patronisation. She mimics not only the difference in their speech but also their grammatical 'inaccuracy'. Her own position of ideological authority and use of Standard English makes her affectionate mimicry problematic. If we compare it with Vaughan's relationship with language strong similarities emerge. While Vaughan is Welsh, like Monica she is of privileged class. In her use of a dialect that was not her own but that of her social 'inferiors', might Vaughan also be committing a form of mimicry?[38]

The relationship between language and social class is explored in *The Invader*. Daniel Evans is aggrieved when the Squire refuses to accept his version of events after the Squire's shepherd, who has been coursing Daniel's sheep, breaks his arm fleeing from the farmer. Daniel believes that his class has some bearing on the perceived authority of his story:

> 'Treating me like dirt,' he muttered as he clattered home. 'Not so much as giving me *Mr. Evans*! Refusing to take my word, because it wasn't the "word of a gentleman." Oh yes, I do know how the quality talk among theirselves. But what is a gentleman without money? Only a poor come-down-in-the-world as no one is ready to believe. When I am owning the money and the land and the house of a gentleman, then, maybe, they'll be thinking as I've got *"the word of a gentleman"* too! (p.22)

In this passage Daniel's title, 'Mr. Evans', is denied him because of his lower social status. The authority of his words is less powerful due to his class, as he is not a 'gentleman'. The language of the 'quality' is distanced and separate from him as they 'talk among theirselves', though, interestingly, not entirely closed off from his hearing. Daniel aspires to money and property but also the greater authority in language that his higher status could award. The higher the social status, it seems, the greater their power over language.

The relationship between language and colonialism is complicated when the additional factor of class is also present.

As Bill Ashcroft et al. point out in its application to Caribbean literature:

> Some of the clearer examples of switching between codes occurs in texts which directly describe pidgin and Creole forms. The most significant feature of their use in the literature is that they become a common mode of discourse between classes. But class in the post-colonial text is a category occasioned by more than an economic structure; it is a discourse traversed by potent racial and cultural signifiers.[39]

Such a complex tension between language, ethnicity and class can be seen at work in *The Invader*. The novel depicts many characters with varying social and ethnic backgrounds, reflected in their use of language. The Welsh working class speak in Radnorshire dialect, Miss Webster speaks in feminist jargon, Fay uses modern English slang, the Squire talks in old literary English and Monica and the Doctor in Standard English. The narrator uses Standard English as well and so awards authority to the English doctor and Monica, who are effectively speaking on an equal footing with the narrator. This is further complicated by the implied presence of a readership, some of whom will also use Standard English. Vaughan's fiction is largely preoccupied with the lives of working-class characters but there is a gap between their language and that of the narrative, which is conceivably shared by the educated English reader. Vaughan was writing about a class that was lower than her own and so, despite being Welsh, she does not share their dialect; in fact, linguistically, she is closer to the English reader than the characters she portrays. Despite Vaughan's attempt to question the privilege of Standard English, the fact that it is the language of the narrative undermines this. There is no reason why Vaughan, in belonging to one class, cannot write about another, but it inevitably creates a tension in the novels that is not suitably resolved.[40]

If we return once more to Heller's idea that code switching is a 'boundary levelling or boundary maintaining strategy' we will see that Vaughan uses language constantly to deconstruct and reconstruct the boundaries of identity. While she recognises the differences between the English-speaking and Welsh-speaking Welsh, she uses the hybridised Radnorshire dialect along with other devices to create a more unified and stable Welsh identity, levelling the boundaries that create difference. She is not a Welsh-speaker herself but she includes many characters that are and she is surprisingly non-judgemental in her treatment of the language. In fact she seems to find the tension between the two languages much less problematic than many male Welsh writers writing in English such as Gwyn Thomas, Dylan Thomas and R.S. Thomas.[41] This is, in part, due to the different gendered relationship with language but owes also to Vaughan's social class which excludes her from the debate and from the decision to 'choose' a language. Though she firmly identified herself as Welsh, her class means that there is no question of her speaking Welsh; it is simply not expected of her and is a matter for the lower classes. She also uses language to maintain the boundary of difference with the English, though in her recognition of her English audience she makes occasional breaches in this boundary to include them when she deems it necessary. To illustrate her use of language, the re-examination of the following extract from *The Invader* proves useful. Here, Miss Webster encounters the Jones family and the boundaries created and dismantled by language can be seen:

> 'Is there a man here who can help with my car?' Miss Webster asked, without those preliminary remarks on weather, health and condition of agriculture which the custom of Wales demands.
> 'What's on the old car then?' Mrs. Jones demanded.
> 'What's on it?' Miss Webster repeated. 'I don't understand.'
> 'You're a foreigner, are you? Maybe German now? We've heard a terrible lot about them Germans these last few years.'
> 'German! Good heavens, no! Can't you tell I'm English?'
> 'You don't seem able to understand English, whatever.'
> (p.95)

While both characters are speaking English, Vaughan makes their difference clear. The Englishwoman is firmly established as foreign. The reference to German is also very interesting. It is used to present Miss Webster as an outsider but, significantly, this novel is set very soon after the First World War and its subplot depicts a character that has returned from active service, so that the reference to German is also a subtle appeal to the English reader that they share common interests and identities as well. While the Welsh and the English are different they have also recently been united in their struggle against a different outside 'other'. The passage also relies on the linguistic differences between social classes. The comical situation seems to privilege, or normalise, the language of working-class Wales but neither of the characters in the situation are privy to this humour; rather, it is shared by the narrator and the reader, who are using or reading Standard English. The author's own class position and consequent use of language problematise her attempt to award authority to the language used by her working-class characters. Language and its relationship with social class create a boundary between her and the characters she depicts. While Vaughan endeavours to negotiate and renegotiate the ideal Welsh identity, linguistically, at least, it is ultimately one that she cannot fully share.

NOTES

1   All Vaughan's novels were reviewed in newspapers from many parts of the world. As a brief example, *The Battle to the Weak* (1925) was reviewed in *The Age*, (Melbourne, Australia) April 4th 1925, *Chicago Evening Post*, June 4th 1926; *Her Father's House* (1930) was reviewed in the *Daily News*, (Colombo, Sri Lanka) June 21st 1930, *Daily Malta Chronicle*, June 6th 1930, *Tasmanian Mail*, (Hobart) July 16th 1930, *Cape Times*, (Cape Town) August 1st 1930, *Standard*, (Buenos Aires) August 26th 1930; *The Soldier and the Gentlewoman* (1932) was reviewed in *Irish Times*, (Dublin) May 14th 1932, *Daily Mail and Empire*, (Toronto, Canada) June 18th

1932, *Rhodesia Herald*, (Salisbury), July 8th 1932, *New Zealand Herald*, (Auckland) July 2nd 1932; *The Curtain Rises* (1935) was reviewed in *Egyptian Gazette*, (Alexandria) July 18th 1935, *Madras Mail* August 24th 1935.

2   Benjamin Heath Malkin, *The Scenery, Antiquities and Biography of South Wales*, (1804), quoted by Roy Palmer in *The Folklore of Radnorshire* (Herefordshire, Logaston Press, 2001), p.48.

3   See Llywelyn Hooson-Owen, *The History of the Welsh Language in Radnorshire since 1536*, (MA thesis, University of Liverpool, 1954), p.195. All further references are to this edition. As Hooson-Owen states 'the period of most rapid decay of the language was that from 1750-1820' after which it was almost completely eradicated from the eastern and central parts of the county.

4   See W.H. Howse, *Radnorshire* (Hereford: E. J. Thurstone, 1949) p.305. All further references are to this edition. Although Vaughan lived in Builth Wells, which is in Breconshire, she seems to have felt a great kinship with the neighbouring county of Radnorshire.

5   Hilda Vaughan, 'A Country Childhood', *The Radnorshire Society Transactions*, 1982 9-18 (15).

6   Monica Heller (ed.), *Codeswitching: Anthropological and Sociolinguistic Perspectives* (Berlin: Mouton de Gruyter, 1988), p.1.

7   Glyn Jones, *The Dragon Has Two Tongues: Essays on Anglo-Welsh Writers and Writing* (London: J.M. Dent and Sons Ltd., 1968), p.44.

8   Homi K. Bhabha, *The Location of Culture* (London: Routledge, 1994), p.148. All further references are to this edition.

9   Hilda Vaughan, *The Battle to the Weak* (New York and London: Harper Brothers, 1925), p.14. All further references are to this edition and are given parenthetically in the article.

10 Hilda Vaughan, *The Candle and the Light* (London: Macmillan & CO., 1954), p.76. All further references are to this edition and are given parenthetically in the article.

11 Hilda Vaughan, *The Invader* (London: William Heinemann, Ltd., 1928), p.16. All further references are to this edition and are given parenthetically in the article.

12 Gwenllian in *The Soldier and the Gentlewoman* is another character who baffles others as she transcends the categories of identity. Dick listens to an exchange between his wife and the lodge-keeper: 'Gwenllian could speak Welsh as fluently as he.

Her voice became more resonant and flexible when she spoke the language of her race. Dick had often been amused to hear her in dramatic conversation with the people' (p.91). His amusement is soon soured as 'Silent and constrained, he listened to her in astonishment, using their dialect, rolling her Rs, raising her voice at the end of every phrase' (p.111). Dick has hitherto been accustomed to hearing Gwenllian speak in the Standard English that her class demands. Gwenllian's ability to adapt her identity is shocking to him. [Hilda Vaughan, *The Soldier and the Gentlewoman* (London: Gollancz, 1932).]

13   Hilda Vaughan, *Her Father's House* (London: William Heinemann, 1930), p.7. All further references are to this edition and are given parenthetically in the article.

14   Hilda Vaughan, *Iron and Gold* (1948; Dinas Powys: Honno, 2002), p.94. All further references are to this edition and are given parenthetically in the article

15   Bill Ashcroft, 'Is that the Congo? Language as Metonymy in the Post-Colonial Text', in *World Literature in English*, 29/2 (1989), 3-10 (5).

16   Howse, *Radnorshire*, p.275.

17   Hilda Vaughan, *Harvest Home* (London: Victor Gollancz, 1936), p.97. All further references are to this edition and are given parenthetically in the article.

18   Howse also comments that Radnorshire dialect 'is shared to a greater or less extent by certain other counties – Herefordshire, Shropshire, Cheshire, and Worcestershire for instance, – and derives largely from the old Kingdom of Mercia. [See W.H. Howse, 'The Speech of Radnorshire, *The Radnorshire Society Transactions* 22 (1952) 58-63 (58).]

19   Roy Palmer, *The Folklore of Radnorshire* (Herefordshire, Logaston Press, 2001), p.55.

20   W.H. Howse, *Radnor Old and New* (Kington: Mid-Border Books, 1989), p.44. All further references are to this edition.

21   Hilda Vaughan, *A Thing of Nought*, in *A View Across the Valley: Short Stories by Women From Wales c.1850-1950*, ed. Jane Aaron (1934; Dinas Powys: Honno, 1999).

22   Anon. quoted by Hooson-Owen, *History of the Welsh Language in Radnorshire*, p.14.

23   Ngugi wa Thiong'o, *Writers in Politics: Essays* (London: Heinemann, 1981), pp.59-60.

24   An 1892 edition of *Cymru* quoted in Hooson-Owen, *History of the Welsh language in Radnorshire*, pp.45-6.

25 Hilda Vaughan, *The Curtain Rises,* (New York: Charles Scribner's Sons, 1935), p.278. All further references are to this edition and are given parenthetically in the article.

26 Dr J Gwenogvryn Evans in *Western Mail*, September 25th, 1926.

27 Bill Ashcroft, Gareth Griffiths and Helen Tiffin, *The Empire Writes Back: Theory and Practice in Post-colonial Literatures* (London: Routledge, 2002), p.65.

28 Elizabeth Gordon and Mark Williams, 'Raids on the Articulate: Code-Switching, Style-Shifting and Post-Colonial Writing', *Journal of Commonwealth Literature*, 33, no. 2 (1998), pp.75-96. All further references are to this edition.

29 See Gordon and Williams, *Journal of Commonwealth Literature*, pp.75-96.

30 Vaughan did not speak Welsh herself and notes that were written for *Here Are Lovers* contain a glossary sent to her from a friend. The glossary contains a mixture of Radnorshire dialect, Welsh and agricultural terms with translations of 'A tidy step', 'Rammas' (which she uses in *Harvest Home*), 'Tŷ un nos', 'Cawl', 'Diawl' and 'Druan fach i' 'and a few such tags of Welsh all possible especially in the mouths of elders.' There is also a note that tells Vaughan that the Mari Lwyd was 'quite alive at your date'. The extensive glossary is many pages long and suggests that Vaughan received copious advice in this area from others. [Reproduced by kind permission of Mr Roger Morgan.] Many misspelled or misused Welsh words can be found in the texts. For example, while the word 'duwch' is used correctly in *The Battle to the Weak* and *The Invader* it is repeatedly spelled 'ddwch' in a later novel, *Iron and Gold*. In *Harvest Home* the name 'Gwydion' is spelled 'Gwyddion' in her mistaken retelling of the tale of the sorcerer in *The Mabinogion*. Of course these mistakes may not be Vaughan's; it is equally possible that these errors in Welsh language words were due to the English typesetters and publishers who printed her novels. Wherever the blame may lie, its effect is to undermine the language's value.

31 *World Today*, March 1925.

32 Kirsti Bohata, *Postcolonialism Revisited* (Cardiff: University of Wales Press, 2004), p.115.

33 Letter from W. Robertson Nicoll at *The British Weekly*, dated February 1st, 1921. Reproduced by kind permission of Mr Roger Morgan.

34 Hilda Vaughan, speech entitled 'Why authors are cads', given at the Sunday Times Book Exhibition at Grosvenor House, London on 20th November, 1934. The speech is unpublished and is part of Vaughan's personal papers reproduced by kind permission of Mr Roger Morgan.

35 *Cambrian Leader*, March 14th, 1925.

36 In fact the supremacy of English is challenged in *The Battle to the Weak* as well as Rhys' uncle suggests that Esther should be taught Welsh as 'she would soon pick it up' (68). Here, the suggestion is that the Anglicised Radnorshire inhabitants could learn or re-learn Welsh thus reversing the process of anglicisation.

37 Bhabha, *The Location of Culture*, p.91.

38 This 'mimicry' of the working-class Welsh can be seen in other writing by Welsh female authors in English. For example in *The Rebecca Rioter* Amy Dillwyn narrates the novel using the Gower dialect of her working-class protagonist who is also often imagined to be speaking in Welsh. See Amy Dillwyn, *The Rebecca Rioter: A Story of Killay Life* (1880; Dinas Powys: Honno, 2004).

39 Ashcroft, Griffiths and Tiffin, *The Empire Writes Back*, pp.74-5.

40 This is not a new problem, of course. It also arises in the work of Charles Dickens and Elizabeth Gaskell but in Vaughan's case the added factor of the postcolonial paradigm further heightens the tension.

41 Of course their perspectives on language are all quite different but they have all struggled with the conflict between the two languages of Wales in one way or another.

Tales of the *Boneddigion*:

Nigel Heseltine's Gentry Context

Rob Gossedge
Cardiff University

Until recently Nigel Heseltine seemed to be one of the forgotten literary voices of Wales. His short surreal satires of
gentrified life have attracted little critical attention while
his name warranted little more than a mention in most surveys of English-language Welsh literature of the twentieth
century.[1] Yet in the 2006 volume of *Welsh Writing in English* Rhian Davies and M. Wynn Thomas both published
essays which aimed to recuperate Heseltine's reputation.[2]
Davies's biographical study was the result of many years'
research into the writer's life and that of his more famous
father, the composer Philip Heseltine, better known by his
pseudonym, Peter Warlock. Thomas's essay, on the other
hand, sought to locate Heseltine's work – particularly his
unpublished manuscript, 'Tales of the Landless Gentry'
(written around 1947) – within the context of Wales's rich
tradition of border writing, a corpus which includes works
by Geraint Goodwin, Margiad Evans, Raymond Williams
and Emyr Humphreys. This present essay follows on from
these two studies but seeks to situate Heseltine's published
fiction – especially his *Tales of the Squirearchy* (1947) –
within the context of the fiction of and about the Welsh
gentry, or *boneddigion*.

Heseltine (1916-1995) was himself a member of the
Welsh squirearchy – at least until he sold the family estate
in 1947. Estranged from his father and unsure of the identity of his mother, Heseltine was raised by his paternal
grandparents at the family seat of Cefn Bryntalch in Montgomeryshire, where he was inculcated into a class which
was already of diminishing importance in rural Welsh life.
Like many of the Anglicised gentry he was sent to school in
England and described his time at Shrewsbury Public

School as a 'tribal education'.[3] Refusing to be fitted into a respectable career as a member of the Welsh gentry, Heseltine became a writer, an intrepid traveller and, in Ireland where he lived through most of the Second World War, a theatrical producer.[4] His first book was an account of his journeys through Albania (1938) and this was followed by poems, short stories, translations, several published and unpublished novels and a steady flow of travel writing, as well as many articles and critical reviews. By the early 1940s Heseltine's reputation had become established enough for his work to be included in several London-published anthologies of short stories and verse.[5] During the mid-1930s he became a confidant of Keidrych Rhys, the founder and editor of the progressive journal, *Wales*. In addition to being one of the journal's most frequent contributors, Heseltine briefly became its editor in 1939. His finest published work is his *Tales of the Squirearchy* (1946), a unique, and humorous account of the *boneddigion* in their final, exhausted years.

The political and social dominance of the Welsh squirearchy had been broken long before Heseltine was born. After three centuries occupying the role of parish sovereigns, the gentry had been politically disenfranchised in the latter half of the nineteenth century by the rise of a radical Liberalism that was, in Wales, closely aligned to Nonconformism. Their suzerainty had been gradually eroded by a succession of General Elections beginning in 1868, as well as the Reform acts of 1867 and 1884, which extended male suffrage to the working classes of the counties, and by the County Council act of 1888, after which local administrative power passed from the justices of the peace, who were almost all of the landowning class, to elected councils.[6] In the following century the gentry relinquished their hold on the ownership of land. First to go were the big aristocratic estates, such as those owned by the Marquis of Bute and the Duke of Beaufort; then followed the sales of many smaller landholdings, many of which were no more than 200 acres.[7] Between the passing of the County Council Act and the disestablishment of the Welsh Anglican Church in 1920 there occurred the largest transfer of property since the Dissolution of the Monasteries (the event which consolidated the political and economic ascendency of the gentry in sixteenth-century Wales).[8] After the Second World War (when Heseltine inherited and sold his own estate) the gentry, as Kenneth O. Morgan has stated, 'subsided as if they had never been.'[9]

The *boneddigion*, like their Anglican Church, were not only disenfranchised, they were, as Gwyn A. Williams defined it, internally exiled from modern Wales.[10] The squirearchy was expelled from the country's history as it was rewritten by their former tenants from the Nonconformist heartlands, educated and empowered by the schools and university colleges which had been established in the last decades of the nineteenth century. The Welsh gentry also largely absent in the extraordinary burgeoning of Welsh writing produced in both languages in the twentieth century. The literary scene Heseltine entered in the 1930s was dominated by prose writers such as B.L. Coombes, Jack Jones, Lewis Jones, Richard Llewellyn and, in Cymraeg, Kate Roberts, whose cultural landscapes were industrial and working class. As Katie Gramich has noted, such was the influence of these writers that authors emerging from the gentry and bourgeoisie (such as Hilda Vaughan and Margiad Evans) were often compelled to write from a working-class viewpoint.[11] In contrast, works that did focus on the gentry, including Joseph Keating's *Son of Judith* (1900) and Rhys Davies's 'The Chosen One' (1967), were written outside of the squirearchy – Keating had worked as a collier; Davies was the son of a grocer.[12] Only rarely did writers from the gentry actually write about their own class: examples include Eiluned Lewis's bestseller *Dew on the Grass* (1934) and Herbert M. Vaughan's less well-known *The South Wales Squires* (1926).[13] But Lewis's and Vaughan's works were essentially nostalgic idylls of the squirearchy – *Dew on the Grass* is a semi-autobiographical account of Montgomeryshire gentrified life, written from a child's point of view; *The South Wales Squires* is a memoir of the gentry and estates Vaughan had known in his youth. Perceiving his position to be an isolated one, Vaughan stated that his work was written 'solely from the point of view of the Welsh landlord, that cock-shy of all and sundry.'[14]

Heseltine's satiric tales are different. Heseltine knew little of industrial Wales and, unlike Hilda Vaughan, his only attempts at lower-class ventriloquism were essentially parodic and made at the expense of servants and gamekeepers. And while his *Tales of the Squirearchy* were written, like *Dew on the Grass* and *The South Wales Squires*, from within the gentry, rarely had a writer of the gentry been so vitriolic in the condemnation of his peers. Brutal, greedy and decrepit, Heseltine's *boneddigion* are depicted in a style possessed of the brutal humour of Caradoc Evans, along with the surrealism of the young Dylan Thomas, with whom Heseltine had a difficult and competitive relationship. As satires they are remarkably bitter; as tales of black humour they are extremely dark.

'No money and thirty acres of land': Heseltine's portrait of the squirearchy

By 1946, when the *Tales* appeared in print, Heseltine had been living in Ireland for several years. Initially joining the RAF, he had apparently broken his pelvis bone when visiting Rhys's home in west Wales, and Rhian Davies has suggested that he may even have deserted.[15] Heseltine's father had died in 1930, his grandmother in 1943; as a result of the financial untenability of maintaining the estate (especially as Heseltine was no longer living in Wales) his solicitor advised him to sell Cefn Bryntalch.[16] His *Tales of the Squirearchy* reflect the chronicle of social decline and economic impoverishment that is the narrative of the *boneddigion* in the twentieth century:

> Mr Thwaite has no money and thirty acres of land; he had a stable without horses, and an estate-carpenter's shop without a carpenter, a fortune-estate map without an estate, a cupboard full of guns with which he shot over his

former estate by the charity of the farmers, and they call him Sir.[17]

But there is no sympathy for the squirearchy in Heseltine's *Tales*; they are, rather, a bloody celebration of the *boneddigion*'s demise. 'Cam-Vaughan's Shoot', the first tale in the collection, is typical of the book. It is an account of a shooting party which descends into violence when Owen, the gamekeeper, leads a revolt against his employer and his fellow squires:

> When the beaters appeared on the edge of the wood, guns and beaters stood still; they stood still and regarded one another [...] Then the General raised his gun and fired, there was nothing else to do. Quickly the loaders ran into the wood and joined the beaters; some of these produced guns from down their trousers. [...] There could be but one result. The beaters came out and beat the wounded till they died.[18]

The victorious tenants, led by Owen, then return to Sir Cam-Vaughan's mansion, which they claim as their own.

Nineteenth-century Montgomeryshire had been the scene for several Chartist and Rebecca manifestations of social agitation. Late in the century workers had risen in Newtown's and Welshpool's flannel mills – one of the chief sources of the county's prosperity in the Victorian period – and the agitation was only ended when the local yeomanry were ordered in.[19] Perhaps Heseltine was recalling this social disturbance when writing 'Cam-Vaughan's Shoot' – the money of his ancestors had, after all, been made in the woollen-flannel industry and his step-grandfather, as well as many other members of the family, had been officers in the county's militia.[20]

And yet 'Cam-Vaughan's Shoot', like all the stories in *Tales of the Squirearchy*, refuses a directly political interpretation of the gentry's demise in favour of farce and Heseltine's pitch-black humour. For instance, the tenantry celebrate their victory over the gentry by singing, not some revolutionary anthem, but the child's song 'Swspan fach' [sic]. Heseltine does not realise the decay of the squirearchy as the result of social or economic change: violence in these stories is casual and does not need to be justified – at least in the perpetrators' minds – by allegiance to political doctrine. Indeed, the brutality of the tenantry is emphasised throughout the stories. The gentry, however, possess no greater moral scruples than the tenants they affect to despise for their barbarity.

The squirearchy's indifference to violent destruction is demonstrated in another story concerned with the gentry's field sports, 'Flaming Tortoises', which was published in the same year as *Tales*, but not collected in that volume. Again, the county's sporting squires assemble in anticipation of a good day's hunting, dressed 'in pinks and tweeds and honourable hats' while a host of 'riff-raff' congregate in order to jeer.[21] Like 'Cam-Vaughan's Shoot' the day descends into anarchy when a renegade member of the county's gentry, Thwaite, arrives mounted on a camel which he has borrowed from a visiting circus. The camel antagonises the other steeds, as well as their riders, causing them to wreak havoc upon the land: limousines are destroyed, valuable horses are lost and an entire farm is demolished. Yet the day is not ruined by such devastation. Indeed, the fox-hunters drive away remarking on a 'good day's sport'.[22]

The decline of the Welsh gentry, Heseltine's tales imply, is brought about not by political emancipation or dialectical change but by their moral dissolution. Although Heseltine did not possess the moralism of such great satirists as Swift or, indeed, Caradoc Evans, he nonetheless locates the cause of the *boneddigion*'s demise in their greed, hypocrisy and social irresponsibility. Often their destruction appears as the product of personal folly – a not inconsiderable factor in the death of the historical gentry. The fortunes of Cefn Bryntalch declined because of the megalomaniac building project of Heseltine's great-grandfather; while his own father bequeathed his estate to a friend, thus disinheriting his son – a substantial sum was required to extricate the estate from the will.[23] Other members of the family,

Heseltine later claimed, exhausted their wealth on race-horses which never won.[24]

Another of the *Tales* which presents a resolutely apolitical account of the gentry's demise is 'Gothic Halls', a story more recently anthologised in John Davies's *The Green Bridge* (1988).[25] Here, the squires of Cariad, led once again by Cam-Vaughan, attempt to get one of their number, John Belial, elected:

> With a bushel of true-blue-tory-ribbon in his button-hole, Cam-Vaughan, rich and unambitious [...] caught up the threads of discourse, the backbone of argument! 'Shall the county be given over to reform?' And from the potted princelings around came shouts of 'No!'
> 'Reform is for hot-heads'.[26]

The election quickly descends into farce: the 'squireens' attack the rival socialists with boxspanners and try to manipulate the result as best they can, for this is a place 'which the Lord forgets on election-day.[27] Yet the efforts of the gentry are to no avail and the socialist John Evans wins the seat. However, this is not so much a political victory as an instance of political travesty – for the women who count the votes accidentally burn the slips and make paper darts from the last of them. Arbitrarily they decide to give the result to Evans. Drunk and excited, the crowd then burn down the town hall.[28]

The second half of the story involves the sale of Belial's estate, items of which include:

> Genuine sideboards from the Paris exhibition, 1859, organ from Crystal Palace, 1868, 5-ton chandeliers from dismantled Chateau du Bonsoir, France: real marble staircase from dismantled Palazzo della Figa, Italy: coats-of-arms of principal extinct families of Wales, selection of useful armour.[29]

There is little that is ancestral about Belial's home. Built 'A.D. 1850', it is furnished with materials scavenged from across Europe, its 'useful armour' purchased in Liverpool.

Nothing is Welsh, except for the heraldic devices, which do not belong to the Belial family anyway. Heseltine presents a portrait of the Welsh squirearchy in all their assumed pomp and fraudulence. Heseltine's own family were only recent members of the *boneddigion*, their money made in industry, their ancestors sheep farmers from Mochdre.[30]

'Aliens in birth, in religion, in politics and in language' is the traditional view of the gentry in Wales as claimed by the Welsh-language writers.[31] Heseltine's sketches of the squirearchy fully conform to this opinion. In birth, the squires hold themselves as not only a class above, but a nation apart from their tenants. They frequently display contempt for Nonconformism, believe that the Welsh language is all 'rot' and their political views are summed up in Cam-Vaughan's title as 'descendent of Welsh kings and chairman of the English Conservative Association in Wales'.[32] Likewise, the myth of the gentry's benevolent paternalism is contrasted by Heseltine's portrait of them as unfailingly mercenary and mean. In 'The Life and the Burial', Cam-Vaughan, while attending a funeral, works out the potential profit on a prospective loan on the back of a prayer book; in 'Rich Relations' an affluent mother refuses to give her impoverished son (a portrait of Peter Warlock and his mother) more than his train fare back to London; and in 'Gothic Halls' Belial is forced to make an insincere appeal to his fellow squires in order to sell his property: one pays half a crown for a 20-foot sideboard, another buys a chandelier. There are no other bids.

In the remaining stories, Heseltine expands on the other failings of the *boneddigion*, satirising their prejudices and belief in their superiority through juxtaposing their respectable appearance with their often criminal behaviour. In 'The Milk of Human Kindness' the squirearchy manipulate their position as Justices of the Peace to effect a desirable verdict against the local nonconformist preacher. When their methods result in a chapel-going farmer's refusal to lend Cam-Vaughan a prize ram, the squirearchy, in what is a typical pattern in the *Tales*, plot to ransack the farmer's house. In 'Lords A-Leaping', the gentry also respond badly when one of their employees decides to race one of his horses against the squires' own. When the employee's horse wins ('not by accident, but by deliberate ill-will and ingratitude'), he is promptly sacked.[33]

Economic decay is matched by physical decrepitude in several of the stories. There is the old woman in 'The Word Burning' who, nearing death, decides to burn all her possessions – images of the Virgin Mary, Jesus Christ, the Bible, 'some of the hundreds of bunches of letters, some of the ten thousand photographs, the bills, the dead visiting-cards'.[34] Her servant even thrusts her own hands into the fire. Rhys Davies's 'The Chosen One' (1967) tells a similar tale, if less surreally. Then there is Elizabeth Cramp-Sturgeon in 'Eve of Something will be done in a Week'. She, too, is old but remains sexually lascivious. She spends her time penning a lusty novel of wicked Welsh squires pursuing local peasant girls. The novel is a displacement of her own sexual lusts, as she can no longer command her manservant, Parks, to sleep with her. Her sexual frustrations leave her, at the end of the story, in a state of hysteria:

> Then Elizabeth Cramp-Sturgeon began to run through the sounding halls of her house, and she ran until the evening she fell from exhaustion and lay sobbing and sweating on the boards of the sounding halls of her house.[35]

The sexual activities of the squirearchy are a constant feature of the *Tales*' narratives. Thwaite, the most common protagonist in the *Tales*, is continually driven by his sexual amourettes, among them Miss Menzies, with whom he flirts while his father is dying, and the 'pretty wife' of a cousin, whom he lusts for during his father's funeral.[36] There are also the gentrified family in 'Boring Story' who, while seemingly respectable, are slowly broken up by their various extramarital affairs and elopements with unsuitable men. The daughter of the family is initially content playing hockey and attending county dances; but then she meets, and eventually elopes with, the distinctly middle-class

Charles France, 'the heir to Bragg's Hotel'.[37] Soon after, the
mother absconds with Albert, the footman. Only Colonel
Blinding is left, and he ends up killing his mother with a
hatchet and is sent to a lunatic asylum.[38]

'And they were left in darkness':
the context of Heseltine's *Tales of the Squirearchy*

Heseltine's portrait of the raucous, drunken, lecherous and
otherwise thoroughly dissolute squirearchy was not
unknown in Wales – at least not in Welsh-language literature – though rarely were they characterised quite so vio-
lently. Such attacks were familiar in the anti-landlord propaganda of the nineteenth century: in the writings of
Samuel Roberts, Thomas Gee and T.J. Hughes, in newspapers like *Baner ac Amserau Cymru* ('The Banner and
Times of Wales') and *Y Genedl Gymreig* ('The Welsh
Nation').[39] The latter, for instance, published a series of
articles in 1893 which attacked the *boneddigion*, which
were included in the minutes to the *Royal Commission on
Land in Wales* (1893-6):

> Besides being useless and immoral, spending money on
> horses and harlots, they are merciless tyrants. They cruel-
> ly oppress those who work hard to keep them. This dou-
> bles and trebles their sin.

> Carousal and pleasure are the chief items, and the money
> of Wales is spent in foreign countries upon every excess
> and ungodliness. The lords impoverish the land, and carry
> our wealth to other countries.

> See this lordling in the midst of racehorses, look at the
> other swaggering in the gaudy rooms of the West of Lon-
> don, see the third amidst the harlots of Paris, and the
> fourth playing away his wealth in the vile dens of Monte
> Carlo.[40]

While different in tone, these are the same attributes with
which Heseltine characterises the squirearchy in his *Tales*.
Attacks on the gentry were not just limited to Nonconformist journalism, however. Gwyneth Vaughan's *Plant y*

Gorthrwm (1908), for example, described the effects of a village following the great election of 1868, which broke the power of the Tory landlords.[41] Vaughan's novel was one of several to memorialise the 'Martyrs of '68': those tenants who had refused to follow their landlords' instructions and instead voted for the Liberals. In vengeance hundreds of these disobedient tenants were evicted.

Despite the similarity in the Welsh-language attacks on the gentry and Heseltine's portraits of a dissolute, alien squirearchy, the *Tales* do not represent the mere transposition of the opinions of Thomas Gee, T.J. Hughes, Samuel Roberts and Gwyneth Vaughan into English-language literature. Unlike these writers, Heseltine did not have the alternative social model of the *gwerin* as a support for his vilification of the existing squirearchy. Rather, Heseltine's satires are best understood in relation to the literary representations of the squirearchy in English-language writing at this time. Unlike Welsh-language writing, the English-language tradition was much less severe on the gentry. Historically, this was the case because it was the squirearchy, along with the Anglican class and a small number of urban bourgeoisie, who composed the vast majority of pre-twentieth century Welsh literary texts in English.[42] And so, in the nineteenth century the squire-tenant feudal system was often characterised as a benevolent social model of paternalistic landlords and their contented tenants.[43] The early English-language historiography was similarly biased in favour of the *boneddigion*. The earliest antiquarian travel books were usually written by members of the Welsh squirearchy, such as Thomas Pennant and Henry Penruddock Wyndham.[44] This was no less true in the early twentieth century: Jonathan Williams's *A General History of the County of Radnor* (1905), for example, is essentially a history of the county's gentrified families, replete with illustrations of county estates, public men and heraldic devices.[45] The work, suitably, is dedicated to the Lord Lieutenant of Radnor, as well as being patronised by the Crown.

During the first half of the twentieth century, English-

language literature, written predominantly in the industrial south, remained unconcerned with the land question, as
the squire here occupied a much smaller social role than in
the rural, Welsh-speaking areas. There were exceptions: the
West-Walian romances of Allen Raine, written with a consciously panoramic view of Welsh village society, which
included the gentry, and *Son of Judith* (1900) by Joseph
Keating, Wales's first English-language working-class novelist, which focused on the decline of the squirearchy in the
nineteenth century. Nonetheless, the gentry novel was rare
in English-language writing and when they did appear after
the First World War they continued to portray the
squirearchy as members of a cohesive society.

One example is Eiluned Lewis's *Dew on the Grass*, published twelve years before the *Tales*. It is set in Pengarth, a
family estate similar to Lewis's own Montgomeryshire
manor (not far from Cefn Bryntalch). It is a place of
sycamores, tree houses, rickety outbuildings perfect for
playing hide and seek, where the 'railway company oblig-
ingly allowed the midday train to stop at Pengarth Halt
whenever the children's father wished to take his family to
the sea.'[46] Many of the adventures Lucy, the novel's gentrified protagonist, undertakes involve encounters with assort-
ed members of the lower-classes, none of which threaten her
dominant position within this rural idyll. There is Ned
Lovell, 'a half-gipsy' who teaches Lucy how to catch fish and
is full of folksy wisdom: 'No use whatever in book-larnin' he
tells Lucy, 'No one ever learnt nothing from old books. You
listen to what the river says, my little dear, and watch Ned
catch a trout for supper.'[47] Similarly, Lucy meets a local
farmer and asks him whether he gets bored working the
land. He replies, 'Well now, I dunno [...] I dare say you get
tired of your book-learning now and then'. 'Dreadfully', says
Lucy. 'Especially French verbs.'[48] She also meets a poacher
who, after Lucy spills her blackberries, gives her a pocket
handkerchief of mushrooms.

The only time an element of social threat appears in the
novel is when Lucy encounters a tramp from Cardiff, a rep-

resentative of the industrial south which forms an 'unknown country' for the Mid-Walian gentry.[49] This tramp is less respectful than the lower classes of Montgomeryshire – refusing, for instance, to address the heroine as 'Miss Lucy' – and brings with him the menaces of poverty, unemployment and social disaffection. On arriving at the Rectory, he asks Lucy's friend, David, for a pair of boots and some food; but David refuses, telling the southerner not to approach the house as 'Mary Ellen's busy and Aunt Hetty's scared of tramps'. The tramp responds angrily, saying that he is 'an honest man', that David has no right to call him names and blames 'the rotten country' and the 'Unions' for his misfortunes. Lucy, however, pacifies the man, inviting him to sit and procuring bread and treacle for him – her gentrified manner being enough to quell social threat. 'I hate tramps; they smell horrid', says David as the man from the south leaves. 'Poor, poor man' says Lucy.[50] Lewis's gentrified novel, while acknowledging the social divide between the land-working and 'book-larnin' classes, focalises them through the naive, nostalgic view of the precocious Lucy. Far from offering a critique of the class system, this nostalgia allows the novel to assert the 'naturalness' of such differences. Here in Pengarth gentry and tenant live peacefully – or would do if only they were left alone by the industrial, dangerous south.

Another writer who came from and set his work among the *boneddigion* was Herbert M. Vaughan. In his best-known work, the informal history of *The South Wales Squires* (1926), he mounted a spirited (and often inadvertently comic) defence of his class, mingled with resentment at their dispossession. An obituary for the gentry, Vaughan's *South Wales Squires* rails against the 'social tyranny' that was inflicted upon his 'little understood but much maligned' class.[51] The book fully conforms to the 'carefully cultivated genre of panic, persecution, and paranoia' that characterised the writings of so many aristocratic and gentrified authors, poets, and politicians in England in the late nineteenth and early twentieth centuries.[52] He also included a 190-page compilation of anecdotes concerning the eccentric figures of the gentry Vaughan knew as a young man. They include Ford Hughes, who rented a squalid house in Union Street, Carmarthen, but would, like a vampire, travel at night to visit one of his country seats before returning to Carmarthen by dawn; Colonel John 'Blundy' Howell whose response to every joke was to bellow 'Haw! Haw! Very superior'; and Sir Owen Scourfield, an early train-spotter, of whom 'it is said...that during his honeymoon he got left behind at Cardiff station, forgetting poor Lady Scourfield in the excitement of inspecting the rolling stock'.[53] Ignoring the mass evictions and political manipulations which characterised the public history of the nineteenth-century squirearchy, the gentry are presented as a class of naive, though essentially good-natured, 'old squires' who were unable to resist the 'malevolent forces' of 'a certain type of Welsh Nationalist'.[54] As Byron Rogers notes in his foreword to the book's 1988 reprint, for Vaughan the gentry's only fault was that they were too poor to keep up their estates.[55]

Heseltine's *Tales of the Squirearchy* was written in opposition to such memorialisations of the Welsh squirearchy as a benevolent, patrician class. Although the louche amoral style of the *Tales* sometimes resembles the upper-class satires of Evelyn Waugh's early fiction (as well as that of the Anglo-Welsh Anthony Powell and Ronald Firbank), Heseltine never produced a Welsh *Brideshead Revisited* (1944). The *Tales* reject any similarly elegiac account of the *boneddigion*'s demise. For Heseltine, the squirearchy passed into history leaving behind only traces of their avarice, brutality and absurdity.

'O bitter benighted bloody Welshman': the influence of Caradoc Evans and Dylan Thomas

In attempting to present the myth of a benevolent, patriarchal gentry as essentially fraudulent Heseltine was greatly influenced by Caradoc Evans. Thirty years earlier Evans had similarly portrayed the ideal of the classless *gwerin* as a false myth, choosing instead to present the rural society of his youth as characterised by 'money worship [and] endemic brutality.'[56] Of course, works like *My People* (1915) and *Capel Sion* (1916) were not only more accomplished than the *Tales*, they were produced in the face of greater hostility than Heseltine ever knew and were much more important in terms of the development of Welsh literature in English. Nonetheless, Evans's anti-*gwerin* tales form a discernable archetype for Heseltine's subversion of the gentry myth.

Evans's influence is apparent throughout the *Tales* – in the casual violence and murder ('Cam-Vaughan's Shoot'), in the hypocrisy of the Church and Chapel ('Milk of Human Kindness') and in figures such as 'the wretched and deformed' Ella Williams, who is sexually used by the local men who 'take her for her idiot grin' ('Break Away if You Can', a story not collected in the *Tales*).[57] Stylistically, Evans's influence is detectable in Heseltine's stripped vocabulary, the repetition of key words and long sentences devoid of subordinate clauses – a style mirroring that of the Old Testament – and the Biblical imagery which is evident throughout the *Tales*' descriptions of Cariad:

> Here you see us live, here are no tumbling valleys or hills where the wind roars like a trumpet, but low hills, and worn hills, and choked drains in the fields where the Haran runs like the rain returns to the sea.[58]

Like their predecessors, the *Tales* use the Old Testament to invest the landscape with symbolic detail. Heseltine's 'Break Away if You Can' uses the symbol of the Biblical Haran, from where Abraham is commanded to leave in search of Canaan (Genesis 12.1-6), as a signifier of enclosure: Beth, the story's narrator, 'could leap over' this stream when she was twenty; but now, aged thirty, the Haran has become an impassable river. Abraham was instructed to leave the land of his fathers; Beth is constrained by her father who commands her to tend to the diminished estate while he drinks whisky in the local hotel bar. The landscape colludes with the patriarchal masters. Like Caradoc Evans's rural scenes, Heseltine's Cariad is constructed of conspiring, almost anthropomorphic, images of constraint and deprivation.

Heseltine's indebtedness to Evans's work is also perceptible in the comedy of the *Tales*. John Harris has listed Evans's use of comic modes as 'teasing irony, religious burlesque, violence and humour juxtaposed, black comedy of the grotesque'.[59] Heseltine uses precisely the same concoction, albeit with a heady dose of the absurd thrown in for good measure. In many ways it is Caradoc Evans's later stories – the stories being published in *Wales* and *Pilgrims in a Foreign Land* (1942), which were appearing around the time Heseltine began writing – which exert the strongest the strongest on the *Tales*.[60] For in these works, like those of Heseltine, the grotesque often collapses into the surreal. Evans's blackest humour is recalled in Heseltine's 'The Word Burning' in which the dying squiress, desiring martyrdom but still revelling in her unquestioned authority over her servants, commands her handmaid to place her hand in the fire. When her servant obeys, the Anglican squiress despises her for her submissiveness and humility.[61]

Usually the *Tales*' most overtly comic moments arrive with the appearance of Thwaite, the renegade squire. He is an ambivalent figure, partly resembling Heseltine himself in his indifference to the personal sufferings of his own class, yet he remains resolutely of the gentry. In 'Gothic Halls', for instance, Thwaite drives round the county, ostensibly drumming up support for the Tory candidate, John Belial, but in fact giving lifts to the rival Socialists.[62] Throughout the *Tales* he seems to possess the qualities of the trickster: his presence inevitably leads to some disaster or violence. He is disliked throughout the county of Cariad, whether for his class ('Constable's Ruin'), his drunken behaviour ('The Life and the Burial'), or his sexual lustfulness ('The Milk of Human Kindness'). Cariad's gentry, who despise him with more vehemence than do the tenants and the 'small bourgeoisie of Llanpumpsaint', articulate their feelings in tones distinctly reminiscent of Caradoc Evans:

> There is no need to shout the disgrace of Thwaite: he has been found lacking in the milk of human kindness. He has shown himself without the milk of human kindness by his recent behaviour. He has not behaved according to the traditions of his class, he has not acted with *esprit de corps*; he has behaved contrary to other people, he has behaved contrary to the principles on which good breeding, on which Kindness or the dealing in a magnanimous way with inferiors is based. Thwaite does not acknowledge his inferiors: and he has no reverence! He has none of the milk of human kindness possessed by the inhabitants of the county of Cariad, who conform.[63]

While Evans's stories exposed the brutality and greed of rural society masked beneath Nonconformist pronouncement, Heseltine attempted to show that same culture of violence and avarice as veiled by a sense of gentrified respectability. Evans had written of the tyranny of Nonconformism as the *Baner* and *Genedl* had written of the squirearchy; it was relatively simple for Heseltine to reverse this and employ Evans's rhetoric against the gentry once again.

Heseltine, as befitting an aggressive and subversive writer, found as much stylistic inspiration in what he disliked as in what he admired. Apart from Caradoc Evans, one of the most notable influences on Heseltine's work was Dylan Thomas. Like Heseltine, Thomas was another frequent contributor to and occasional editor of *Wales* and, as Rhian Davies has pointed out, their involvement in the journal was a source of rivalry and unpleasantness.[64] Heseltine's reviews of Thomas's work were lacklustre at best. In 1937 Heseltine criticised Thomas's *Twenty-Five Poems* as lacking poetic maturity. Later that year he claimed that David Jones's *In Parenthesis* (1937) was 'more likely to make our national peculiarities international than the mouthings of D.T.' – a comment which impelled Keidrych Rhys, as editor, to insert 'Oh dear me!' in brackets.[66]

It also seems likely that Thomas makes a brief, unflattering appearance in *Tales of the Squirearchy*, in the form of the anonymous poet with 'a pot-belly', 'full o' beer', who is searching for his 'twenty-sixth poem'.[67] The descriptions of 'The Poet' in 'Constable's Ruin' bear distinct similarity to Thomas's self-portraits. Compare, for instance, Heseltine's 'In the poet's head is his tongue like a flame in a tube of brass', with Thomas's declaration of himself as 'the brassy orator' with 'the foxy tongue'.[68] At one point 'The Poet' starts to tell a story, beginning 'when I was sixteen...' which is interrupted by the irascible Thwaite: 'You're always sixteen [...] Prodigy of sixteen published poems [...] Always sixteen, always new'.[69] Indeed, aged sixteen, Thomas had begun his career as a writer, starting as a junior reporter on the *South Wales Daily Post*. He also began to keep the 'Notebooks' in this year, which contained the majority of the poems he would publish in his lifetime.[70] Thwaite, in his rant against the poet from the South, continues:

> 'This is the man', said Thwaite, 'acclaimed in U.S.A. and abuses his own kind. Welsh poet of sixteen staggers with Cymric thunderbolts. He staggers, we applaud. O bitter benighted bloody Welshman! Your own kind doesn't know you.'[71]

Yet if this is a portrait of Thomas, Heseltine's satire seems a little misplaced as several of Heseltine's *Tales* bear similarity to Thomas's early 'Jarvis' stories. One story in particular, 'Skirt in Long Strips', seems to be a direct rewriting of Thomas's 'The Tree', included in his 1939 collection, *The Map of Love*.[72] As Stephen Knight has pointed out, several of Thomas's early modernist stories 'read like a surreal version of Caradoc Evans's rural darkness' – which could also serve as a description of Heseltine's *Tales*.[73]

With such similarities and indebtedness, the obvious question is why did Heseltine create such an unpleasant portrait of Thomas? Professional rivalry and personal jealousy certainly may have played a part, as Rhian Davies has noted, but it is worth considering that Heseltine's work resembles Thomas's surreal 'Jarvis' stories, rather than the later tales of childhood and 'Welsh whimsy', which were of great attraction to London publishers.[74] Perhaps the aggressively nationalist (at times) Heseltine perceived in Thomas's transition from modernist writer to author of the English-friendly *Portrait of the Artist as a Young Dog* a certain 'selling-out' of his Welshness. Certainly he has the drunken Thwaite say to 'The Poet': 'you make your living out of being Welsh.' But, as 'The Poet' says to Thwaite, '[y]ou don't make your living at all'.[75]

'A Very Un-British Book': Heseltine's position in twentieth-century Welsh fiction

By the time of the publication of *Tales of the Squirearchy* Heseltine appears to have been set to become a major literary figure in post-war Wales. In addition to the *Tales*, he had published two volumes of verse (1938, 1941), a series of translations of Dafydd ap Gwilym's poetry (1944), several pieces of travel writing and had contributed to some of the most prestigious literary journals of the day. During this time he also wrote at least two plays, made a translation of Georg Buchner's *Wozzek*, completed an unpublished novel – which again focused on the gentry's decay – and finished a sequel to the *Tales*, called 'Tales of the Landless Gentry'.[76] Yet Heseltine was unable to fulfil his early promise, despite continuing to publish throughout the next forty years, chiefly in the form of travel writing – though a novel, *The Mysterious Pregnancy*, was published in 1953 and his memoir, *Capriol for Mother*, appeared in 1992.

There is little doubt that English-language Welsh literature lost an important literary voice when Heseltine abandoned Wales in favour of the Irish theatre and, from the 1950s, 'a successful career in remote places' – a career which allowed Heseltine to indulge his enormous appetite for travel and exploration.[77] Yet, even without the temptations of the exotic and perilous, the fact that he did not remain a 'Welsh writer' is the natural conclusion to a literary career which was concerned with the decline, disestablishment and whole-sale eradication of an entire social class. By the time he began writing his short stories of gentrified Welsh border life, the time of the squirearchy had already passed. He was him-self the last of a line of squires whose fortunes had been made in industry and who had set themselves up as lords of the manor in the nineteenth century.

Tony Brown, in an article on the Welsh short story, has noted how the form often articulates the experience of 'the marginalised, the isolated, the lonely'.[78] In Wales in the twentieth century, the short story has generally been patro-nised by lower- or lower-middle class writers. Whether written by men or women, in English or in Welsh, and whether reflecting rural or industrial experiences, the short story has repeatedly been used by writers who possessed neither time nor leisure enough to compose novel-length works. As a short-story writer from the squirearchy, Nigel Heseltine appears almost wholly separate from the corpus of shorter fiction produced in the last century. Yet to read Heseltine's stories is to perceive the marginality of the *boneddigion* in the last century. This sense of unromantic alienation is especially evident in 'Homecoming' (1946), one of Heseltine's final stories on the dispossessed Welsh gentry. It concerns a squire's son who, like Heseltine, has left Wales for many years. Now an old man, he returns to the county of Cariad and reflects on his country, the extinct families he knew in his youth, the ruined estates and his inheritance, which fastens him 'like a chain, pulling me back across the world':

> 'What is the future?' I thought, and thought how the future rushed on you like a river and left you suddenly old and lonely like an old stone standing unwanted in the land of your fathers.[79]

Yet Heseltine's *Tales* are not worthy of attention just because of their unusual subject matter. For, like Caradoc Evans before him, Heseltine challenged many of the roman-tic assumptions made about Wales, independent of his own preoccupations with the Welsh squirearchy. First among these is that Wales is somehow a classless nation – that ties of nationhood, religion, political faith, language and community are more important than socio-economic differences. Glyn Jones wrote in *The Dragon Has Two Tongues* (1968) of how no Welsh or Anglo-Welsh writer made the subject of the class struggle the 'personal subject of his work'.[80] But Heseltine's fiction seems to belie Jones's words. Throughout the *Tales* Heseltine realises a class war being waged between squire, tenant and bourgeois. There is no pursuit of justice in the aims of the dissolute Cam-Vaughan, the 'dark' and 'evil' Owen or the conceited, anonymous bourgeoisie of Llanpumpsaint; but the war is being fought nonetheless and with great conviction and bitterness. Like Evans's expose of the myth of the *gwerin* (itself a powerful reaction to the squire-tenant feudal model), Heseltine's political panorama of the mid-Wales rural life subverts the notion of Wales as a classless nation, in which economic struggles are 'impersonal'.

Nigel Heseltine, then, was one of the most unusual of twentieth-century Welsh writers: a member of the disappearing squirearchy, whose work celebrated their demise. His largely-forgotten *Tales of the Squirearchy* parodied both earlier and contemporary writers and continues to challenge current conceptions of the social make-up of Wales. In its extreme comedy, brutal satire and modernist style, Heseltine's work exists on the periphery of both Welsh and British fiction. As Heseltine wrote of Flann O'Brien's *At Swim-Two-Birds*, his *Tales of the Squirearchy* is 'a very sly, unkind, un-British book.'[81]

NOTES

1   As a poet Nigel Heseltine receives mention in Keith Turner, *Fishing by Obstinate Isles: Modern and Postmodern Poetry and American Readers* (Chicago: Northwestern University Press, 1998), p.26; Andrew Duncan, *Centre and Periphery in Modern British Poetry* (Liverpool: Liverpool University Press, 2005), p.304. As a writer of prose he has been referenced in Glyn Jones, *The Dragon has two Tongues: Essays on Anglo-Welsh Writers and Writing* [1968], ed. Tony Brown (Cardiff:

University of Wales Press, 2001), pp.39, 49, 128; Glyn Jones and John Rowlands, *Profiles: A Visitor's Guide to Writing in Twentieth-Century Wales* (Llandysul: Gomer, 1980), p.370; Tristan Jones, *A Steady Tale* (London: Sheridan House, 1982), p.12. More recently Stephen Knight, in *A Hundred Years of Fiction* (Cardiff: University of Wales Press, 2004), p.171, has compared Heseltine's 'brief fantastic satires', written with a 'ferocious wit and pared-down modernist style' , favourably with the large number of romance novels published in the wake of Richard Llewellyn's phenomenally successful *How Green Was My Valley* (1939). I would like to acknowledge my grateful thanks to Stephen Knight, Katie Gramich and an anonymous reader for *Welsh Writing in English* for their comments and suggestions on earlier versions of this article.

2 Rhian Davies, 'Scarred Background: Nigel Heseltine (1916-1995), A Biographical Introduction and a Bibliography', *Welsh Writing in English* 11 (2006): 68-101; M. Wynn Thomas, ' "A Grand Harlequinade": The Border Writing of Nigel Heseltine', *Welsh Writing in English* 11 (2006): 50-67.

3 Nigel Heseltine, *Capriol for Mother: A Memoir of Peter Warlock and his Family* (London: Thames, 1992), p.8.

4 Heseltine's memoir, *Capriol for Mother*, contains many details of the writer's early life in Wales; for an account of Heseltine's later life see Rhian Davies's 'Scarred Background'.

5 Davies's 'Scarred Background' contains a bibliography of Heseltine's published and unpublished writings (98-100).

6 For accounts of the squirearchy's diminution in the second half of the nineteenth century see Gwyn A. Williams, *When was Wales? A history of the Welsh* (Harmondsworth: Penguin, 1985), pp.197-218; John Davies, *A History of Wales* (Harmondsworth: Penguin, 1994), pp.430-69; Philip Jenkins, *A History of Modern Wales, 1536-1990* (London: Longman, 1992), p.289.

7 The sales of these estates were necessitated through reduced relative incomes rather than by legislation. Indeed, the 1893-4 Royal Commission into Land in Wales and Monmouthshire, though it remains an important document on the Welsh squirearchy, had done little to curtail the power of the landlords.

8 David Cannadine, *The Decline and Fall of the British Aristocracy* [1990], revised edition (London: Papermac, 1996), p.704.

9 Kenneth O. Morgan, *Rebirth of a Nation: Wales 1880-1980*, vol. 6 of *The History of Wales* (Oxford: Clarendon Press, 1981), p.187.

10 Gwyn A. Williams, *When was Wales?*, p.219.

11 Katie Gramich, 'Introduction' to Eiluned Lewis's *Dew on the Grass* [1934] (Dinas Powys: Honno, 2007), pp.7-20 (p.14).

12 Joseph Keating, *Son of Judith: A Tale of the Welsh Mining Valleys* (London: G. Allen, 1900); Rhys Davies, 'The Chosen One' [1967], in *The Green Bridge*, ed. John Davies [1988] (Bridgend: Seren, 2003), pp.133-63.

13 Herbert M. Vaughan, *The South Wales Squires* [1926] (Carmarthen: Golden Grove, 1988).

14 Vaughan, *The South Wales Squires*, p.83.

15 Davies, 'Scarred Background', 83.

16 Heseltine, *Capriol for Mother*, p.26; Davies, 'Scarred Background', 83-4.

17 Heseltine, 'Data on the Squirearchy', in *Tales of the Squirearchy* (Carmarthen: Druid Press, 1946), pp.44-53 (p.51).

18 Heseltine, 'Cam-Vaughan's Shoot', *Tales*, pp.7-11 (pp.10-11).

19 Pauline Philips, *A View of Old Montgomeryshire* (Swansea: Christopher Davies, 1977), pp.138-45.

20 Heseltine, *Capriol for Mother*, p.12.

21 Heseltine, 'Flaming Tortoises', *Wales*, Winter, 1946: 25-46 (29, 32).

22 Heseltine, 'Flaming Tortoises', p.42.

23 Heseltine, *Capriol for Mother*, pp.37, 90.

24 Heseltine, *Capriol for Mother*, pp.24.

25 Heseltine, 'Gothic Halls', in *The Green Bridge*, ed. Davies, pp.25-30.

26 Heseltine, 'Gothic Halls', *Tales*, pp.54-60 (p.54).

27 Heseltine, 'Gothic Halls', p.55.

28 Heseltine, 'Gothic Halls', p.57.

29 Heseltine, 'Gothic Halls', pp.58-9.

30 Heseltine, *Capriol for Mother*, p.5.

31 Vaughan, *The South Wales Squires*, p.193.

32 On their views of Nonconformism see 'The Milk of Human Kindness', *Tales*, pp.28-42; Cymraeg is described as 'rot' in 'The Life and the Burial', p.15; Cam-Vaughan's political views are given in 'Gothic Halls', p.53. Unlike the characters of his *Tales*, Heseltine was a Welsh-speaker, a fact made more unusual in that not only was the gentry notoriously unable to speak the language of their tenantry, but the east of Montgomeryshire was almost universally English-speaking by the twentieth century. While living in Dublin during the 1940s he produced a series of prose translations of Dafydd ap Gwilym's poetry:

Twenty-five Poems (Dublin: Cuala Press, 1944).

33 Heseltine, 'Lords A-Leaping', *Tales*, pp.82-90 (p.87).

34 Heseltine, 'The Word Burning', *Tales*, pp.76-81 (p.77).

35 Heseltine, 'The Word Burning', p.81.

36 Heseltine, 'The Life and the Burial', *Tales*, pp.12-19 (pp.12, 18-19).

37 Heseltine, 'Boring Story', *Tales*, pp.61-8 (p.66).

38 Heseltine, 'Boring Story', p.68.

39 Davies, *A History of Wales*, p.411.

40 Translations of extracts from *Y Genedl Gymreig* February-March, 1893, included in the official 'Minutes of Evidence taken before the Royal Commission on Land in Wales and Monmouthshire' (Vol. II, pp.913-4). Quoted in Vaughan, *The South Wales Squires*, pp.196-7.

41 Gwyneth Vaughan, *Plant y Gorthrwm* (Cardiff: The Educational Publishing Company, 1908).

42 See Raymond Garlick, *An Introduction to Anglo-Welsh Literature* (Cardiff: University of Wales Press, 1970) and Garlick and Roland Mathias, *Anglo-Welsh Poetry, 1480-1990* (Bridgend: Seren, 1993).

43 Stephen Knight, *A Hundred Years of Fiction*, p.9.

44 See Henry Penruddock Wyndham's *A Gentleman's Tour through Monmouthshire and Wales* (London: T. Evans, 1775) and Thomas Pennant's *A Tour in Wales* (London: H. Hughes, 1778-81). Pennant was of Flintshire gentry stock; Wyndham, though born in Wiltshire, was of Welsh ancestry. See also M. Wynn Thomas, 'Introduction', in *Welsh Writing in English*, vol. 7 of *A Guide to Welsh Literature* (Cardiff: University of Wales Press, 2003), pp.1-6.

45 Rev. Jonathan Williams, *A General History of the County of Radnor* (Brecknock: Davies and Co., 1905).

46 Lewis, *Dew on the Grass*, p.61.

47 Lewis, *Dew on the Grass*, p.52.

48 Lewis, *Dew on the Grass*, pp.94-5.

49 Lewis, *Dew on the Grass*, p.63.

50 Lewis, *Dew on the Grass*, pp.171-2.

51 Vaughan, *The South Wales Squires*, pp.218, 73.

52 Cannadine, *Decline and Fall of the British Aristocracy*, p.31.

53 Vaughan, *The South Wales Squires*, pp.113-4, 44, 100.

54 Vaugham, *The South Wales Squires*, pp.7, 192.

55 Byron Rogers, 'Foreword', *The South Wales Squires*, pp.xi-xvi (p.xii).

56   John Harris, '"Our Antagonist is our Helper": An Introduction', in Caradoc Evans, *Selected Stories* (Manchester: Carcarnet, 1993), pp.7-17 (p.9).

57   Heseltine, 'Break Away if You Can', *Penguin New Writing* 28 (July 1946): 9-19 (18).

58   Heseltine, 'Break Away if You Can', 9.

59   Harris, '"Our Antagonist in our Helper"', *Selected Stories*, p.13.

60   Caradoc Evans's 'Your Sin Will Find You Out' was published in *Wales* 8-9: 214-19, an issue edited by Heseltine. It was republished in *Pilgrims in a Foreign Land* (London: Andrew Dakers, 1942).

61   Heseltine, 'The Word Burning', p.80.

62   Heseltine, 'Gothic Halls', p.54.

63   Heseltine, 'Milk of Human Kindness', p.28.

64   *Wales* 6/7 (one issue) was jointly edited by Keidrych Rhys and Dylan Thomas. Issues 8/9 and 10 were edited by Heseltine. Rhian Davies gives a summary of the relationship between Heseltine and Dylan Thomas in 'Scarred Background', 78-80.

65   Heseltine, Review of *Twenty-Five Poems* by Dylan Thomas, *Wales* 2 (August, 1937): 74-5.

66   Heseltine, Review of *In Parenthesis* (1937) by David Jones, *Wales* 4 (March, 1938): 157.

67   Heseltine, 'Constable's Ruin', *Tales*, pp.97-111 (pp.99, 101).

68   Heseltine, 'Constable's Ruin', p.97; Dylan Thomas, 'I, in my intricate image' (1937), l. 3; 'When, like a running grave', l. 9, in *The Dylan Thomas Omnibus: 'Under Milk Wood', Poems, Stories and Broadcasts* [1995] (London: Phoenix, 2000), pp.29-32, 18-9.

69   Heseltine, 'Constable's Ruin', p.98.

70   Glyn Jones, *The Dragon has Two Tongues*, p.166.

71   Heseltine, 'Constable's Ruin', p.98.

72   Thomas, 'The Tree', *The Dylan Thomas Omnibus*, pp.139-45.

73   Knight, *A Hundred Years of Fiction*, p.123.

74   Knight, *A Hundred Years of Fiction*, p.124

75   Heseltine, 'Constable's Ruin', p.98.

76   For a complete bibliography of Heseltine's published and unpublished works see Rhian Davies, 'Scarred Background', 97-100.

77   Heseltine, *Capriol for* Mother, p.35; Rhian Davies, 'Scarred Background', 84-88.

78   Tony Brown, 'The Ex-centric Voice: the English-Language Short Story in Wales', *North American Journal of Welsh Studies* 1.1 (2001): 25-40 (26).

79 Heseltine, 'Homecoming', in *Celtic Story: no. 1*, ed. Aled Vaughan (London: Pendulum Publications, 1946), pp.144-157 (p.152).

80 Glyn Jones, *The Dragon Has Two Tongues*, p.14.

81 Heseltine, Review of Flann O'Brien's *At Swim-Two-Birds*, *Wales* (Autumn, 1943): 308.

The Welshness of William Emrys Williams:

strands from a biography

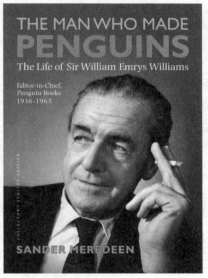

Malcolm Ballin
Cardiff University

William Emrys Williams (1896-1977) was a significant British figure in the field of popular education and became a human powerhouse in the field of cultural transmission, but one whose influence has until now been largely disregarded. It is salutary to consider to what extent Williams sought to emphasise his links with Wales and how others who knew him treated his Welshness as a factor in the way they constructed his identity. These lines of enquiry can suggest ways in which notions of Welshness reverberated in the epi-centre of British literary and cultural life in the middle of the twentieth century. It will be necessary, too, to discuss whether the recent neglect of William Emrys Williams may be linked in any way to his Welshness.

This essay takes as its focus a recent scholarly biography of Williams by Sander Meredeen.[1] Williams's Welshness comprises one significant strand within Meredeen's comprehensive treatment of a multi-faceted life, and the project of this essay is to disentangle it from this context and to examine its significance. Life-writing about cultural figures within Wales has frequently carried substantial emotional resonance, supported by recognisable literary tropes. Readers of biographical articles in the *Anglo-Welsh Review* often encountered attributions of remote places of birth, with sources of fervent national sentiment around links to humble origins in rural Wales; the role of early education in encouraging self-expression is often emphasised, together with emotional and formative affiliations to Welsh non-conformity.[2] It will be seen that these characteristic formations recur in relation to Williams but that they are received in contradictory ways in different contexts. They are exploited positively by Williams himself and his friends – but they are also interpreted in negative ways by some of his critics. At a time when there were numbers of Welsh figures at the heart of the British cultural establishment the phenomenon of Welshness could become something of a two-edged sword. Before attempting any analysis of this phenomenon, however, it will be helpful to summarise the main features of Williams's career, as set out in Meredeen's biography.

Sander Meredeen's book is called *The Man Who Made Penguins*. This choice of title emphasises the key role that Bill Williams filled as the Editor in Chief of Penguin Books for the thirty years between 1936 and 1965. For the whole of this period Williams acted as a major influence on Allen Lane, the founder of the firm. Lane's original intention was not much more than the production of reprints of high quality books. He turned to Williams as a source of literary and intellectual support and for strategic advice.[3] Then in his thirties, Williams had already built a substantial reputation in the Workers Educational Association, succeeding Barbara Wootton and R.S. Lambert as the editor of the movement's magazine *Highway* from 1930 and becoming Secretary to the

British Institute of Adult Education in 1934. By this time, Williams had published several books on English literature, directed to schools, including a course on précis, a critical study (*Shakespeare to Hardy*) and a set of selections from George Borrow. From 1935 he ran the *Art for the People* project which for the first time took travelling exhibitions around outlying areas of Britain.[4] He persuaded Allen Lane to start the Pelican imprint to run alongside the Penguin logo: thus creatively instituting 'a parallel series of cheap books on a wide range of intellectual interests – philosophy, psychology, history, literature, science.'[5] He therefore brought to his role at Penguin Books a deep personal commitment to the concepts of adult education, community development and cultural democracy. The cultural effect of the popular availability of Penguins and Pelicans was crucial. In Meredeen's words, reflecting his own experience, 'Williams changed the reading habits and filled the bookshelves of a whole generation.'[6]

Over these thirty years, alongside his continuous running commitment to Penguin Books, Bill Williams was also to perform another series of formative roles in the cultural life of working people in Britain. During the Second World War, he directed the Army Bureau of Current Affairs, which ensured the regular briefing and continuing access to education of a largely conscript army. Williams had to contest a deep-seated opposition to such liberalisation among many high-ranking military figures who feared that encouraging free discussion would provoke indiscipline. This expansion of the horizons of many voters was credited by some (and blamed by others) for encouraging growing political and social awareness and consequent shifts of opinion among serving soldiers.[7] There was 'a dangerous rumpus' over discussions of the Beveridge Report.[8] Although Williams denied any party political intent, R.A. Butler asserted that the influence of the ABCA 'virtually won over' the serviceman's vote for Labour in 1945.[9] Throughout the war, too, Williams wrote regular monthly columns as the radio critic of the *Listener;* after the war he performed a similar role for the *Observer* and also wrote early television criticism for the *New Statesman*.

Williams was at the forefront of a new drive to initiate public funding of the arts. He played a major part alongside John Maynard Keynes in establishing the ground-breaking Council for the Encouragement of Music and the Arts, [CEMA] working as its Director for Art from 1942-45. After the war he became Secretary General of its massively influential successor, the Arts Council of Great Britain, for twelve critical years from 1951 to 1963, working closely alongside chairmen such as Kenneth Clarke. From 1963-1970 he was Secretary to the National Arts Collection Fund. Williams gained several conventional accolades: in 1946 he was made CBE and was awarded the American Medal of Freedom for his wartime contributions; he was knighted in 1955.

In many respects, however, Williams was a controversial figure. Meredeen deals in some depth with the tensions that Bill Williams both experienced and to a substantial degree generated between two contradictory philosophies of public involvement in artistic life. He was by instinct drawn to the concept he characterised as 'the grain of mustard seed' which sought to promulgate artistic and literary works widely through the community, working especially actively outside the metropolitan centres.[10] The best examples of this process are in his seminal contributions to Worker's Education, in the entirely innovative *Art for the People* project and in his influential work for the Army Bureau of Current Affairs. The 'mustard seeds' approach continued under the Council for Encouragement of Music and the Arts, alongside such supportive initiatives as the commissioning of original murals for the cheap British Restaurants of the day. CEMA also financed many regional performances of opera, ballet and live music.

On the other hand, during his lengthy period at the Arts Council, the exigencies of financing under various governments forced upon him a more highly selective approach that he encapsulated in the phrase 'Few but Roses'.[11] While Williams always sought to include 'regional roses' in this prescription the bulk of the Arts Council's efforts were in practice directed at supporting and establishing national institutions, such as the Royal Shakespeare Company, Covent Garden and the National Theatre. His tenure has therefore attracted both praise and blame, accusations of elitism from some and counterbalancing suggestions of populist philistinism from others. Some saw him as cunning, ruthless and driving; others described him as far more relaxed. Jeremy Lewis, the biographer of Allen Lane, even characterised him (amazingly enough considering the rate of his activities) as 'endearingly idle, a man for the broad brushstrokes who left others to fill in the details'.[12]

In addition, Williams had a complicated personal life. His early, life-long marriage to the distinguished economist Gertrude Rosenblum was affectionate and mutually supportive. The private memoir of Williams's career that Gertrude wrote after his death (*Educator Extraordinary*) supports the view that this was an exemplary life-long union.[13] Matters were, however, complicated by Williams's passionate relationship with Estrid Bannister – once identified in the *Sunday Telegraph Magazine* as 'the naughtiest girl of the century.' Meredeen devotes a full chapter to 'Bill and Estrid', showing that 'she remained Williams's mistress, close friend and travelling companion for... twenty years.' It is apparent that his wife knew about and  decided to tolerate this long-term infidelity. She was, however, far less complaisant about her husband's relationship with his secretary, Joy Lyons, to whom he had dedicated his selections from Hardy. In a dramatic gesture, Lyons destroyed the text of his autobiography on the night of Williams's death, before killing herself. In tune with the conventions of the period, these entanglements never became the topic of press comment at the time. However, they were probably known about within the tight social and cultural circles surrounding the Arts Council.

These personal contradictions are bound up to some extent with the perception of Williams as an outsider, 'on the edge' perhaps, someone not always wholly comfortable in the centres of metropolitan power. As will be seen, these perceptions are in turn related to his position as a Welshman, designated as such both by his own choice on some occasions and in the terms of his critics on others. The ambivalence that features in his characterisation of himself as a Welshman becomes instructive. At the beginning of *The Location of Culture* Homi Bhabha argues that the ' "in between" spaces provide the terrain for elaborating strategies of selfhood... that initiate new signs of identity.'[14] It is time for us to explore in some more detail the role of these more personal 'in between spaces' in the life of William Emrys Williams, the cultural mandarin, public servant of the arts and practitioner of cultural democracy.

II

The first 'in between space' is that of his birth. William Emrys Williams was born on October 5 1896. His obituary in *The Times* some eighty years later on April 1 1977 asserts authoritatively that 'he was born at Capel Isaac, a village in Carmarthenshire. His father, Thomas Owen Williams was a carpenter; his mother a farmer's daughter from nearby Llandilo (*sic*).'[15] This account was confirmed by the then current entry for him in the *Oxford Dictionary of National Biography* which added the following somewhat problematic comment: 'Living in Wales until his eighth year, he was brought up to speak Welsh and retained marked Welsh characteristics throughout life.'[16] The *DNB* entry assumes that this statement explains itself; it is not elaborated on in any way. So far, so typical: we can immediately recognise another impeccable account of humble Welsh origins, working along very much the lines of many of those somewhat stereotypical life stories familiar from the *Anglo-Welsh Review*. In 1963 Professor Gwyn Jones confirmed the account of Williams' birth in his formal address to the University of Wales on the occasion of Bill Williams being awarded an Honorary Degree of Doctor of Letters. 'William Emrys Williams', he declared 'was born in a Carmarthenshire village and is Welsh of the Welsh.'[17] Things are, however, not quite so simple.

Gertrude Williams's private memoir of her late husband, provides an alternative story, supplied with equal conviction:

> He was born in 1896 in a small farm in Morfa Bychen [Bychan] a neighbouring village to Criccith [Criccieth] the village where Lloyd George was born, a few miles inland from Portmadoc [*sic*].[18]

This preserves the account of Williams' rural Welsh authenticity but adds an intriguing geographical connection with an even more famous Welshman. The source of this account is obscure. Sander Meredeen assumes that Gertrude is recollecting early family sources, perhaps provided by Williams himself.[19] The jolting fact, however, is that – according to a birth certificate obtained by Meredeen from the Family History Centre – Williams' mother, Annie, registered his birth on November 6 1896 at 'the Hulme sub-district of the Chorlton Registration District in the counties of Manchester and Lancaster.' The family address is given as '16 Raglan Street, South Manchester.'[20] It is not perhaps entirely unusual for people to romanticise some of the circumstances of their birth but the factual discrepancies do bring one up short when so much of Williams's proclaimed *persona* seems to have stemmed from the notion of being born as 'Welsh of the Welsh.'

However, these 'in between spaces' are not all difficult or dubious. Williams could indeed fairly trace his ancestry and his links with Welsh craftsmanship from his paternal grand-father, William Williams, a ship's carpenter, born in Beddgel-ert in 1815.[21] According to the 1881 and 1891 censuses, this is where the family link with Morfa Bychan originated. The hamlet was the site of his grandfather's farm, Garreg Wen Bach, located near a larger establishment with a similar name which is traditionally regarded as the birthplace of David of the White Rock. William Emrys Williams' father, Thomas, was born here and acquired his trade as a joiner in a local apprenticeship. His mother Annie did indeed origi-nally come from a Carmarthenshire farm near Llandeilo. Thomas and Annie Williams then became part of the well-documented *diaspora* that took many rural Welsh craftsmen to the larger centres of population in England, in search of work at the turn of the nineteenth century.[22]

William Emrys Williams had three sisters, two of whom died in infancy. Despite his Manchester birth registration, Williams apparently did attend the village school in Morfa Bychan (almost certainly Welsh-speaking) for around eight years before the family made its more permanent move to Manchester in 1904.[23] A large part of the family's life there centred around the Booth Street Congregational Chapel and Thomas Williams conceived an early ambition that his son should make a career in that ministry.[24] His education up to the postgraduate stage (age twenty-three) was conducted with this in mind.[25] The Sunday school and the visiting preacher were undoubtedly formative influences. Williams prided him-self on his facility with language and associated this with his Welsh background. A schoolboy essay celebrated the way 'the Cymry have clung tenaciously to all their traditional lore and legend' and quoted freely from Taliesin as cited in Borrow's *Wild Wales*.[26] In 1927 Williams published his *Selections from George Borrow,* the first of half a dozen similar anthologies from English authors that he was to produce over the next thirty years. In an article about D.H. Lawrence, written for *Highway* half a century later, William Emrys Williams vividly recalled the character of much Welsh sermonising, adding however a sardonic hint of reservation:

> Those who follow this passionate and volcanic writer through his poems or stories or essays will have no diffi- culty in discovering his 'message' – except perhaps on those not infrequent occasions when, carried away by fer- vour, he is inclined to lapse into the incoherence of a revivalist preacher. The parallel comes particularly to mind because I remember as a youth in Wales listening so often to some celebrated preacher who became rapt to such an extent that he temporarily abandoned his discourse in favour of passages of sheer incantation.[27]

Kenneth Morgan has attributed some of the political effec- tiveness of those he terms 'fluid people', such as Dr Thomas Jones – who was to be Williams' mentor – and Lloyd George, to the persuasive use of Welsh speech rhythms inculcated early in life.[28] Meredeen argues convincingly that much of Williams's own influential talent as a formidable committee member and successful institutional manager stemmed from his early practice in organised debate. He quotes a conver- sation with the historian, Peter Stead, who took the view that the long affiliation of Welsh youngsters to the setting of the Congregational chapel 'served as a training ground for debate and argument on the widest range of issues, both theological and secular.'[29] These early influences were soon to be reinforced (and also simultaneously undermined) in the course of further education at University and later in a theological college.

Commencing his undergraduate studies at Manchester University in 1914, Williams never seems to have contem- plated volunteering for army service during the First World War. Nor does this seem to have involved him in any criticism or controversy. The institutional pacifism of Welsh non-con- formity would have made that crucial decision more likely. At Manchester, reading for a degree in English, Williams came under the influence of Charles Harold Herford, an inspiring teacher of English and a perceptive literary critic, who had previously taught Thomas Jones at Aberystwyth. Herford was originally a Renaissance scholar but in later life wrote mainly about the Romantics.[30] His influence on Williams' literary taste and intellectual development was decisive. Bill Williams wrote some fluent undergraduate poems to his future wife, Gertrude Rosenblum, published in the Manchester under-graduate magazine *The Serpent*:

> They did not sing of you in Babylon:
> They garnered gold and ivory and lace;
> And fought: and loved a little and were gone;
> O they have died who never saw your face.[31]

These opening lines echo William Morris and Tennyson and his future publications were to feature selections from Wordsworth, Browning and Hardy. It is possible to detect here a stage in his intellectual development that begins to run against the grain of his conventional non-conformist Welsh upbringing. Herford co-opted Williams (as he had Thomas Jones before him) into Arnoldian concepts of impartiality and objectivity. Williams began to see himself in membership of a critical cultural community with its bases in class and edu-cation and a mission to achieve the amelioration of manners among both upper-class Philistines and industrial Barbarians. This grasp of the potency of cultural authority was to be a crucial element throughout his later career. Writing about Arnold, the critic Daniel G. Williams explores the importance of his conviction that, in his time, 'any major literary or his-torical work was likely to reach "a very large proportion of the governing elite" '. This made the act of publication not merely part of a coterie activity, but rather a decisive mis-sionary intervention in society. Daniel Williams has also recorded the emphasis, developed during the nineteenth cen-tury, that Britishness could embrace 'a highly respectable Welsh identity that could nevertheless be contrasted to Eng-lishness.'[32] These cultural presumptions recur throughout the future intellectual history of William Emrys Williams.

At the same period during his Manchester University years, Williams was introduced to active Labour Party politics by his intellectually superior fiancée and his initially difficult involvement with her orthodox Jewish family at once widened his horizons and complicated his early career decisions.[33] Following his graduation in 1918, with only a disappointing pass degree, he still persisted in undertaking postgraduate work in divinity at a Congregationalist training establishment: the Lancashire Independent College. However, within a year of starting this course, the clear pre-set path his father had set for him towards the Congregational ministry was to be abandoned. He was to proclaim growing doctrinal doubts and by the middle of 1919 he had resigned from the LIC and was working as a volunteer with the YMCA in London. In the same year he was married to Gertrude, who was by now exploiting her own first class degree as a Tutor in Economics at Bedford College, and he had secured a teaching appointment as Senior English Master at Leytonstone High School for Boys. He seems to have been a very successful teacher. Remarkably, considering the indifferent quality of his first degree, in his six years at Leytonstone Williams produced half a dozen educational books on literary topics, all of them published by Methuen. *The Craft of Literature* (1925), *First Steps to Parnassus* (1926) and *A Progressive Course of Précis and Paraphrase* (1927) established a developing authority in the teaching of English that was reinforced by a broad critical commentary (*Shakespeare to Hardy*) and then by his selections from George Borrow.[34] *Plain Prose* (1928) completed a remarkably prolific output, especially for a writer scarcely yet out of his twenties.

During these years Williams was also working as an evening-class tutor for the Workers' Educational Association and in 1928 he persuaded the Extramural Department of London University to appoint him as a full-time staff tutor in English Literature. A year later he became editor of *Highway,* the monthly journal of adult education. William Emrys Williams emerges in this role as a substantial force, both entering into the contemporary polemics of the adult education movement and also recruiting a remarkable set of contributors to his magazine. These included Virginia Woolf, R.H. Tawney, Ivor Brown, Dover Wilson and G.D.H. Cole. At the same time, he appears to become more focused on a career that will give him a British national profile. His tenure as editor of *Highway* and his later role as Secretary of the Workers Educational Association took place in the aftermath of the failure of the General Strike in 1926, and continued up to 1939. It encompassed the controversies around the Spanish Civil War and was marked by the continuation of that 'intense and bitter resistance' the WEA put up to essentialist Marxist influences that had been associated with the Plebs League and the Central Labour College ever since 1909.[35] By the end of Williams's tenure, the WEA's approach, described by one commentator as 'ameliorative and not revolutionary' and strongly influenced by *Highway*'s contribution, had become the dominant force.[36] Thomas Jones asserted that Williams's journalistic skills transformed *Highway* into 'the poor man's *New Statesman.*'[37]

Working jointly with A.E. Heath, Professor of Philosophy at University College Swansea, Williams produced an influential 1936 study on the educational formations of WEA students, *Learn and Live*. This consulted numbers of WEA students and explored the conflicted mix of cultural and political motivations among them, revealing the social insecurities of many participants.[38] These were themes which Williams, in Meredeen's words, 'hammered away at' in successive editorials in *Highway*.[39] Jonathan Rose, in his detailed account of the Williams-Heath survey, says

> One of the most commonly cited motives for pursuing adult education was very Arnoldian: 'Disinterstedness.' This involved not only the effort to overcome bias, though it certainly included that. It meant as well that education should be pursued with no thought of competitiveness or economic gain, that education must be acquired for its own sake in an environment where students helped each other.[40]

Fears among WEA students about losing touch with their working class roots and of alienation from family also figured prominently in this research. These responses, reflecting as they did some of the key elements in his own family history and intellectual development, must have produced some plangent personal resonances for Williams.

It was at this stage in his career that Williams came increasingly under the benevolent influence of Thomas Jones. The one time junior clerk in an ironworks store in Rhymney had become a career civil servant and had been appointed Cabinet Secretary by Lloyd George in 1916. He subsequently worked as the trusted confidant of four Prime Ministers. Tom Jones (TJ) acted as a significant figure in international negotiations over Irish independence, over the Treaty of Versailles at the end of the First World War and during the appeasement controversies of the 1930s. By the time he came to play a crucial part in the life of William Emrys Williams, however, Jones had retired from the Civil Service and was primarily engaged in cultural and philanthropic work. He was especially active in the large-scale charitable benefactions of the American-financed Pilgrim Trust, in the artistic collections of the Davies sisters in Gregynog, in preserving the journal *Welsh Outlook,* in the formation of CEMA and in the foundation and management of Coleg Harlech.[41] Both Welshmen had begun life with the intention of becoming clergymen, but had been diverted into secular social and cultural roles. TJ's biographer, E.L. Ellis, claims that Jones's influence, through the Pilgrim Trust, secured the promotion of Williams's role in *Art for the People.*[42] One of the earliest exhibitions was at Coleg Harlech. She describes his protégé as 'a young man of Welsh working class origin clearly marked for greater things' and also asserts that TJ was the main advocate of Williams's fitness for the role of Director of the Army Bureau of Current Affairs.[43] Meredeen traces detailed contacts and frequent correspondence between these two Welshmen during the next twenty years, mainly over key appointments and nominations in fields such as the Army Bureau of Current Affairs, the foundation of CEMA and the establishment of the Arts Council of Great Britain.[44]

In the course of his career Williams cultivated other influential expatriate Welshmen working in the arts, including Walford Davies, Gwyn Jones, B. Ifor Evans, Huw Weldon and Wyn Griffith.[45] In his wartime *Listener* reviews he explored Welsh themes through the broadcasting work of

Walford Davies and Wynford Vaughan Thomas. His ambivalence about the actor Emlyn Williams betrays some contradictory feelings about Wales. In his article, 'A Couple of Winners' in the *Listener* on October 3 1940 he says that

> So ardently and persuasively did he [Emlyn Williams] gen-
> eralise from his own experience that one forgot for the
> moment how very few clever little Welsh boys ever get to
> college. The corn may be green all right but it does not
> always get a chance to ripen.... There were many points in
> his talk in which he spoke for all Welshmen. One was his
> account of his racial susceptibility to language – which he
> illustrated by absolutely vibrating examples. Another was
> the candid admission of the dexterity with which a Welsh-
> man can turn black to white. As a broadcaster, Emlyn
> Williams has got everything the microphone takes: an indi-
> vidual manner of talking, a beautifully-paced rhythm and
> an artful sense of impromptu.[46]

'Clever little Welsh boys' meet here amid the ripening corn, demonstrating their instinctive command of language and their gift for manipulating opinions. Just two weeks later, however, in a further article in the *Listener* on October 17, this time entitled 'The Celtic Touch', Williams has unac-countably changed his mind about Emlyn Williams:

> After his first postscript I cried him up to the skies. But
> after his last I like him less. Partly, perhaps, because, as his
> fellow countryman, I begin to discern that too-easy mas-
> tery... of the art of rhetoric. Is he becoming the equivalent
> in postscripteers of the notorious Welsh pulpiteers? Is he
> fingering the stops of sentiment too brazenly? Is he going a
> bit *Wurlitzer*? The Welsh have this pull over the Irish – that
> they can do their blarney without kissing a stone: they can
> bamboozle you with these rope-tricks into seeing a stone
> that isn't there. It is for such incoherent reasons as these
> that I hope Emlyn Williams will abandon virtuosity and
> resist temptation.[47]

The swiftly changing emotional mix of attraction and repul-sion here surely reflects deep-felt personal sensitivities and may also betray a canny insight or even some self-doubt on Williams' part about the way in which he himself may have been perceived by some non-Welshmen. In the second article he also has some parallel observations about the broadcasting capabilities of his friend and mentor Dr Thomas Jones:

> His voice has the Welsh qualities of colour and vibration; it is decisive yet responsive to each turn of thought. It is what you might call a gesticulating voice. I do not mean to suggest that he waggles his spectacles or waves his arms at the microphone. I mean that he brandishes his sentences rather than delivers them. He has that rarest of microphone gifts, one which even such aces as Churchill lack, the gift of rhythm.... There is some power of divination in that little black box – and Dr Tom Jones is the sort who can look it in the face and speak what is in his heart.[48]

On this occasion Williams clearly struck a sympathetic note in the consciousness of Gunner Keidrych Rhys, the editor of the 'National Magazine', *Wales,* who was then stationed in the army at an anti-aircraft station in the South of England. Rhys read these comments on Thomas Jones and wrote to Williams, saying that

> I think every true Welshman would appreciate your remarks... And that is something to be thankful for these days because most of our 'New Wales Society' feel that the Principality doesn't get her due share of 'attention' in papers and periodicals! That is not due to any lack of writers I assure you.[49]

Williams passed on Rhys's comments to Jones, adding, significantly enough, 'Latterly I have felt a need to be a Welshman in more than blood and association: I'd like to help with the cultural movements in Wales.'[50] But Williams had by now already moved a long way, geographically and psychologically, from Wales and his involvement with Wales was never again much more than peripheral and nostalgic. He did get involved in fighting the cause for the retention of Coleg Harlech during the war, but this was probably a worker's education issue rather than a national one.[51] It seems that Welshness had again become confined to 'in between spaces' in his life.

III

The Welshness of William Emrys Williams belongs, however, not only to his own projection of himself but also to an equal extent to the view of him taken by others. A repeated *leitmotif* of this kind appears throughout the different strands of his multifarious career. Consider Jack Morpurgo's ostensibly sympathetic account of Williams at age forty, at the outset of his work for Allen Lane and Penguin Books:

> William Emrys Williams was a Welshman to every letter of his unmistakably Welsh name, even if he did come from Manchester. The rich rhythm of his Welsh voice, cunningly modulated by a controlled stammer freed him from the suspicion that hung over so many of the Oxonian and metropolitan popular educators of that era.... He was mercurial, as eager to make friends as to make enemies, and his earnest political opinions like his devout concern for public understanding, was tempered by commercial shrewdness. Unlike Krishna Menon or Beales [his rivals] he was essentially a polymath.[52]

The sense of the acceptability to working people of his provincial persona is seen as a determining factor in his success as a popular educator. But the key terms here are the invocation of his 'unmistakably Welsh name' and then of 'Manchester', 'cunningly modulated', 'mercurial', 'devout' 'shrewd' and 'polymath.' They are all unstable terms, especially in the context of Morpugo's emphasis on Williams' typical Welshness, registering at once as apparently positive but potentially negative. They suggest brilliance but they infer unreliability. Perhaps, Morpurgo seems to hint, there is too much Celtic cleverness here, self-proclaimed as 'devout', and too little of that English virtue, 'bottom.' I do not believe that Morpurgo's account is deliberately intended to be unflattering. But, maybe inadvertently, he still sows seeds of doubt. Other personal attacks on Williams were far more directly malicious.

There was an early damaging controversy at the Arts Council when Williams was suspected by some, and accused openly by others of 'devious and manipulative' behaviour, in allegedly intriguing to bring about the premature resignation of his predecessor as Secretary General, Mary Cecilia Glasgow.[53] Among a number of other aspersions about Williams and Tom Jones, the journalist Norman Lebrecht, in his history of Covent Garden, asserts that Glasgow was replaced by 'W.E. Williams, one of Tom Jones's antediluvian Taffia'.[54] A later anonymous civil servant's account of the affair, writing some twenty years later, maintains the tone of depreciation: 'I have always had the impression that the process by which Sir William Emrys Williams supplanted Miss Mary Glasgow as Secretary-General would not bear too close scrutiny. There was a vast amount of intrigue.'[55] In his waspish history of the Arts Council, published in 1998, Richard Witts, the irreverent musician and sociologist, adds the typically colourful accusation that Williams 'hated his predecessor, Mary Glasgow, and had her pushed out.'[56]

Meredeen considers these allegations judiciously. He counters them by pointing out that Williams was aged fifty-five at the time (and so scarcely 'antediluvian') and that Mary Glasgow herself had strongly supported Williams' original nomination to the Arts Council. Consideration of him as her successor did not begin until a full five months after her unexpected resignation. He also cites detailed documented contemporary accounts from the proceedings of a specially convened appointments sub-committee of the Arts Council that had begun its considerations seriously divided but had finished some five months later by unanimously recommending Williams' appointment.[57] It is, of course, not unprecedented for public appointments to be controversial or for there to be persistent rumours about skullduggery in high places. The question for consideration here is to what extent the Welshness of William Emrys Williams affected the nature of this controversy.

Norman Lebrecht has other views about Welshmen in

London, especially clearly illustrated in the context of his account of the foundation of CEMA in 1940. Thomas Jones is described as 'oleaginous', a producer of documents characterised by 'manipulative disingenuousness.' He is accompanied by his 'Welsh cronies, the composer and popular broadcaster, Sir Walford Davies and the adult education propagator, William Emrys Williams.' After failing to secure the appointment he wanted, Jones 'trickled off to oblivion' (presumably in Wales). Later, William Emrys Williams is called 'The Taffia epoch general secretary' and it is reported that 'Taffia Bill Williams was now in sight of his pension.'[58] The random scatter of these depreciatory terms throughout Lebrecht's book has a cumulative effect, creating a generalised assumption of the existence of a corrupt, self-seeking group, sharing unpleasant national traits.

Richard Witts, who also displays a high degree of personal animus against Williams, invariably chooses to refer to him by his nickname, 'Pelican Bill', and describes him thus:

> He was stocky, well built but not tall, his hair routinely Brylcreemed, and he wore double-breasted suits, "a cross between a headmaster and a bank manager – standard professional wear of the fifties". Pelican Bill had a stammer, which appeared at moments of tension. He wore tiny specs over which he would view you like a magistrate. In the CEMA days he was known as Bill or Billy and he cultivated that style. Williams was born into a working-class family from Carmarthenshire which moved to Manchester. His father was a journeyman joiner, his mother a farmer's daughter.
> Fervently socialist in the thirties he drifted languidly to the centre and by degrees a certain snobbery pervaded his outlook. He had married Gertrude Rosenblum, who became professor of social economics at London University, and they lived a full, elevated society-parading life together.[59]

Witts goes on to accuse Williams of deliberately fomenting the McCarthyite persecution of Tom Russell, the Communist Managing Director of the London Philharmonic, and of doing so deliberately, calculating that this disreputable manoeuvre

would secure his knighthood. Witts' account radiates several kinds of prejudice, partly class induced, partly racial, but also invoking some cruel stereotypes of aspiration and provinciality. Williams' presumed lower-class choice of hair dressing, his suspect bourgeois suits, his affected spectacles are linked with his humble origins, 'fervent beliefs' 'languid' social drifting and with the final exaggeration of a *nouveau riche* 'parading' lifestyle. This strident *ad hominem* criticism by Witts, is actuated by his own declared preferences for the 'cool' and the 'hip' and even seems coloured by a frisson of sexual jealousy. But it cannot be separated from the image of Williams as a Welshman, presented here as pompous, self-indulgent, endemically self-seeking, unreliable, and ill at ease in the heart of the metropolitan establishment. Elsewhere in the book, Witts describes other eminent Welshmen in terms touched by a similar animosity:

> [Thomas] Jones had his fidgety fingers in the arts as Hitler
> had fathomed. His musical crony was the composer Wal-
> ford Davies, one of those fake Welshmen like Lloyd George
> who served the principality well.[60]

It does appear that Lebrecht's 'antediluvian Taffia' were
the objects of some jealousy and prejudice.

It may, indeed, not be too fanciful to see some of the parallels between Williams' career and the earlier trajectory
taken by Lloyd George as contributing added colour to
these rumours, encouraging among the enemies of these
Welshmen a number of wish-fulfilling fantasies of misuse of
power and moral ambiguity. Both men were from North
Welsh stock, both brought up in Manchester, both raised in
the ambience of Welsh nonconformity. They were driven
hard by ambition, and they were noted for irresistible personal charm. Both were known to be serial adulterers
(although this was treated with public discretion in the
practice of the time) and both had well-founded reputations
for the cunning circumvention of opposition. The presence
of numbers of influential Welshmen in government had the
consequence that the key parameters of the debates and
accusations around the imagined characters of Welshmen
were well rehearsed over thirty years. Thomas Jones's own
article on 'Welsh Character' in *The Listener* in 1934
emphasised the intense local differences within Wales, and
the great variety of Welsh manners. It identified the non-
sensical nature of any Herderian claims to a homogenous
national culture or 'racial purity.' The key common factor
that Jones eventually isolates is one that has by now
become a commonplace in this study: 'a natural gift of
ready speech and a delight in its exercise':

> Much of a Welshman's talk is like the play of a kitten with
> a ball of wool, a tossing and twisting of ideas into a tangle
> of shapes by under – and over-statement, for the sheer fun
> of provoking slow and stolid listeners... Lying is a sin
> which sticks between buying and selling. English horse and
> cattle dealers have bargained in Welsh fairs from time

immemorial. 'It is naught, it is naught saith the buyer: but when he is gone on his way, then he boasteth.' Conquest and defeat breed lies.... The Welsh... are artists, deviously honest, and they give a finish and colour to their statements beyond what the occasion demands in the eyes of plain people.... This play of the fancy, this dramatic power, this mastery of a language steeped for. a thousand years in poetry... may be abused, and there are notorious occasions where fluency has proved fatal.[61]

In this article, Thomas Jones tackles head-on the reputation of the Welsh for suspected dishonesty. This stems, he suggests, from aspects of the tortured history of Welsh relations with the English, from longstanding and sometimes misunderstood rural traditions about the techniques of bargaining over livestock. He emphasises the psychological insight that 'conquest and defeat breed lies.'[62] In 1934 this appears as an unexpectedly early anticipation of postcolonial theory *avant le lettre*, identifying within the 'deviously honest' some of that characteristic 'sly civility' which is to be later diagnosed by Homi Bhabha as the voice of 'the litigious lying native' in a more obvious colonial setting. Similar characteristics have been perceived by Stephen Knight (rather to his own surprise) as operating in the contemporary works of Gwyn Thomas, such as *Sorrow for My Sons,* published in 1937 and *Where Did I Put My Pity* (1946).[63] In line with the Arnoldian construction discussed earlier, Raymond Williams identifies the central argument of Gwyn A. Williams's book *The Welsh in Their History* (1982) as the survival of the Welsh 'by anchoring themselves in various forms of Britishness.'[64] The tensions generated between Welshness and Britishness meet together in a recognisable syndrome. The ghost of this psychological state surely lurks behind the ascriptions of Welsh character in the exemplary case of William Emrys Williams who, throughout his life, sought satisfaction and fulfilment in a British rather than a Welsh career scope.

IV

Given all his unquestionable achievements, there is a nagging residual question about why Williams should be so little known today, thirty years after his death, and why attempts to revive interest in him have met with difficulties. Bringing Williams in from the edge of Welsh consciousness has been up to now rather an uphill task. When Sander Meredeen approached the existing management of Penguin Books to discuss the possibility of their publishing the story of their former Editor in Chief he had difficulty in finding an editorial employee there who owned to even knowing who Williams was. Nor has it been possible to negotiate the publication of the book by a Welsh publishing house. This may well say something about the development of a resistance in the devolved Wales of today to the ambitions of those who make their lives in a British rather than primarily in a Welsh context. Those engaged with the grand narratives of Welsh identity and history can find it difficult to come to terms with the co-option of brilliant Welsh agents into a primarily British cultural scene. Different 'structures of feeling' are involved in these conflicted areas of identity formation. A persistent anxious theme in biographical articles from the *Anglo-Welsh Review* centred on the kind of question posed about the painter, Will Roberts: 'How does a Welsh artist escape provinciality and yet remain Welsh?'[65] One answer, in his case and in that of others facing a similar dilemma, has been to secure a countervailing recognition outside Wales as well as within it. And those striving subjects who have worked to manage their own transition to a wider sphere of ambition may suspect Welsh devotion to myths of origin as redolent of the tribal or xenophobic aspects of a crude nationalism.

Robert Browning proclaimed 'the dangerous edge of things' as the primary focus of human interest.[66] But 'the edge' may indeed be dangerous, a risky path away from the centre, the site of a road to oblivion. Thomas Jones recovered some of his standing within a Welsh pantheon by his later dedication to Welsh causes. Some of the cultural issues that have appeared to operate to associate William Emrys Williams with his Welshness in both positive and negative terms can also be seen to resonate in judgements about other public figures from Welsh backgrounds. Under this rubric it would be interesting to consider, within the changing terms relevant to their different times, the career histories and personal legacies - not only of Lloyd George, Thomas Jones and William Emrys Williams – but also of other prominent British Welshmen, such as Aneurin Bevan, Neil Kinnock or Alun Michael.

NOTES

1   Sander Meredeen, *The Man Who Made Penguins: The Life of Sir William Emrys Williams*. (Stroud, Darien-Jones, 2008). I should acknowledge my personal interest, in that the writer was a personal friend and I was involved in editing the final draft of the book, following his death in 2007.

2   Numerous examples of such biographical writing appear in articles in the *Anglo-Welsh Review* through the late 1950s, 1960s and the early 1970s. Some typical examples that illustrate the tropes mentioned here include: Islywyn Jenkins, 'Idris Davies: Poet of Ryhymney' in *AWR*, IX, 23 (1957), 13-125; David Wynne, 'Alun Hoddinot' in *AWR*, XIII, 31 (1963), 44-55; Kathleen Raine, 'Vernon Watkins: Poet of Tradition', in *AWR*, XIV, 33, (1964), 20-38; Alun Page, 'Valiant for Truth: some comments on part of the elegy for John Edward Daniel by Gwenallt', in *AWR*, XIX, 43 (1970), 32-43.

3   Meredeen, 78-79.

4   Ibid., 66-73.

5   William Emrys Williams, *Allen Lane: A Personal Portrait* (London, Bodley Head, 1973) 48.

6   Meredeen, 78.

7   Ibid., 143.

8   E.L. Ellis, *T.J.: A Life of Dr Thomas Jones C.H.* (Cardiff: University of Wales Press, 1992), 443.

9   Ibid., 444.

10 Meredeen, 62, cites Williams's original use of this phrase in his 1938 essay, 'The Changing Map of Adult Education': 'The grain of mustard seed principle is more dependable than the beanstalk principle.' Also see 218 and 242.

11   Meredeen, 171. In an Arts Council Report for 1950/51, Williams's first use of 'Few but Roses' was to support the argument that 'high standards can be built only on a limited scale', attributing the phrase to the Greek poet, Meleager.

12   Meredeen, 235-40; Jeremy Lewis, *Penguin Special: The Life and Times of Allen Lane*. (London: Viking, 2005) 118.

13   See Meredeen, esp. 49-50 and 114. Also see Gertrude Williams, *W.E. Williams, Educator Extraordinary: A Memoir,* (London, Penguin Collectors Society, 2000) *passim*

14   Homi Bhabha, *The Location of Culture.*(London and New York,: Routledge, 1994), 1.

15   Meredeen, 10.

16   *Oxford Dictionary of National Biography*. (Oxford: Oxford University Press,1986).

17   Meredeen, 10.

18   Gertrude Williams, 16.

19   Meredeen, 10.

20   Ibid.

21   Ibid:, 15.

22   Kenneth O. Morgan, *Rebirth of a Nation: A History of Modern Wales*. (Oxford; Oxford University Press, 1998), 6.

23   Meredeen, 17.

24   Ibid., 19.

25   Ibid., 38.

26   Ibid., 24.

27   *Highway,* June-September 1950.

28   Kenneth O. Morgan, *Modern Wales: Politics, Places and People*. (Cardiff: University of Wales Press, 1995) 474.

29   Peter Stead in conversation, quoted in Meredeen, 19.

30   *Oxford Dictionary of National Biography,* 1949 edition, 423

31   WEW, 'For G.', *Serpent,* Manchester University Unions, 1918.

32   Daniel G. Williams, *Ethnicity and Cultural Authority: From Arnold to Dubois*. (Edinburgh; Edinburgh University Press, 17-19).

33   Meredeen, 29, 36.

34   Meredeen, 47-49.

35   Jonathan Rose, *The Intellectual Life of the British Working Classes*. (New Haven and London: Yale Nota Bene; Yale University Press, 2002), 272, 302-4) Peter Stead, *Coleg Harlech: The First Fifty Years*. (Cardiff; University of Wales Press, 1998, 12).

36 See Richard Lewis, *Leaders and Teachers: Adult Education and the Challenge of Labour in South Wales: 1906-1940.* (Cardiff: University of Wales Press, 1993), 191-233 for an account of the WEA's progress during this period.

37 E.L. Ellis, 443.

38 W.E. Williams and A.E. Heath, *Learn and Live: The Consumer's View of Adult Education,* Boston, Marshall Jones, 1937.

39 Meredeen, 60.

40 Rose, 282-7, 283.

41 Meredeen, 55; Ellis, 335-58.

42 Ellis, 434.

43 Ibid., 433-44.

44 Meredeen, 134, 145, 172.

45 Meredeen, 12.

46 *Listener,* October 3 1940.

47 *Listener,* October 17 1940.

48 Ibid.

49 Letter K. Rhys to Williams, October 25 1940, quoted in Meredeen, 205.

50 Letter W.E. Williams to Thomas Jones, November 4 1940, quoted in Meredeen, 206.

51 Stead, *Coleg Harlech,* 86.

52 J.E. Morpurgo, *Allen Lane: King Penguin.* (Harmondsworth: Penguin, 1979) 116.

53 Meredeen, 180.

54 Norman Lebrecht, *Covent Garden: The Untold Story: Dispatches from the English Culture Wars: 1945-2000,* (London: Simon and Schuster, 2000) 79.

55 Treasury Minute July 23 1957, PRO, cited in Meredeen, 180.

56 Richard Witts, *Artist Unknown: An Alternative History of the Arts Council* (London: Little Brown, 1998) 210.

57 Treasury Minutes January 12 and 13 1951, PRO, cited in Meredeen, 169 and 170.

58 Lebrecht, 22, 24, 166, 198.

59 Richard Witts, 353-4.

60 Ibid., 38.

61 *Listener,* January 31 1934.

62 Ibid.

63 Homi Bhabha, *The Location of Culture,* 99-100; Stephen Knight, *A Hundred Years of Fiction: Writing Wales in English.* (Cardiff: University of Wales Press, 2004) 98.

64   Daniel G. Williams, *Who Speaks for Wales, Nation, Culture, Identity: Raymond Williams*. (Cardiff: University of Wales Press, 2003) 65.

65   Philip Barlow, 'The Work of Will Roberts', *Anglo-Welsh Review*, XII, 30, 1962, 32-5, 32, 47.

66   'Our interest's on the dangerous edge of things./ The honest thief, the tender murderer/ The superstitious atheist...' Robert Browning, 'Bishop Blougram's Apology' in J.W. Harper (ed.) *Men and Women and Other Poems* (London; J.M. Dent, 1988) 80 – 104, 89, ll. 396-8

WORKS CITED
Primary Sources: William Emrys Williams

'Legends of the Welsh', *Manchester Central High School Magazine* (1913)

'For G.', *The Serpent*, (Manchester: Manchester University Unions, 1918)

The Craft of Literature. (London: Methuen, 1925)

First Steps to Parnassus. (London: Methuen 1926)

George Henry Borrow: Selections, chosen and edited by William Emrys Williams. (London: Methuen, 1927)

A Progressive Course of Precis and Paraphrase (London: Methuen, 1927)

Plain Prose: The elements of a serviceable style (London: Methuen, 1928)

A Critical Commentary on "Shakespeare to Hardy" (by Sir Algernon Methuen). (London: Methuen, 1928)

Learn and Live: The Consumer's View of Adult Education., by A.E. Heath and W.E. Williams (Boston: Marshall Jones, 1937)

'The Changing Map of Adult Education' in *Adult Education in Great Britain and the United States. (*London, BIAE, 1938)

Critic on The Hearth 'The Spoken Word', regular column of radio criticism in *The Listener*, May 1939 – June 1944

William Wordsworth, selected by W.E. Williams. (Harmondsworth: Penguin, 1943)

Tennyson, Alfred, selection and extracts, selected by W.E. Williams (Harmondsworth: Penguin, 1948)

David Herbert Lawrence: Selected Poems, chosen with an introduction by W.E. Williams. (Harmondsworth: Penguin, 1950)

Robert Browning: A selection by W.E. Williams. (Harmondsworth:

Penguin, 1954)
Thomas Hardy: A Selection of poems, chosen and edited by W.E. Williams. (Harmondsworth: Penguin, 1960)
The Reader's Guide, edited by Sir W.E. Williams. (Harmondsworth: Penguin, 1960)
Allen Lane: A Personal Portrait. (London: Bodley Head, 1973)

Secondary Sources: criticism and comment

Barlow, Philip. 'The Work of Will Roberts', *Anglo-Welsh Review,* XII, 30, 1962, 32-5, 32
Bhabha, Homi, *The Location of Culture.* (London and New York: Routledge, 1994)
Ellis, E.L., *T.J.: A Life of Dr Thomas Jones, CH.* (Cardiff: University of Wales Press, 1992)
Jones, Thomas, 'Welsh Character', in *The Listener,* January 31 1934
Knight, Stephen, *A Hundred Years of Fiction: Writing Wales in English.* (Cardiff: University of Wales Press, 2004)
Lebrecht, Norman, *Covent Garden: The Untold Story: Dispatches from the English Culture Wars: 1945-2000.* (London: Simon and Schuster, 2000)
Lewis, Jeremy, *Penguin Special: The Life and Times of Allen Lane.* (London: Viking, 2005)
Lewis, Richard, *Leaders and Teachers: Adult Education and the Challenge of Labour in South Wales: 1906-1940.* (Cardiff: University of Wales Press, 1993)
Meredeen, Sander, *The Man Who Made Penguins: The Life of Sir William Emrys Williams.* (Stroud: Darien-Jones, 2008)
Morgan, Kenneth O. *Modern Wales: Politics, Places and People.* (Cardiff: University of Wales Press, 1995)
—, *Rebirth of a Nation; A History of Modern Wales.* (Oxford, Oxford University Press, 1998)
Rose, Jonathan, *The Intellectual Life of the British Working Classes.* (New Haven and London: Yale Nota Bene; Yale University Press, 2002)
Stead, Peter, *Coleg Harlech: The First Fifty Years.* (Cardiff: University of Wales Press, 1977)
Williams, Daniel G. (ed.), *Who Speaks for Wales? Nation, Culture, Identity: Raymond Williams.* (Cardiff: University of Wales Press, 2003)
—, *Ethnicity and Cultural Authority: From Arnold to Dubois.*

(Edinburgh: Edinburgh University Press, 2006)

Williams, Gertrude: *W.E. Williams: Educator Extraordinary: A Memoir.* (London: Penguin Collectors' Society, 2000)

Witts, Richard, *Artist Unknown: An Alternative History of the Arts Council.* (London: Little Brown, 1998)

The *London Kelt* 1895 – 1914:

Performing Welshness, Imagining Wales

Tomos Owen
Cardiff University

The Welsh community in London by the turn of the twentieth century reached the peak of what Emrys Jones has
termed its 'Victorian Heyday'.[1] The *London Kelt* was a newspaper published in London catering for what appears to be
a distinctive and vociferous Welsh milieu in the city. It began
publication in 1895 and ceased due to the First World War.
The emergence of the *Kelt* can be related to a broader context of Welsh activity in London at the time. The *Cymru
Fydd* movement's influence was at its height and derived
from the same location: according to Kenneth O. Morgan
'Its very name suggested the forward-looking optimism of a
new, rebellious generation [...A]s in similar nationalist
movements, its initial impetus came from émigré Welshman,
the first *Cymru Fydd* society being formed in London in
1886.'[2] At the same time, the Honourable Society of Cymmrodorion, the society of Welsh intellectuals, writers and busi-
nessmen in London, began to mount a campaign for the
establishment of a National Library and Museum.

The National Eisteddfod – the institution which stands as
the epitome of Welsh-language culture – twice visited London in the years around the turn of the twentieth century,
in 1887 and again in 1909. Given this context, the *Kelt* can
be read as both reflective and constitutive of this broader
Welsh milieu in London. Clearly, the emergence of the *London Kelt* in 1895 indicates that the London-Welsh community had created a space and felt a *need* for such a publication, at a time when Wales and Welsh issues were beginning
to command increasing attention on the British political
agenda. Linking each of these movements, events and institutions is their location in London and their collective imagining and re-imagining of Wales. Increasingly obvious in all

spheres of Welsh life in London at the turn of the twentieth century is a vocal, performative quality – Welshness is being constructed and asserted in the very act of its performance and articulation.

The *London Kelt* was joined in print in October 1896 by another publication catering for immigrants from one of the other three nations of the British Isles in the city, namely the *London Scot*, 'A Weekly Journal for Scots Folk' – as is proclaimed by the subtitle of the paper. Walter Wellsman, writing of the 'Births and Deaths of London Newspapers and Magazines' in the *Newspaper Press Directory* of 1897, remarks that,

> Undeterred by the fate of former papers published in London for Scotchmen residing in the metropolis, the *London Scot* has been launched. There is certainly room of such a paper, and its career will be watched with interest.[3]

These remarks stress the importance of space-creation for minority groups in the city: previous publications catering for the London Scottish have failed, but, by 1896, there is 'room' for the *London Scot* to occupy. In this regard, it becomes clear that the Welsh community in London is also involved in a similar project of space-creation. The *Kelt* is a significant part of the process of carving out and contributing to a distinctive Welsh niche in the city.

A glance through the back-numbers of the paper from its inception in 1895 reveals varied forms of writing – journalistic, critical, literary, and in both languages – indicative of a community coming to terms with a peculiar experience of exile. The typical content and format of the paper suggest that this hybridity was both a source of comfort and bewilderment for the London Welsh. Though the form, and indeed the language of the *Kelt* changes repeatedly during the paper's lifetime, several features remain constant throughout: 'General Notes', consisting of brief news items; 'Reports', consisting of longer pieces describing London-Welsh activities of note which had taken place the preceding week – these include concerts, public meetings or lectures, and

eisteddfodau; 'Musical Notes'; short stories, poems and historical essays; 'London Notes', detailing the activities of the
London-Welsh; 'Welsh Notes', giving descriptions of the current affairs deemed to be of the greatest relevance in Wales.
In addition to this, every week's issue carried information
regarding the activities of the London-Welsh chapels, as well
as an extensive correspondence section. Taken in its entirety,
therefore, the *London Kelt* stands as a monument to the
vibrancy of Welsh activity in London, and of the way the
Welsh community in the metropolis comes to position itself
in relation to its current London location and the real-and-
imagined Wales left behind; indeed, even the marginalia of
the paper – in the form of advertisements and notices – can
be incorporated into the thesis that the Welsh in London at
the turn of the last century are engaged in the project of
imagining Wales and a distinctive Welsh identity into existence from London. All of this testifies to the split identity of
the Welsh in London; indeed, in this respect, the pages of the
Kelt become the space where the bifurcated nature of the
London-Welsh condition can be debated and negotiated.[4]

The initial correspondences, both between members
responsible for setting up the publication, and from those
early readers who wrote to the first editor, T.J. Evans, indicate that the London Welsh felt that it was time that this
significant and influential community of émigrés was given
its own voice. Initial editions of the newspaper reflect the
concerns of a community confronted with its own peculiar,
split identity, and the responsibility of that exiled community towards the home left behind. This sense of the oblig-
ation towards the Wales left behind can be detected in the
initial editorial in the first edition of the *London Kelt*, published on Saturday 12 January 1895:

> To all our fellow countrymen where-ever located, and to
> all who have the advancement of Wales at heart GREETING.
> In this journal from week to week, we hope to have a per-
> sonal word with you all, and gather together on one home-
> ly hearth, the deeds and doings of the children of our land.
> To those in this metropolis we will endeavour to have

> short bright news from every district in Wales supplied by
> local correspondents; while the doings within our own
> circle in London will be chronicled for the information of
> the 'good old folks back home.'[5]

This editorial indicates that the *Kelt* is setting out to become
a galvanising force for the 'scattered citizens' of Wales; it is
the 'advancement of Wales' which is the factor which unites
the readership. The London-Welsh community, exiled from
its home, is confronted by the metropolis, which is implicitly in this extract a dark place, illuminated only by the
'bright news from every district of Wales'. The dark,
labyrinthine city is a familiar trope in the Gothic fictions of
the late nineteenth century, including the work of the Anglo-
Welsh writer, Arthur Machen. Raymond Williams notes that,
by this period, 'A predominant image of the darkness and
poverty of the city, with East London as its symbolic example, became quite central in literature and social thought.'[6]
Both London and Wales are thus, in this editorial, invoked
for their symbolic signification; this excerpt establishes an
axis between versions of Wales and London which are both
real and imagined. In the darkness of the metropolis, the
source of comfort to the London Welsh is the placing of
Wales at the forefront of the collective consciousness: the
'homely hearth' in this case is the shared idea of Wales
engendered by the *London Kelt*. Present here also is an indication of the bifocal nature of the *London Kelt*, looking back
to Wales on the one hand as a source of comfort, while
deriving a sense of confidence to perform in the London
arena, for the benefit of those 'countrymen' back in Wales,
a bold and vibrant version of Welshness.

The axis imagined here between London and Wales as a
familiar contrast between country and city is recurrent in,
though not specific to, much of the work of Welsh writers
in London in this period. Along with the *Kelt*, the work of
Ernest Rhys, Arthur Machen, W.H. Davies and Caradoc
Evans at this time all involve a re-imagining of Wales from
a London perspective. The final paragraph in the editorial
goes some way to identifying precisely how the London

Welsh regarded their exile. By indicating the dual objective of the newspaper – i.e. providing news about the London-Welsh for the interest of Welsh people back in Wales as well as including news from Wales for the benefit of the London Welsh – the complex nature of this particular exiled position becomes clearer. The *Kelt* also often carries reports of the activities of other exiled Welsh communities, such as reports of eisteddfodau in places like South Africa, Australia and America. Nevertheless, news from Wales is clearly a source of comfort, a link with the home from which these exiles have emerged. Even the fact that this news is provided by 'local correspondents' is significant: the presence of actual people still living and working at home is deemed worthy of mention; the imagined home is coupled with a physical, concrete reality.

Conversely, and perhaps even more importantly, the inclusion of news from among the London Welsh themselves is also a source of solace. By inscribing for themselves their own particular history, the London Welsh effectively participate in an act of self-validation, for which the 'good old folks back home' are both a real and an imagined audience. This process may be seen as a late-nineteenth century manifestation of what Gwyn A. Williams describes as 'The Welsh or their effective movers and shapers... repeatedly employ[ing] history to make a useable past, to turn the past into an instrument with which a present can build a future.'[7] The useable Welsh past is in many regards a London-based construct produced through chapel service and political meeting. Kenneth O. Morgan notes how the Cymru Fydd movement was characterised by a politics concerned with 'education, literature, music, and art, with debating societies and reading rooms as much as with electioneering. It resembled continental cultural nationalism... in being based to a considerable degree on the intelligentsia.'[8] In this regard, it is a brand of cultural nationalism which Anthony D. Smith characterises as 'culture communities, whose members were united, if not made homogeneous, by common historical memories, myths, symbols and traditions.'[9] The symbols and traditions mentioned by

Smith are certainly performative acts but, arguably, so too is the very act of remembering and (re)calling a lost past.

This initial editorial calls to mind Benedict Anderson's argument regarding the importance of newspapers and print culture to the forging of a national consciousness. Anderson suggests that the newspaper could be described as a 'one-day bestseller', whose

> obsolescence... on the morrow of its printing... creates this extraordinary mass ceremony: the almost precisely simultaneous consumption ('imagining') of the newspaper-as-fiction...The significance of this mass ceremony... is paradoxical. It is performed in silent privacy, in the lair of the skull. Yet each communicant is well aware that the ceremony he [sic] performs is being replicated simultaneously by thousands (or millions) of others of whose existence he is confident, yet of whose identity he has not the slightest notion.[10]

In perusing the pages of the *London Kelt*, one can easily imagine a community of London-Welsh people using the paper to participate in just such a 'mass ceremony' wherever they happened to be living in the widely dispersed districts of the great metropolis. For, as Emrys Jones has pointed out in his history of the London Welsh, on their arrival in London the Welsh of the early nineteenth century settled 'everywhere and anywhere, as they had done for two centuries... There was never a need for enclaves of ghettos, although some parts of London may have been more attractive than others.'[11] Perhaps because of their peculiar kind of relationship with the host community – Jones evocatively describes them as 'familiar strangers'[12] – the Welsh in London have always been dispersed throughout the city; there has never been a Welsh equivalent to Brick Lane. Nevertheless, despite the dispersal of the Welsh far and wide throughout the city the *London Kelt* stands as a monument to how this community endeavours to come together along certain lines. As we have seen, the paper is replete with reports of, and advertisements for, concerts, recitals, eisteddfodau or meetings. There are abundant signals that the Welsh in London –

organised along lines of religious, political or cultural interest (though these categories invariably overlap) – are concerned to come together and create a space for themselves.
Yet, more than providing a mere reflection of this endeavour
to create a Welsh space in London, the pages of the *London
Kelt* in many ways *are* that space.

The twin objectives of the *Kelt* may be considered in the
light of another term used by Anderson (and borrowed from
Walter Benjamin), namely that of 'homogeneous time'.[13]
Benjamin suggests that 'universal history' is written by
means of an 'additive' method: 'it musters a mass of data to
fill the homogeneous, empty time'.[14] Anderson sees 'The
idea of a sociological organism moving calendrically through
homogeneous, empty time' as 'a precise analogue of the
idea of the nation, which is also conceived as a solid community moving down (or up) history',[15] giving the example
of how 'An American will never meet, or even know the
names of more than a handful of his 240,000,000-odd fel-
low-Americans. [...] But he has complete confidence in
their steady, anonymous, simultaneous activity.'[16]

Upon its publication every Saturday, the *London Kelt*
strives to fill the 'empty time' of the intervening week with
news from London and Wales for the benefit of readers in
both locations. The *Kelt*'s twin objectives, outlined in the
first editorial, brings about four different effects: firstly, the
London-Welsh, scattered throughout the city, are able to
come together on the 'homely hearth' and see themselves
as a more unified or galvanised community of exiles; secondly, that same London-Welsh community is able to imagine Wales and the Welsh from London, simultaneously a
source of inspiration and comfort; thirdly, and conversely,
those Welsh readers in Wales are able imagine into being a
community of their countrymen in the metropolis; fourth-
ly, the Welsh readers in Wales are brought together in the
same collective enterprise of Welshness. Via the *Kelt*, the
network of 'children of our land' distributed in Wales, London and beyond, is highlighted, and a concept of Welshness
is imagined into being.

With this in mind, the significance of the *London Kelt* to the Welsh community in London becomes clearer. Anderson notes how 'the newspaper reader, observing exact replicas of his own paper being consumed by his subway, barbershop, or residential neighbours, is continually reassured that the imagined world is visibly rooted in everyday life'.[17] Not only does the content of the newspaper provide news about the activities of the Welsh in London, but the very act of reading contributes to the maintenance of this Welsh identity in the city. Consuming the paper, then, becomes part of the project of performing Welshness in London.

London is the home of the oldest Welsh community outside Wales. Emrys Jones states that 'the Welsh were the first ethnic minority in the city' (p.4): another reason for the widespread dispersal of the Welsh within the city is the fact that there has been a Welsh presence in London for so long. The city has been an attraction as a place of opportunity and advancement, for the Welsh as much as for any other group. Welsh numbers in London at the time were greater than ever before – an advertisement in the *Kelt* suggest a figure of c. 70,000 either Welsh-born or first-generation London Welsh.[18] It is no co-incidence, therefore, that this is the period when the London Welsh are at their most vociferous. An important feature of the *Kelt*, most clearly visible in opinion columns and correspondence sections of the paper, is the way in which the paper serves as a forum in which the Welsh in London are able to debate and discuss their responsibilities towards Wales. This is something which is clearly occurring on a national level through the activities of the Cymru Fydd movement; yet opinion columns in the *Kelt*, and the responses to these columns, often show how these broader concerns regarding the responsibilities of the London Welsh towards 'the good old folks back home' are manifested at a local, personal level.

The second issue of the *Kelt*, for example, laments the fallen condition of the Welsh language in the London-Welsh chapels' literary societies, particularly that of the King's

Cross society, which according to the author, 'Ogwenydd', was using more and more English and less and less Welsh in its programmes and proceedings.[19] The response to this article is a quite striking example of how the readership of the *London Kelt* comes to debate its position and relationship with the Welsh language and the importance (or otherwise) of London-Welsh parents passing the language on to their children. Some correspondents argue that Welsh is the single most important link between the London-Welsh and Wales; others suggest that the new London environment makes understanding and use of Welsh less important. Still others stress the importance of bilingualism: indeed, one humorous response, from the tongue-in-cheek 'Taffy' articulates the hybrid condition of the London Welsh particularly amusingly by saying that '...os bydd y *Kelt* yn methu nid ar yr Editor bydd y disgrace yn disgyn ond ar y London Welsh at large' ['If the *Kelt* fails then the disgrace won't fall solely on the Editor but on the London Welsh at large'].[20] It may only be a mischievously-intended note, sent under an ironic nom de plume, but Taffy's letter can also be incorporated into the body of writing which articulates the split, plural nature of the Welsh voice in London - combining both Welsh and English in this instance; perhaps, given the number of London-Welsh choir concerts, chapel services and cymanfaoedd canu (singing festivals), it is appropriate that the Welsh voice in London is made up of so many different elements. It is notable that the code-switching 'Taffy', though combining Welsh and English, is nevertheless able to conceive of the 'London Welsh at large'. The most striking development of the debate over which language the London-Welsh should use is the fact that the *Kelt* itself changes from its initial bilingual content to become a Welsh-only publication in January 1897, before returning once more to bilingual content by the end of its publication history. Arguably, nothing demonstrates more dramatically than this the fact that the *Kelt* itself is both a forum where debates over Welsh identity can be conducted, as well as an active participant in such debates.

The invocation of a shared memory of 'home' is a prominent feature of the editorial content of the London Kelt but, somewhat unexpectedly, even in the marginalia of the paper it proves to be a source of comfort and inspiration to the exiled readership. Such marginalia, existing as they do literally on the margins of the pages of the London Kelt, can be read as a kind of interface between Wales and London which not only asserts a sense of shared experience and identity, but, by virtue of many of the Welsh products which are advertised, constitute an almost physical direct link with Wales from London. This imagined Wales is sometimes even blessed with medicinal properties. An advert reappearing frequently in the pages of the Kelt, and not one which has been found reproduced in Welsh-based publications or periodicals,[21] proclaims the virtues of 'Hugh Davies's Cough Mixture – The Great Welsh Remedy'. The advertisement is a striking example of the richness of the London Kelt as an archive providing a reflection of the London-based imagining of Wales at the turn of the twentieth century:

HUGH DAVIES'S
COUGH MIXTURE
NO MORE Difficulty of Breathing
NO MORE Sleepless Nights
NO MORE Distressing Coughs

DAVIES'S COUGH MIXTURE for COUGHS
DAVIES'S COUGH MIXTURE for COLDS
DAVIES'S COUGH MIXTURE for ASTHMA
DAVIES'S COUGH MIXTURE for BRONCHITIS
DAVIES'S COUGH MIXTURE for HOARSENESS
DAVIES'S COUGH MIXTURE for INFLUENZA
DAVIES'S COUGH MIXTURE for COLDS
DAVIES'S COUGH MIXTURE for COUGHS
DAVIES'S COUGH MIXTURE for SORE THROAT
DAVIES'S COUGH MIXTURE – most Soothing
DAVIES'S COUGH MIXTURE – warms the Chest
DAVIES'S COUGH MIXTURE – dissolves the Phlegm
DAVIES'S COUGH MIXTURE for SINGERS
DAVIES'S COUGH MIXTURE for PUBLIC SPEAKERS

THE GREAT WELSH REMEDY
13½d. and 2/9 bottlesSold Everywhere.
Sweeter than Honey.Children like it.
HUGH DAVIES, Chemist, MACHYNLLETH[22]

So proclaims the advertisement – this is a potent *elixir vitae* indeed. It is clearly significant that Wales is invoked in the notice as the source of this medicine. Contrasted with the displaced urban readership of the *Kelt*, the source of Hugh Davies's wonderful cough mixture is rural Powys; the implication is that London has a very literal suffocating effect on its Welsh inhabitants, and that the cure emerges out of the pure, wholesome homeland. The stifling or chok-ing effects of London were obviously very much a physical reality at the time: then, as now, pollution is commonly connected with descriptions of the city. There is also a sym-bolic level to this kind of asphyxiation, where London is an impediment to easy breathing and a healthy way of life: it is a place of irritation, disease and physical discomfort.

One of the most prominent images connected with Lon-don in the nineteenth century is, of course, the London fog. Peter Ackroyd in his biography of the city even suggests that 'fog is the greatest character in nineteenth-century fic-tion,'[23] adding that '...Victorian fog is the world's most famous meteorological phenomenon' (p.432). Novels such as *Bleak House* and *The Strange Case of Dr Jekyll and Mr Hyde* – as well as, slightly later, much of the work of the Arthur Machen – present the city through the film of pol-lution, smog and mist. Strangely, this fog endows the city with a sense of grandeur, power and mystery: it is, as Ack-royd suggests, 'London at its most shadowy and powerful, powerful precisely because of the shadows which it casts' (p.436).

Yet whereas the fog may lend the city a sense of power and mystery, there is also a strong element in late nine-teenth-century London writing which likens this foggy metropolis to hell itself. It is implicitly in opposition to such an infernal image that the 'Great Welsh Remedy' is positioned. Set against the hellish metropolis is the godly, bucolic nation of the Welsh. A mixture 'sweeter than honey' deriving from such a pure source can have only positive effects on the vocal prowess of the growing numbers of London-Welsh singers and orators.[24]

The advertisement, along with much of the other content of the *London Kelt*, alludes to the highly vocal nature of the London-Welsh. As previously touched upon, its pages are replete with reports and announcements for various London-Welsh public events, including concerts, lectures, eisteddfodau, and public meetings. The advertisement for Hugh Davies's cough mixture can thus be seen to invoke the performative character of London-Welsh life. The assertion that Davies's Cough Mixture is ideal for 'Singers' and 'Public Speakers' is clearly directed towards those in London who performed their Welshness at the events and gatherings described so extensively in the pages of the *Kelt*.

Other incarnations of this and similar products often carry endorsements from preachers and religious figures. In this way, the dominant presence of Welsh Nonconformity in London is clearly discernible. Rhidian Griffiths has described the importance of the chapel in the religious life of the London Welsh, noting that worship through the medium of Welsh had occurred since at least the early eighteenth century. The number of Welsh causes in London increased from the middle of the nineteenth century, reaching its peak early in the twentieth, so that the *Kelt* emerges at the very time when the rate of growth of London-Welsh chapels was approaching its height.[25] Every issue carried information on the activities of the chapels, from the names of the preachers billed to appear on the following Sunday to reports of the meetings of the various denominations held the previous week. Reports and notices concerning these various weekly meetings and eisteddfodau hint at Griffiths' suggestion that the London-Welsh chapels were 'more than places of worship' and that, instead, 'they... offered from generation to generation a meeting place and a focus of social activity that, by reflecting something of Wales, recreated for those far from home an oasis of Welshness, a surrogate homeland'.[26]

Religious practices clearly contribute significantly to the self-fashioning of a Welsh identity in London. Attending the Sunday chapel service not only brought Welsh individuals together in a particular place at a particular time but the communal act of worship itself could be seen to contribute to the forging of a Welsh Nonconformist identity. Such a forging of a shared identity through religious practice has been documented among other exiled groups in the late nineteenth century. Anne-Marie Fortier, for example, has discussed the 'formation of an Italian émigré culture in London'[27] through a series of communal performative acts around St Peter's Italian church in London: 'written renditions of former Little Italy, where the church stands, a Weekly Mass; the annual procession; a first communion'.[28] 'As performative acts,' writes Fortier, 'these episodes are part of regulatory practices that produce social categories and the norms of membership between them.'[29] Similarly, this performativity is a centrally important aspect of the cultural, religious and political life of the London Welsh in this period. Chapel activity stands as a means of gathering in a physical space – perhaps a substitute for the 'homely hearth' imagined by the *Kelt*'s first editorial – to assert a communal religious and national identity. As James Loxley, taking his lead from Judith Butler's thinking about the construction of gendered identity, remarks, 'culture is a process, a kind of making, and we are what is made and remade through that process. Our activities and practices, in other words, are not expressions of some prior identity... but the very means by which we come to be what we are.'[30]

Griffiths' analysis of the role of the London-Welsh chapels, and his argument that they reflect Wales and recreate 'a surrogate homeland' may be extended further by reference to the evidence of the pages of the *London Kelt*. While a shared affiliation with Wales is the factor which unites the London Welsh, it becomes clear that their actions are not

merely a recreation or reflection of Wales, but a new performance of those values held to be Welsh. Gwyn A.
Williams remarks in the concluding passage of his 'History
of the Welsh' that 'The Welsh as a people have lived by making and remaking themselves in generation after generation,
usually against the odds, usually within a British context'.[31]
In this instance, the London location of this Welsh culture
provides the late-nineteenth century context for this making
and remaking, this performance or willed imagining of
Wales and Welshness.

In an 1897 interview, the editor of the paper, the journalist, politician and historian W. Llewelyn Williams, is
quoted as stating that one of the *Kelt*'s aims is 'to bring the
English and Welsh literature into closer communion',
because 'the Welsh language as a medium of national
thought has given birth to work of which no country need
feel ashamed'.[32] The inclusion of short stories and poetry
are significant features (which require much further and
more detailed research and analysis than is possible here),
particularly in the early years of the *Kelt*'s life, because it
pre-dates by some twenty years the publication of Caradoc
Evans' first volume of short stories, *My People*, which, until
recently, has been commonly regarded as a starting-point for
Welsh fiction in English in the twentieth century. The literary content of the *Kelt* indicates that Evans' 1915 volume
owes a debt to a previous generation of Welsh writers thinking through the condition of exile in which they found themselves, and how this exiled condition relates to the Wales
from which they emerged.

Ernest Gellner, in response to his question 'What is a
Nation?', identifies two generic types of human group formation, contrasting the factors of 'fear, coercion, compulsion' on the one hand with 'will, voluntary adherence and
identification, loyalty, [and] solidarity' on the other.[33] This
second category corresponds more appropriately with the
performative character of Welshness in London at the turn
of the last century: there is a conscious self-fashioning at
work, and it can easily be argued that the London-Welsh

experience is a kind of willed imagining of a Welsh identity. At a time when Britain's control over its empire is the cause of increasing anxieties, the end of the nineteenth century sees the Welsh voice emerge in London, through its literature, culture, politics and religion. The *London Kelt* is both the platform for and the projection of that voice.

NOTES
1   See Emrys Jones, 'Victorian Heyday' in *The Welsh in London 1500-2000* (Cardiff: University of Wales Press on behalf of the Honourable Society of Cymmrodorion, 2001), pp.110-26.
2   Kenneth O. Morgan, *Wales in British Politics 1868-1922*, (Cardiff: University of Wales Press, 1991), pp.104-5. See also Dewi Rowland Hughes, Cymru Fydd (Caerdydd: Gwasg Prifysgol Caerdydd, 2006).
3   Walter Wellsman, 'Births and Deaths: London Newspapers and Magazines' in the *Newspaper Press Directory* (London: 1897), p.16.
4   Much of the literature of late-nineteenth-century London, particularly that of the 1890s Gothic, is concerned with contemporary anxieties regarding the 'split' self. Stevenson's *The Strange Case of Dr Jekyll and Mr Hyde* (1886) and the London-Welsh author Arthur Machen's *The Great God Pan* (1894) are two texts which debate late-Victorian anxieties regarding the essentially split nature of the human condition in the wake of emergent theories of Darwinian science and Freudian psychoanalysis.
5   'To our Readers', *London Kelt / Newyddiadur Cymry Llundain*, 12 January 1895, p.3
6   Raymond Williams, *The Country and the City* (New York: Oxford University Press, 1973), p.221.
7   Gwyn A. Williams, *When Was Wales? A History of the Welsh* (Harmondsworth: Penguin, 1985), p.304.
8   Kenneth O. Morgan, *Wales in British Politics 1868-1922* (Cardiff: University of Wales Press, 1991), p.104.
9   Anthony D. Smith, *National Identity*, (Harmondsworth: Penguin, 1991), p.11.
10 Benedict Anderson, *Imagined Communities, Reflections on the Origins and Spread of Nationalism*, revised edition (London: Verso, 2006), p.35.
11 Emrys Jones, 'The Early Nineteenth Century' in Emrys Jones (ed.), *The Welsh in London: 1500-2000* (Cardiff: University

of Wales Press on behalf of the Honourable Society of Cymmrodorion, 2001), pp.88-109 (92).

12 Emrys Jones, 'Conclusion' in Emrys Jones (ed.), *The Welsh in London: 1500-2000*, pp.193-204 (193).

13 Benedict Anderson, *Imagined Communities*, p.24. The phrase 'empty, homogeneous time is taken by Anderson from Walter Benjamin, 'Theses on the Philosophy of History' in *Illuminations*, tr. Harry Zorn and ed. Hannah Arendt, (London: Pimlico, 1999), pp.245-55.

14 Walter Benjamin, *Illuminations*, p.254.

15 Benedict Anderson, *Imagined Communities*, p.26.

16 Benedict Anderson, *Imagined Communities*, p.26.

17 Benedict Anderson, *Imagined Communities*, pp.35-6.

18 John Davies estimates that by 1901 'London accounted for 35,000' of the Welsh-born inhabitants of England, including '4,000 natives of Cardiganshire who were predominant in the dairying business.' See John Davies, *A History of Wales* (Harmondsworth: Penguin,1994), p.443.

19 'Ogwenydd', 'Yr Iaith Gymraeg yn ein Cymdeithasau Llenyddol', *London Kelt*, 19 January 1895, p.9.

20 *London Kelt*, no.5, 9 February 1895, pp.11-2.

21 This is by no means confirmation that the advertisement appears only in this London-based Welsh newspaper; the *Kelt* is a vast and largely unexplored archive and the author would be delighted to be corrected on this or any other points.

22 *London Kelt* no. 278 27 January 1900, p.2.

23 Peter Ackroyd, *London: The Biography* (London: Vintage, 2001), p.434.

24 When considered in conjunction with the vibrant London-Welsh dairy trade of the period, Wales from London indeed appears quite literally as a land of milk and honey.

25 Rhidian Griffiths, 'The Lord's Song in a Strange Land' in Emrys Jones (ed.), *The Welsh in London 1500-2000* (Cardiff:University of Wales Press on behalf of The Honourable Society of Cymmrodorion, 2001), pp.161-183.

26 Rhidian Griffiths, 'The Lord's Song in a Strange Land', p.182.

27 Anne-Marie Fortier, 'Re-Membering Places and the Performance of Belonging(s)' in *Performativity and Belonging*, ed. Vikki Bell (London: SAGE Publications, 1999), pp.41-65.

28 Anne-Marie Fortier, 'Re-Membering Places', p.43.

29 Ibid.

30 James Loxley, *Performativity* (London and New York: Rout-
    ledge, 2007), p.118.
31 Gwyn A. Williams, *When Was Wales?*, p.304.
32 *Kelt Llundain*, Mai 1, 1897, t.8.
33 Ernest Gellner, *Nations and Nationalism*, 2nd edn (Oxford:
    Blackwell, 2006), p.52.

'Passionate and simple':

R.S. Thomas and Irish Writing

Sam Perry
University of Leicester

I

R.S. Thomas's connection with the Irish literary scene of
the late 1930s is described in his autobiography *Neb*,
where he tells of his relationship with Seamus O'Sullivan's
The Dublin Magazine, a publication well known in Wales
for its hospitality to Anglo-Welsh writing. Richard Burnham
has pointed out that between 1939 and the mid-50s
Thomas contributed over twenty poems to this periodical
and, whilst visiting O'Sullivan in Dublin during the winter
of 1938, was introduced to a number of Ireland's leading
writers.[1] The account Thomas gives of this meeting provides a useful insight into his thinking at the time:

> The girl he had started to court was a recognised artist with
> experience of art school in London and also of Italy. Look-
> ing at her paintings, he identified with the artistic life. She
> had already exhibited her work in galleries in London, and
> he too yearned to prove himself in his field. He heard of an
> editor of a magazine in Dublin, Seamus O'Sullivan, who
> had the reputation of being kind to young writers. He sent
> a poem or two, and before long one of them was accepted.
> He arranged to visit the editor when the latter was staying
> with his brother in Bryn-y-neuadd, Llanfairfechan, and he
> was able to spend a whole day in their company. Later he
> went to Dublin to see him, where he met other poets such
> as Austin Clarke, who was considered to be Ireland's fore-
> most poet after W.B.Yeats. As everyone knows, the Irish
> are talkers, and the young poet felt quite shy and taciturn
> in their midst, but their company satisfied some urge with-
> in him.[2]

Thomas sets his visit firmly within the context of youthful literary ambition.Yet there is reason to believe that his eagerness to engage with the Irish literary community was also related to his dissatisfaction with the genteel atmosphere of the parish at Chirk where he was curate, and his later decision, at the age of twenty-nine, to leave the anglicised lowlands and return to "the true Wales of my imagination".[3] After all, it was whilst he was living at Chirk that Thomas discovered the work of visionary writers like Fiona Macleod (the female pseudonym of William Sharp) and W.B. Yeats, men who, towards the end of the nineteenth century, had looked to inspire a Celtic cultural revival through work which appealed to a powerful sense of Celtic history, myth and legend:

> Another author who influenced him at this time was Fiona Macleod. One of his books came to his attention accidentally and it echoed the hiraeth for the west that he was experiencing at the time. He went to look for other books by the same author and for months he was under the spell of the Hebrides of which the author wrote. He was already familiar with the early work of W.B. Yeats in poetry and prose, and the two writers soon came to represent exactly the life that he would like to live among the peat and the heather on the west coast.[4]

Such was Thomas's hunger for this new life that he journeyed first to the Hebrides and later to Galway in search of the communities of which Sharp, J.M. Synge and Yeats had written. At Galway, glimpses of Irish language and custom occasionally broke the surface through the smell of peat fires and snatches of Gaelic conversation – at one point Thomas

> [...] was passed by cart after cart on its way home to the west. As each cart passed him the driver greeted him in Irish. This, and the smell of the peat in his nostrils, raised his spirits and filled him with new hope. This was the country of which Yeats had sung, a land of common folk, their language Irish and their ways traditionally Celtic.[5]

Of course, the vision of Celtic life put forward by Sharp and Yeats is heavily romanticised, as Thomas discovered when, having made the trip to the Hebrides, a relentless Scottish drizzle ensured that "he did not get one glimpse of Fiona Macleod's magical land".[6] But the young poet was not to be dissuaded. In fact, Thomas's trips to Scotland and Ireland seem to have strengthened his belief that he had found the model for the life he wished to lead, a life rooted in the traditions of the Celtic past, where identity was unproblematic, growing from a rich cultural heritage, rooted in a particular place. This is evident from the work Thomas produced at Manafon and Eglwysfach where, as Tony Brown has observed, in a number of poems and essays Thomas suggests that an equivalent to the lost life of the native Gaelic communities had once existed in the upland pastures of Wales.[7] In 1968, by which time Thomas had moved to Aberdaron, a small coastal parish situated on the tip of the Llŷn Peninsula, he published 'The Mountains', an essay that finds him wandering out into the wild land-scape of Snowdonia and evoking "the summer pastures of the Celtic people":

> There is Eden's garden, its gate open, fresh as it has always been, unsmudged by the world. The larks sing high in the sky. No footprints have bruised the dew. The air is some-thing to be sipped slowly. Coloured drops depend from the thorn. This is the world they went up into on May Day with their flocks from *yr hendre*, the winter house, to *yr hafod*, the shieling. They spent long days here, swapping englynion over the peat cutting.[8]

The life of the *hafod* lies at the heart of Thomas's idealistic vision of the "true Wales", since he imagines it as an exis-tence which is imaginatively rich, a communal, pastoral mode of living that moves the fulfilled self into a state of profound spiritual awareness through its contact with the natural world. This passage also shows Thomas's aware-ness of the centrality to the *hafod* of Welsh cultural tradi-tions like the writing of *englynion*, a short verse form characterized by complex patterns of rhyme and alliteration. With the notable exception of Barbara Prys-Williams's analysis of *The Echoes Return Slow* (1988),[9] the extent to which Thomas's search for identity as a man was bound up with his search for identity as a writer is something that has tended to be overlooked by previous scholarship, and what I am seeking to show in this essay is how Thomas's engagement with Welsh-language culture during the 1940s and early 50s needs to be seen in the broader context of his interest in Celtic culture generally, and Irish poetry in particular. My initial focus will be the steps Thomas took, in response to the work of Austin Clarke, towards developing what he hoped would be a distinctively Welsh poetry in English. I will then examine the ways in which Patrick Kavanagh's anti-pastoral masterpiece *The Great Hunger* (1942) seems to have acted as an enabling device for Thomas's poetry of the 1940s and 50s, with Kavanagh employing a poetic methodology and register ideally suited to the hill farming culture Thomas encountered at Manafon, Montgomeryshire, the parish to which he moved in 1942, four years before the publication of his first volume, *The Stones of the Field*.

II

In August 1947, R.S. Thomas took part in a radio broadcast for the B.B.C., during which he revealed that

> A growing realisation of the plight of my country, together with the desire to live up to the reputation for difference implied by the terms Welsh and Anglo-Welsh, have been responsible for certain experiments of mine both in subject matter and technique.[10]

Thomas then proceeded to read 'Hill Farmer', a poem into which he had deliberately "tried to introduce a certain amount of internal rhyme and assonance":

> And he will go home from the fair
> To dream of the grey mare with the broad belly,

And the bull and the prize tup
That held its head so proudly up.
He will go back to the bare acres
Of caked earth, and the reality
Of fields that yield such scant return
Of patched clover and green corn.
Yes, he will go home to the cow gone dry,
And the lean fowls and the pig in the sty,
And all the extravagance of a Welsh sky.[11]

Although, strictly speaking, this poem does not abide by the technical rules of *cynghanedd*, the complex patterning of rhyme and alliteration of Welsh cultural tradition, it remains a highly significant piece of writing, because it finds Thomas consciously seeking to relate his poetry to the Welsh poetic tradition. Thus, 'Hill Farmer' can be viewed as one of a number of early poems which reflect Thomas's desire to lose his liminal "Anglo-Welsh" status and establish a more secure, authentic identity as a Welsh writer of specifically Welsh poetry. The point is underlined later in the broadcast, when Thomas reads from 'The Welsh Hill Country' (1946), pointing out that this too displays "a certain amount of characteristically Welsh internal rhyme and alliteration"[12]:

Too far for you to see
The fluke and the foot-rot and the fat maggot
Gnawing the skin from the small bones,
[...]

The moss and the mould on the cold chimneys,
The nettles growing through the cracked doors.[13]

What R.S. Thomas was seeking to do, as he strove to locate himself within the "true Wales", was to find a way of writing poetry in English that at the same time had an *atmosphere* of the Welsh tradition, an English-language poetry that was 'un-English' in its aural and emotive effects. In that same radio broadcast of 1947, Thomas explains that

> The work of poets like Austin Clarke in Ireland has inter-
> ested me. For he has shown how much of the atmosphere
> of old Irish verse can be brought into English by skilful
> counterpointing.[14]

We know from *Neb* that Thomas had met Austin Clarke
during his trips to Dublin to visit Seamus O'Sullivan, and
it is reasonable to assume that part of the reason why fellow Celtic writers like Clarke were of such great interest to
Thomas at this time was that they were artists who had
faced a similar dilemma to himself, namely how a Celtic
writer could continue to express himself through the English language while retaining a sense of his own distinctive
cultural identity. Clarke had come into contact with Douglas Hyde and Thomas McDonagh whilst studying at University College, Dublin, and was subsequently inspired to
attempt to recreate a style of Gaelic poetry in English.[15] In
Literature in Ireland (1916) MacDonagh argues that the
'Irish mode' in poetry is based on the use of assonance and
internal rhyme in traditional Gaelic verse. He also highlights the conversational tone of much modern Irish poetry, what he calls its "grace of the wandering, lingering,
musical voice".[16] Clarke's first extended statement about
assonance comes in a note to *Pilgrimage and Other Poems*
(1929):

> Assonance, more elaborate in Gaelic than in Spanish poet-
> ry, takes the clapper from the bell of rhyme. In simple pat-
> terns, the tonic word at the end of the line is supported by
> a vowel-rhyme in the middle of the next line. Unfortunately
> the internal patterns of assonance and consonance are so
> intricate that they can only be suggested in another lan-
> guage. The natural lack of double rhymes in English leads
> to an avoidance of words of more than one syllable at the
> end of the lyric line, except in blank alternation with
> rhyme. A movement constant in Continental languages is
> absent. But by cross-rhymes or vowel-rhyming, separately,
> one or more syllables of longer words, on or off accent, the
> difficulty may be turned: lovely and neglected words are
> advanced to the tonic place and divide their echoes.[17]

Clarke's aim, as it is expressed here, is not to achieve fuller rhyme or more audible stress, but to achieve assonantal rhyme between a concluding syllable, the final or the penultimate syllable in a line, and a corresponding vowel sound within the following line: rhyme in Irish may be between words at the end of lines, as in English; it may be internal, when a word or words within one line of a couplet rhymes with a word or words in the next, or there may be *aicill*, when rhyme is achieved between the final word of the first line of a couplet and a word in the interior of the next.[18] In practice, Clarke imitates the larger assonantal patterns of Irish poetry by writing a number of recurrent vowel sounds within a line or within a stanza: in this sense assonance, or *amus*, is simply a correspondence of vowel sounds; the consonants need not agree, and the assonating words may be of different lengths. Although Clarke experimented with assonance from the beginning, the best examples of his assonantal poetry are to be found in *Pilgrimage* and 'The Land of Two Mists' section of *The Cattledrive in Connaught* (1925), from which 'The Lost Heifer' is taken:

> When the herds of the rain were grazing
> In the gap of the pure cold mind
> And the water hazes of the hazel
> Brought her into my mind,
> I thought of the last honey by the water
> That no hive can find.
>
> Brightness was drenching through the branches
> When she wandered again,
> Turning the silver out of the dark grasses
> Where the skylark had lain,
> And her voice coming softly over the meadow
> Was the mist becoming rain.[19]

Like Austin Clarke, R.S. Thomas sought entry into his native culture through the imitation of its poetic forms and conventions, and by using some of its linguistic idioms and turns of speech. We have already seen signs of Thomas responding to Clarke's verse experiments in 'Hill Farmer' and, in a late interview with Molly Price Owen, he cited the Irish poet as one of the chief technical influences upon his early work:

> When I was younger, learning to write seriously, I was quite influenced by the Irish poets, people like Austin Clarke and he, I suppose with a knowledge of Irish, he was very keen on assonance and dissonance and I produced several poems pursuing the same theme – 'The Ancients of the World'. It was vowel technique, and vowel sounds appealed to me at that time.[20]

As well as 'The Ancients of the World' (1952) Thomas's comments implicate another uncollected poem from this period, 'Song', which was published in *The Dublin Magazine* in the spring of 1948. This poem also features in the B.B.C radio broadcast of 1947, where Thomas describes it as "an experiment in prosody", one which has "a strangely un-English sound about it"[21]:

> Up in the high field's silence where
> The air is rarer, who dare break
> The seamless garment of the wind
> That wraps the bareness of his mind?
>
> The white sun spills about his feet
> A pool of darkness, sweet and cool,
> And mildly at its mournful brink
> The creatures of the wild are drinking.
>
> Tread softly, then, or slowly pass,
> And leave him rooted in the grasses;
> The earth's unchanging voices teach
> A wiser speech than gave you birth.[22]

If we deal with the internal rhymes first, we can see that the "ere" sound of "where" in the tonic place at the end of line 1 raises that of "air", "rarer" and "dare" in line 2, and looks ahead to the "bareness of his mind" in line 4, where assonantal rhyme is also achieved between "That" and "wraps". In the second stanza the "ee" of "feet" divides its echoes between "sweet" in line 6 and "creatures" in line 8, before being picked up again in the final couplet of stanza 3, where we have "teach" and "speech". Here rhyme between vowel sounds is entwined with the alliteration of consonants, a technique that Clarke employs to great effect in 'The Lost Heifer', and Thomas uses the same ploy to heighten the full rhymes of "brink" and "drink" in stanza 2 and "pass" and "grass" in stanza 3. Thus, Thomas responds to Clarke's assonantal counterpointing by retaining rhyme between words at the end of lines, as in the English tradition, while keeping to traditional English iambic tetrameter, but then complicates this structure by incorporating a series of assonantal and consonantal rhymes. Equally, given the instability that surrounded Thomas's identity, we can see how these experiments with techniques derived from traditional Irish poetic forms can be viewed as quite deliberate attempts to establish a Celtic identity through the act of writing, to cast off the legacy of his anglicised upbringing and, as he puts it in his early review of 'Some Contemporary Scottish Writing' (1946), "strike that authentic note".[23]

III

This movement away from the anglicised culture of Thomas's youth also underlies his creative response to the work of a very different Irish poet. In 1993 Sandra Anstey observed that a significant amount of Thomas's verse remained uncollected.[24] She went on to point out that many of Thomas's earliest poems – his work began appearing in literary periodicals in 1939, seven years before the publication of *The Stones of the Field* – exhibit a pronouncedly Georgian style of writing.[25] This was something which Thomas was to lament, attributing the tendency to a highly conservative poetic education:

> In the late twenties, at a time when I should have been in touch with what Eliot, Joyce and Pound were doing, I was

receiving my ideas of poetry via Palgrave's *Golden Trea-sury*, and through such Georgian verse as was compulsory reading for my examinations in English. I was also a confirmed open-air nature lover so that such verses as I then achieved myself were almost bound to be about trees and fields and skies and seas. No bad thing if I had been familiar with the poets who knew how to deal maturely with such material, Wordsworth and Hardy for instance. But my efforts were based on the weaker poems of Shelley and the more sugary ones of the Georgians.[26]

It is a measure of Thomas's attachment to the Georgians that, when *The Stones of the Field* appeared in 1946, the influence was still present. 'Frost', which is quoted in full here, was among those poems which Thomas subsequently chose not to collect from his first volume:

> Thoughts in the mind's bare boughs sit dumb,
> Waiting for the spring to come:
> The green lispings, the gold shower,
> The white cataract of song,
> Pent up behind the stony tongue
> In stiff tribute to the frost's power.[27]

The opening line strikes one as classic R.S. Thomas, but there is little else to dissuade one from the view that 'Frost' could have been written by any writer of neo-Georgian pastoral. While the synthetic quality of the poetry is epitomised by its clichéd diction, with Thomas's use of the word "lispings" standing out as particularly odd, even more revealing is the fact that 'Frost' is essentially a poem about being unable to communicate, thus reinforcing the sense of an author who has yet to discover his own voice. As Tony Brown has suggested,[28] it is here, within the context of Thomas's dilemma about how he could attempt to write about the Welsh hill-farming culture of Montgomeryshire, that we can begin to appreciate the vital role that Patrick Kavanagh's *The Great Hunger* played in the development of Thomas's poetic methodology and register, Kavanagh himself having broken free from an early attachment to the neo-Georgian style.[29] Before I examine Thomas's response to that poem, however, it is useful to consider the literary framework within which he and Kavanagh were operating.

The most obvious affinity that Thomas's early work holds with that of Kavanagh is that it is a poetry rooted in locality, in region and place. Following the publication of his first collection *Ploughman and Other Poems* by Macmillan in 1936, Kavanagh went to London to seek literary employment and was commissioned to write *The Green Fool* (1938). This turned out to be an autobiography with an anthropological dimension, combining a portrait of the artist with a portrait of his society. The rituals and pastimes, religious practices and superstitions, folklore and dialect of the parish of Inniskeen, County Monaghan, were recorded with an affectionate eye, and although Kavanagh was later to repudiate *The Green Fool* as a work which pandered to the tastes of two metropolitan audiences – a London publisher and readership with stereotyped views of the Irish, and a Dublin literati with romanticised notions of an Irish peasantry – it was his relationship with Inniskeen, the parish where he lived for the first 35 years of his life, which was to become his primary subject. Right from the earliest stages of his life, Kavanagh seems to have had a very clear idea of what it means to be a writer of locality. In his essay 'The Parish and the Universe', he re-evaluates the pejorative term 'parochial', defining the parochial writer as one who "is never in any doubt about the social and artistic validity of his parish."[30] This is certainly true of Kavanagh's own work: his ironically-entitled sonnet 'Epic' (1951) ends by invoking Homer's authority to allay any doubts as to the legitimacy of 'local' art and much of Kavanagh's best poetry is characterised by the way it succeeds in expressing the sights, sounds and smells of a sharply particularized local community.[31] In 'A Christmas Childhood' (1947) "Mass going feet" splinter "the wafer-thin ice on the pot-holes", while "Outside in the cow-house my mother / Made the music of milking" and "A water-hen screeched in the bog."[32] This is a community which still lives according to the cultural rhythms of the distant past; its child poet, inscribing on frost-silvered stone or making his mark on the family doorpost, will inherit the rural rhythms of his parents, and nowhere is this more apparent than in the final, poignant stanza, where familial, cultural and religious registers combine to create an image of profound emotional fulfillment:

> My father played the melodeon,
> My mother milked the cows,
> And I had a prayer like a white rose pinned
> On the Virgin Mary's blouse.[33]

A crucial consequence of Kavanagh's championing of the local was that it brought him into conflict with the previous generation of Irish writers. At the beginning of the century, J.M. Synge, Lady Gregory and Yeats had formed a core grouping in what is now commonly known as the Irish Literary Revival, and these three were to suffer continual assaults from Kavanagh's pen. The essay 'Self-Portrait' sees him condemn the "so-called Irish Literary Movement" as "a thoroughgoing English-bred lie"[34] while, in an article published in the Catholic Sunday newspaper *The Standard* in May 1943, Kavanagh dismisses the Protestant Ascendency as people who operate "totally outside the mainstream of the people's consciousness".[35] Clearly, these comments are laced with sectarian prejudice and are indicative of the fact that Kavanagh's concept of Irish identity was inextricably linked to his rural, Catholic upbringing, where the parish was an homogenous unit, a community of people who not only lived in the same place but also shared the same religion and day-to-day life. As Antoinette Quinn suggests, for Kavanagh,

> Parochial literature was a comic realist art which was grounded in the local, offered an affectionate, particularized portrayal of a small, intimately known community. It was inaccessible to writers of the Ascendancy caste, such as Synge, Lady Gregory and Yeats, who were out-

siders to a communal local consciousness, and it was also anti-metropolitan or, rather, indifferent to the metropolis.[36]

Of course, R.S. Thomas was *not* a native of the Welsh hill country, and his status as an outsider at Manafon is reflected in the detached perspective from which so much of his early poetry is written; we do not get the vivid sense of belonging to a particular place and a particular community which is such a strong feature of Kavanagh's writing.[37] However, this should not be allowed to overshadow the extent to which Thomas's early work is grounded in the local. Indeed, in taking the hilly district of central Montgomeryshire as his focus, Thomas can be seen to be asserting the primacy of the local as a subject for poetry. During a B.B.C. radio broadcast in 1947, Thomas highlights the fact that the landscape of 'A Peasant' (1943) is "not general but localised".[38] Similarly, in an article published the following year, he attacks the idea "that art must be contemporary, meaning that it must deal with the English urban and mechanised civilisation".[39] Ultimately, though, our strongest sense of Thomas as a writer of locality derives from his ability to capture the atmosphere of the lonely farms and smallholdings, the *tyddynnau* where his parishioners lived:

> Evans? Yes, many a time
> I came down his bare flight
> Of stairs into the gaunt kitchen
> With its wood fire, where crickets sang
> Accompaniment to the black kettle's
> Whine, and so into the cold
> Dark to smother in the thick tide
> Of night that drifted about the walls
> Of his stark farm on the hill ridge.
>
> It was not the dark filling my eyes
> And mouth appalled me; not even the drip
> Of rain like blood from the one tree
> Weather-tortured. It was the dark

> Silting the veins of that sick man
> I left stranded on the vast
> And lonely shore of his bleak bed.[40]

A telling selection of detail enables Thomas to evoke the sights and sounds of the sick man's room, lending the poem an uncompromising air of authenticity. The opening image of the "bare flight of stairs" leading into the "gaunt kitchen" with its "wood fire" is accompanied by the sound of the "black kettle's / Whine" and "the drip of rain" from the tree outside. As is often the case with Thomas, an image of the sea is used to heighten a particular mood or tone – a "thick tide of night" threatens to envelop the speaker, anticipating the final image of Evans "left stranded on the vast / And lonely shore of his bleak bed". And yet, this remains a poem in which imagery is ultimately subservient to the presentation of a particular pattern of experience. It draws upon the visits Thomas made to sick parishioners high in the hills above Manafon, and the sense of helplessness and compassion in the speaker's voice as he recalls leaving the house, perhaps for the last time, is deeply moving; the image of "the one tree / Weather tortured" alludes to Christ's death on the cross, a symbol of man's salvation, but the deep sense of guilt and impotence expressed in the final lines makes it clear that the narrator feels he has failed to communicate that message of salvation to Evans, leaving him alone in a hopeless darkness. This is a crucial element in the poem, for it demonstrates Thomas's ability to realise the metaphorical and emotional power of *actual* instances and occurrences, an attribute which was notable for its absence from his earlier, Georgian-influenced verse.

Thomas does seem to have responded strongly to the way Kavanagh introduced a new authenticity to poetic representations of the countryside. In section III of *The Great Hunger*, the narrator, who has been watching Patrick Maguire struggle with his plough amidst a black March wind, suddenly diverts the reader's attention to a close-up of the Inniskeen headland:

> Primroses and the unearthly start of ferns
> Among the blackthorn shadows in the ditch,
> A dead sparrow and an old waistcoat.[41]

It is this same documentary, almost cinematic presentation of hill-farm life that we encounter in R.S. Thomas's early poetry. Midway through 'The Airy Tomb' (1946) we are confronted with the image of

> ...sheep rotting in the wind and sun
> And a hawk floating in a bubbling pool,
> Its weedy entrails mocking the breast
> Laced with bright water.[42]

Such detail is particularly effective when used to capture the soporific atmosphere of rural life. In 'The Village' (1955) our attention is drawn to a "black dog / Cracking his fleas in the sun", while in 'Depopulation of the Hills' (1952) Thomas directs his reader's gaze to a deserted farmstead's "patched roof / Sagging beneath its load of sky".[43] Here, in striking contrast to the distanced abstraction and superficialities of Georgian pastoral, is a poetry that draws its strength from close observation and a refusal to hide from the less palatable social and economic realities of life in the countryside. Thomas is now drawing on his own first-hand, day-to-day knowledge of these realities, a knowledge that, by and large, the Georgian poets simply did not have. It is in this sense that *The Great Hunger* can be said to have had a releasing influence upon Thomas, for in showing him how such realities could be expressed in verse, it enabled him to create his own distinctive pastoral vision, a poetry which expresses an attachment to rural life that is based on a truth to its *real* qualities and which refuses to separate beauty from squalor.

There are signs that Thomas also drew inspiration from the way Kavanagh's narrator records the mannerisms of Patrick Maguire and invites the reader to "wait and watch"[44] the farmer as he goes about his daily tasks: "collecting the scattered harness and baskets"[45] after a day's potato picking, gathering "the loose stones off the ridges"[46], walking among his cattle or "load[ing] the day-scoured implements on the cart".[47] Images like these bear comparison with the opening lines of Thomas's 'Out of the Hills' (1946), where we are met with the image of the hill farmer "ambling with his cattle from the starved pastures" before being asked whether we wish to "follow him down" to the village below. Similarly, in 'A Peasant' the reader is invited to picture Iago Prytherch "Docking mangels... churning the crude earth / To a stiff sea of clods that glint in the wind"[48] and later to "see" the labourer "fixed in his chair / Motionless except when he leans to gob in the fire". As Sandra Anstey has noted, the attention to detail that we get in these early poems is of considerable significance, because it provides clear evidence of Thomas's awakening to the richness of his surroundings at Manafon as a subject matter for poetry, and marks the beginning of his move-ment away from a nature poetry written in the style of the Georgians to one which engages with the full experience of rural life.[49] In short, we are witnessing the emergence of an authentic poetic voice from the shadows of 1940s neo-Georgian pastoral, a poetic "awakening" which was later recognised by Thomas himself:

> My awakening to the possibility of a more robust poetry came with my removal to my first incumbency in the Mont-gomeryshire foothills in 1942. I came in contact for the first time with the rough farm folk of the upland valleys. These were pre-tractor days. Their life was a hard slog in wind and mire on hill slopes with the occasional brief idyl-lic interludes. Their life and their attitudes administered an inward shock to my Georgian sensibility. I responded with the first of my poems about Iago Prytherch, a sort of pro-totype of this kind of farmer. It was called 'A Peasant'.[50]

A measure of the speed with which Thomas took to his new poetic terrain can be gained from the fact that 'A Peas-ant' was first published in *Life and Letters Today* in 1943, less than a year after Thomas made the move to Mont-gomeryshire and not long after he had written his neo-Geor-gian poems of the late 1930s and early 40s.[51] The question lies in how we can account for such a rapid development of methodology and register, and the answer must include the likelihood that Thomas began to read *The Great Hunger* shortly after arriving in Manafon. This seems even more plausible when we consider Thomas's use of the word "peas-ant", for as M. Wynn Thomas has observed,[52] when reading the comments passed by certain critics on the early poems we should bear in mind Raymond Williams's words regard-ing the terms appropriate for a mature discussion of Hardy:

> First, we had better drop 'peasant' altogether. Where Hardy lived and worked, as in most other parts of England, there were virtually no peasants, although 'peasantry' as a gener-ic word for country people was still used by writers. The actual country people were landowners, tenant farmers, dealers, craftsmen, and labourers.[53]

One might add that the 'peasantry' of mid-Wales (a term ultimately derived from feudal social structures) were, like Hardy's rural workers decades before, part of a capitalist economy, a fact of which R.S. Thomas, as their priest, was all too aware. It is by no means implausible, then, that the only reason Thomas uses the term "peasant" in his early poetry is because he had come across it while reading *The Great Hunger*. In fact, while Thomas did buy the Cuala Press edition of *The Great Hunger*, he might first have read parts I, II, III and 26 lines of Part IV, which was published in the London-based journal *Horizon* in January 1942, under the title 'The Old Peasant'.[54] It is a link which has not previously been made, and its credibility is strength-ened by the fact that Thomas himself contributed to *Hori-zon*: his poem 'Homo Sapiens 1941' appeared there in October 1941.[55] It seems almost certain, therefore, given that not only did they share friends and literary acquain-tances but were also publishing in the same journals and often within only a few months of each other, that Thomas would have been alive to the work of Kavanagh and would have read *The Great Hunger* shortly after its publication in April 1942.[56]

IV

One of the things that made *The Great Hunger* so revolutionary was its fidelity to fact at a time when idealisation still coloured attitudes to rural life in Ireland.[57] Antoinette Quinn makes the point that when Yeats died in 1939 the tradition of peasant romanticism was at least a century old and Irish writers could choose from a variety of literary stereotypes. The Irish peasantry had also become a nationalist property in the period preceding Independence, and in the self-consciously chauvinist period that followed. Famously, rioting had broken out at the Abbey Theatre during first week performances of Synge's *Playboy of the Western World* (1907), with sections of a largely nationalist audience incensed at what they mistakenly saw as a realist play which cast slurs upon the Irish peasantry of the West. Speaking in 1943, almost a year after the publication of *The Great Hunger*, Eamon De Valera, Taoiseach since 1932, made a notorious St Patrick's Day address, in which he projected his vision of a contented rural Ireland composed of frugal, pious, Irish-speaking, self-sufficient communities, an Ireland

> [...] joyous with sounds of industry, the romping of sturdy children, the contests of athletic youths, the laughter of comely matrons; whose firesides would be the forums of the wisdom of serene old age.[58]

Patrick Kavanagh, however, had actually worked as a subsistence farmer, and was acutely aware of the gulf which separated cultural and political fantasy from the struggle to wrest a living from a few acres of stony earth. His portrait of the Irish peasantry represents a stark, realist alternative to the more colourful heroes favoured by the Revivalists and Neo-Revivalists, such as Synge's Christy Mahon and

Yeats's Red Hanrahan. The central theme of *The Great Hunger* is the tragedy of Patrick Maguire, a Monaghan farmer whose emotional and spiritual life is nullified by local forms of righteousness and respectability, most notably those of his mother and the Catholic Church.[59]

The emptiness of Maguire's life is implicit in the title of Kavanagh's poem, which suggests a disturbing analogy between the emotional and sexual deprivation that is slowly depopulating and devitalising contemporary Ireland and the famine that ravaged the country in the mid nineteenth century. Kavanagh's anger at the way these contemporary problems have been passed over in favour of a rose-tinted view of the peasantry culminates in section XIII, which opens with a bitterly ironic view of rural contentment:

> The world looks on
> And talks of the peasant:
> The peasant has no worries;
> In his little lyrical fields
> He ploughs and sows;
> He eats fresh food,
> He loves fresh women,
> He is his own master
> As it was in the Beginning
> The simpleness of peasant life.
> The birds that sing for him are eternal choirs,
> Everywhere he walks there are flowers.
> His heart is pure,
> His mind is clear,
> He can talk to God as Moses and Isaiah talked –
> The peasant who is only one remove from the beasts
> he drives.[60]

Kavanagh locates uninformed, metropolitan perspectives within the stereotype of the peasant as a figure who, being poor but content, "has no worries". The artificiality of such idealised notions is implicit in the ironic tone of the narrative, but it is also signalled by the presence of anaphora, a short, simple sentence structure which, when combined with a biblical register, means that each statement reads as an axiom that has been learned by rote. The effect is similar to that achieved by Blake in a number of his *Songs of Innocence*, notably 'The Lamb', and it serves to highlight the limitations of a viewpoint which fails to question conventional views of the world. From the very beginning, the idyllic vision of rural life is seen to be a projection of the desires of the town, the "world" which looks on and "talks of the peasant" and whose representatives in the poem are the travelling tourists.

Kavanagh's fury at the idle talk of the town is reflected in R.S. Thomas's attitude towards what he frequently perceives to be an outside world ignorant to the social and economic realities of life in the countryside. We get an early indication of this in 'The Welsh Hill Country' (1952), the opening line of which could lead one to think that the author is indulging romanticised ideas of rural life. But it soon becomes clear that the verse carries an ironic tone and this strengthens the feeling that, even as he evokes the classic pastoral scene, Thomas is already drawing attention to the unreal nature of such landscape descriptions:

> The sheep are grazing at Bwlch-y-Fedwen,
> Arranged romantically in the usual manner,
> On a bleak background of bald stone.[61]

The artificiality of idyllic portraits of rural life is emphasised by the wonderfully sardonic terms "arranged" and "the usual manner". In the lines that follow it is the refrain "too far for you to see" which reinforces the sense that those who view the Welsh countryside in romantic terms are blind to the realities of rural life: to the "moss and mould on the cold chimneys"; to the "holes in the roof that are thatched with sunlight"; to "the nettles growing through the cracked doors". The refrain appears to be directed both towards and *against* the perspective of the distant, urban voyeur, a reading which is endorsed by 'Iago Prytherch' (1946), where Thomas mocks "the ignorant people" who would view the labourer as "the last of his kind" (CP, 16), and 'There' (1966), in which Thomas, looking back on his early portraits of hill farm life, concludes:

> It was not my part
> To show them, like a meddler from the town,
> Their picture, nor the audiences
> That look at them in pity or pride.[62]

If we return to section XIII of *The Great Hunger*, we can see that another literary stereotype to be invoked by Kavanagh involves the idea of the peasant as a touchstone for Ireland's cultural heritage, a living archive of folklore and song. Continuing in an ironic vein, the narrator declares:

> *There* is the source from which all cultures rise,
> And all religions,
> There is the pool in which the poet dips
> And the musician.
> Without the peasant base civilisation must die,
> Unless the clay is in the mouth the singer's singing is
> Useless.[63]

It seems likely that Kavanagh had Yeats in mind when he wrote these lines. After all, the idea that art thrived upon 'contact' with the earth was one which Yeats had done much to promote – witness his claim, in 'The Municipal Theatre Revisited', that

> John Synge, I, and Augusta Gregory thought
> All that we did, all that we said or sang
> Must come from contact with the soil, from that
> Contact everything, Antaeus-like, grew strong.[64]

In contrast to Yeats, Kavanagh presents us with a world in which the peasant, far from being the embodiment of a mythological fertility derived from the soil of Ireland, is unable to achieve the freedom and independence that, according to the laws of nature, should result from growth and gradual separation:

> The cows and the horses breed,
> And the potato-seed
> Gives a bud and a root and rots
> In the good mother's way with her sons;
> The fledged bird is thrown
> From the nest – on its own.
> But the peasant in his little acres is tied
> To a mother's womb by the wind-toughened navel-cord
> Like a goat tethered to the stump of a tree –
> He circles around and around wondering why it
> should be.
> No crash,
> No drama.
> That was how his life happened.
> No mad hooves galloping in the sky,
> But the weak, washy way of true tragedy –
> A sick horse nosing around the meadow for a clean
> Place to die.[65]

These lines, which bring section XIII to a close, set the sterility of Maguire's existence against the fertility of nature, his inability to break free from his misery encapsulated in the wretched image of "a goat tethered to the stump of a tree." This naturalistic method is one that Kavanagh pursues throughout *The Great Hunger*, with Maguire and his men repeatedly compared to animals: as well as the "sick horse nosing round the meadow for a clean / Place to die", the poem contains the equally savage line: "No monster hand lifted up children and put down apes / As here".[66] An important point regarding Kavanagh's demythologising of peasant life is made by Antoinette Quinn when she observes that the author's satiric presentation of primitivism "does not stop at sneering at tourists or debunking a Revivalist ideology which had been triumphantly proclaimed by Yeats."[67] More fundamentally, it subverts the Wordsworthian ideal of the noble peasant or rural worker, with Maguire stripped of the dignity that is such an essential quality in many of Wordsworth's rural figures. To emphasise this, one need only consider that, along with the animalistic comparisons, Kavanagh's poem contains scenes in which Maguire is reduced to masturbating over the lukewarm hearth of his family home – "He sinned over the warm ashes again" – and fantasising about groping schoolgirls.[68]

So far we have seen plenty of evidence to suggest that *The Great Hunger* acted as an enabling device for R.S. Thomas's poetry of the 1940s and 50s, with Kavanagh employing a poetic methodology and register ideally suited to the hill farming culture Thomas encountered at Manafon. But the Irishman's influence does not end there, for as well as showing Thomas the way in terms of providing him with a sense of how to write about rural life in a much more direct way than his earlier neo-Georgian techniques and tones would allow, it would appear that *The Great Hunger* also provided the thematic substance out of which Thomas moulded his first narrative poem 'The Airy Tomb' (1946). However, before moving on to look at that poem, it is worth considering an earlier piece of work which, with the notable exception of Tony Brown's recent study, has hitherto been overlooked by R.S. Thomas scholarship, a poem which finds Thomas experimenting with some of the techniques and the subject matter that would later go towards the creation of 'The Airy Tomb'.[69] Published in 1944 but never collected, 'Gideon Pugh' tells the story of a bachelor farmer who

> Has a house of his own, but no wife
> To ease the loneliness of his wide bed,
> And the crickets, invisible under the cauldron
> Of simmering broth, are a poor exchange for children.[70]

The parallels that can be drawn with the life led by *The Great Hunger*'s protagonist, Patrick Maguire, are striking – he too is a "lonely farmer", haunted by the absence of wife or child – and our awareness of this affinity is heightened by Thomas's subsequent presentation of Gideon as a man "who works all day, his thoughts trained to one furrow."[71]

The emphasis Thomas places on the sheer monotony of this daily routine – we are told that Gideon's feet "shuffle their way / From hedge to hedge forty times in a day" – evidently owes something to Kavanagh's portrait of a life of drudgery in the fields. But perhaps the most telling sign of Thomas's response to *The Great Hunger* comes in the third and final stanza where, in a manner which overtly recalls the invitations to "Look" and "Watch" that we encounter in Kavanagh's poem, the reader is urged to picture Gideon leaving his home and making his way out into the night in search of company:

> Follow him down, follow him down, he goes,
> Down like a moth through the dark, to the far windows
> To break the wings of his pride, sick with the hunger
> No supper allays.[72]

Thomas's use of the word "hunger" to describe this profound emotional need is a telling reminder of the way Kavanagh's poem subverted the traditional understanding of the word by focusing upon emotional and sexual hunger and unfulfilment rather than the famine that ravaged Ireland during the mid-nineteenth century. These echoes of *The Great Hunger* are all the more resonant for being repeated twice in the final lines of the poem: first via the image of the farmer's "haggard face / With its starved eyes brooding over the place" and, secondly, through the comparison of Gideon's desire to

> The dream of a stone in the grass, the hunger of a tree
> For the soft touch of the sky, of the land for the sea. [73]

V

It was in his introduction to *The Faber Book of Irish Verse* (1974) that John Montague first remarked on the "releasing influence" that *The Great Hunger* had upon writers such as R.S. Thomas and Seamus Heaney.[74] Eight years later, in an article published in the *Irish Times*, Montague went further, suggesting that Thomas "was so impressed by *The Great Hunger* that he rewrote it twice in Anglo-Welsh terms, firstly as 'The Airy Tomb' and then as *The Minister*."[75] This theme is taken up by Patrick Crotty in his essay '"Lean Parishes": Patrick Kavanagh's *The Great Hunger* and R.S. Thomas's *The Minister*'.[76] Crotty argues that "where *The Minister* is concerned the parallels with *The Great Hunger* are almost overwhelming",[77] pointing out that:

> Both poems are of middle length (458 and 753 lines respectively); both are set among materially and culturally impoverished communities; both chart the spiritual extinction of a protagonist who is more sensitive than others in his mileu but who is undone, partly at least, by his own timidity; both use rhyme sparingly and in the main for darkly comic, reductive purposes; both employ cinematic technique and zoom in upon their protagonist after a panoramic opening movement; both measure the protagonist's decline by the cycle of the seasons; both repeatedly compare his lot to that of a farm-horse; both avail of musical terminology to suggest the monotony of rural life; both comment on the irrelevance of their Sabbath observance to the day-to-day lives of the worshippers; both extract dour comedy from the spare-time attempts at intellection of their country-folk; both feature a last-page visit to the protagonist's grave.[78]

There can be no disputing the validity of *some* of these points, but many, like the assertion that "Both poems are of middle length (458 and 753 lines respectively)", fail to give any meaningful sense of a relationship between the poems, and the fact is that when reading *The Great Hunger* one is more struck by the parallels with 'The Airy Tomb' than with *The Minister*. Crotty argues that

> The evidence of 'The Airy Tomb''s debt is suggestive rather than conclusive, and even if such a debt could be proven it would remain incidental to the (somewhat limited) achievement of Thomas's poem.[79]

It is my belief that 'The Airy Tomb''s debt to Kavanagh *is* conclusive, not least because its subject matter – the life on the hills of a farm worker whose existence is unfulfilled – and its direct approach to that subject matter are firmly in tune with that of *The Great Hunger*. We notice too, that whereas *The Minister* was not published until 1955, some thirteen years after *The Great Hunger*, 'The Airy Tomb' appeared just a couple of years later, in 1946.

Although the demise of Twm (or 'Tomos'), the protagonist of 'The Airy Tomb', is not portrayed in quite such graphic terms as those employed by Kavanagh, he is seen to suffer a similar fate to Patrick Maguire in that he is a tragic figure, a destitute farmer who dies alone, wifeless and childless. Sharing the narrative form of *The Great Hunger*, if not its scale (it is less than a third of its length) 'The Airy Tomb' traces Tomos's life from his earliest school days through to his solitary adult existence and eventual death. As well as the obvious parallels in storyline – the unfulfilled life of the worker on a hill-farm – there are striking similarities in the way Kavanagh and Thomas choose to represent the fate of their protagonists. Both poets pay close attention to the life of the spirit and the imagination. In section III of *The Great Hunger*, Kavanagh suggests that the workers are alive to the ability of the landscape to bring forth glimpses of the divine:

> ...sometimes when the sun comes through a gap
> These men know God the Father in a tree:
> The Holy Spirit is the rising sap,
> And Christ will be the green leaves that will come
> At Easter from the sealed and guarded tomb.[80]

R.S. Thomas once quoted these lines in a letter to the novelist James Hanley and, although 'The Airy Tomb''s protagonist is not shown to possess a comparable *religious* impulse, it is suggested that as a child Tomos was blessed with an intuitive feeling for nature.[81] We are told that, at school, Twm's eyes "found a new peace / Tracing the poems which the rooks wrote in the sky." Furthermore,

> ...his grass-green eye
> Missed nor swoop nor swerve of the hawk's wing
> Past the high window, and the breeze could bring,
> Above the babble of the room's uproar,
> Songs to his ear from the sun-dusted moor.[82]

Thus, as in *The Great Hunger*, a more uplifting pastoral note breaks in occasionally upon the dark anti-pastoral tone, keeping before us the tantalising possibility of an alternative, more emotionally and spiritually fulfilling, existence.

But what really brings the poems together is the sadness that is felt at the way the imaginative and spiritual potential of the protagonists is lost to the earth. In the opening section of *The Great Hunger*, the narrator's despairing question "Is there some light of imagination in these wet clods?" expresses Kavanagh's fear that the endless toil of a fourteen-hour day has nullified any creative potential which may once have existed within the minds of the workers. At various points, Kavanagh portrays the Irish peasantry as living in a state of semi-consciousness: reference is made to "the enclosed nun"[83] of Maguire's thought, with the labourer later described, in marked contrast to Yeats's "wise and simple man",[84] as "illiterate, unknown and unknowing".[85] Thomas's poem follows a similar pattern in the sense that Tomos leaves school unable to read or write, and it is not long before the relentless physical demands of making a living from the land have desensitised any latent imaginative potential. Twm's "insensitive mind" remains concentrated upon "the usual jobbery in sty and stable", despite the fact that he is witness to the beauty of the changing seasons. It is a pattern which shows no sign of breaking down as Twm gets older, for as the narrator points out:

> Docking and grading now until after dark
> In the green field or fold, there was too much work
> For the mind to wander.[86]

A related and equally intriguing thematic link resides in the stress that is placed upon the *emotional* poverty of the protagonists' lives. Midway through *The Great Hunger*, the Catholic Church is identified as "the rope that was strangling true love", having engendered within Maguire a stifling repression and timidity which has prevented him from forming relationships with women. This is in spite of the fact that he feels both desire and, more profoundly, the need for love:

> Health and wealth and love he too dreamed of in May
> As he sat on the railway slope and watched the children
>> Of the place
> Picking up a primrose here and a daisy there –
> They were picking up life's truth singly.[87]

If anything, 'The Airy Tomb' takes the theme of emotional starvation to even greater extremes for, unlike Maguire, who wonders "if his mother was right / When she praised the man who made the fields his bride"[88] and "cried for his loss one late night on the pillow", Twm shows little sign of possessing even an awareness of love, regarding it merely as a crude sexual impulse, indistinguishable from "the itch of cattle at set times and seasons".[89] This reductive view of human relationships echoes that described by Kavanagh in *The Great Hunger*, where Maguire inhabits a community in which "Love" has been reduced to "The heifer being nosed by the old bull".[90] Estranged and disinterested, Twm remains utterly unresponsive to the attentions of the girls of the parish, who

>> ...stood at their doors
> In November evenings, their glances busy as moths
> Round that far window; and some, whom passion
>>> made bolder
> As the buds opened, lagged in the bottom meadow
> And coughed and called.[91]

Crotty argues that these lines attest to "a frankness about sexual matters in Tomos's community strikingly at variance with the attitudes and practices of Maguire's Donaghmoyne", thus confirming the distance that separates the two poems.[92] Yet it seems to me that Thomas is drawing, unconsciously perhaps, upon a similar scene from *The Great Hunger*, in which Maguire, "walking / Among his cattle in the Yellow Meadow" meets

> ...a girl carrying a basket –
> And he was then a young and heated fellow.
> Too earnest, too earnest! He rushed beyond the thing
> To the unreal. And he saw Sin
> Written in letters larger than John Bunyan dreamt of.[93]

In both poems, the encounter in the meadow is a microcosm of the lost opportunities suffered by the two protagonists; of the extent to which life has been stifled. But whereas Maguire's desires are frustrated by a combination of his endless toil in the fields and the repressive strictures of the Catholic Church, Tomos's failure to respond to the natural cycle is attributed solely to his inability to conceive of anything beyond the day-to-day running of his hilltop farm. The girls from the village may call,

> But never a voice replied
> From that grim house, nailed to the mountain side,
> For Tomos was up with the lambs, or stealthily hoarding
> The last light from the sky in his soul's crannies.[94]

Surprisingly, one can detect a touch of admiration in the narrator's voice, stemming perhaps, from the fact that Tomos has refused to yield to the social and economic pressures of the wider world. As in 'Out of the Hills' (1946), we can see the Welsh uplands assuming a sense of purity and morality which is set against the malicious gossip of "the lewd tavern".[95] In certain poems from the 1960s, such as 'A Welshman at St James' Park' (1966), Thomas views isolation as a means of preserving individual integrity and it is tempting to see the seeds of that idea being sown here. The same tone emerges in the final lines of 'The Airy Tomb', when the narrator urges us to recognise that

...Twm was true to his fate,
That wound solitary as a brook through the crimson heather,
Trodden only by sheep, where youth and age
Met in the circle of a buzzard's flight
Round the blue axle of heaven; and a fortnight gone
Was the shy soul from the festering flesh and bone
When they found him there, entombed in the lucid weather.[96]

Conclusion

Given the strength of the affinities that have been observed, not just in 'The Airy Tomb' but in a number of R.S. Thomas's early poems, it is clear that his creative response to *The Great Hunger* played a vital role in his development as a poet, in terms of providing him with many of the thematic and methodological tools out of which he moulded the darker shades of his pastoral vision. The transition from an early pastoral lyricism in the style of the Georgians to a poetry that engages with the complex realities of the life he encountered at Manafon was achieved with the help of a writer who had made a similar journey himself and, as we have seen, it was to another Irish poet, Austin Clarke, that Thomas turned for guidance when confronted with the question of how one could be a Welsh writer and yet continue to express oneself in English. Moreover, while this essay has focused on Thomas's relationship with Irish poetry during the 1930s, 40s and 50s, this is not to suggest that the connection ends there. Allusions to the work of Kavanagh, Synge and particularly Yeats crop up throughout Thomas's poetry and prose. Writing of his time at Aberdaron in *The Echoes Return Slow* (1988), Thomas asks:

> Had he like John Synge come 'towards nightfall upon a race passionate and simple like his heart'? Simple certainly. There is an intellectual snobbery.[97]

The abrupt manner in which Thomas undercuts the quotation from Yeats's elegy 'In Memory of Major Robert

Gregory' is a measure of Thomas's bitter disillusionment at failing to realise his communal vision of the "true Wales", a vision that had been shaped by his youthful response to the work of Synge, Sharp and Yeats. In *Neb* Thomas describes how, having retired to Sarn Rhiw, a small cottage overlooking the fierce waters of Porth Neigwl, he would often look across the Irish sea and gaze at the mountains of Wicklow. Ireland clearly continued to exert a powerful hold upon Thomas's imagination and the appeal that it held for him is perhaps best summed up by the following passage from his autobiography, in which he reflects that:

> [...] Naming the areas of Wales as a mother names her children, there takes shape in the mind a unified picture that pleads for the heart's loyalty. The land of Wales has to be loved as well as its people. That is where the Irish beat the Welsh. Éire has stolen their heart away. In one of Yeats's plays, there is an account of an old woman coming to a young man's cottage the day before his wedding, calling on him to follow her. He does so. Later a neighbour asked someone else whether he had seen the old woman. 'No,' said the man. 'But I saw a young, beautiful girl who walked like a queen.'[98]

NOTES

1   Richard Burnham, '*The Dublin Magazine*'s Welsh Poets', *Anglo-Welsh Review*, 27, 60 (1978) 49-63, 52. R.S. Thomas's father, T.H. Thomas, worked on the ferry that ran between Dublin and Holyhead. The poem 'Memories of Yeats whilst traveling to Holyhead' (1946) seems to have been inspired by the thought that Yeats had often made the same journey.

2   R.S. Thomas, *Autobiographies*, trans. Jason Walford Davies (London: Dent, 1997) 45.

3   Of course, the "true Wales" was in fact an *imaginative* construct, born out of a deeply personal and emotional need. This moment of self-recognition marks the point at which Thomas began a conscious movement towards what he felt to be a more authentic, emotionally fulfilling mode of existence, involving the rejection of his English-speaking background and the re-casting of himself according to his own designs as a Welshman.

4   *Autobiographies*, 45. The poet's son, Gwydion Thomas, suggests that it was actually R.S. Thomas's then fiancée, the artist Mildred Eldridge (known as 'Elsi'), who introduced him to Sharp and to works like *Ossian*. Email to Professor Tony Brown, University of Wales, Bangor, October 2005.

5   *Autobiographies*, 47-8.

6   *Autobiographies*, 47.

7   Tony Brown, 'The Romantic Nationalism of R.S. Thomas', *The Literature of Place*, ed. Norman Page and Peter Preston, (Basingstoke: Macmillan, 1993) 156-169, 157.

8   'The Mountains', *Selected Prose*, ed. Sandra Anstey, with an introduction by Ned Thomas, (Bridgend: Poetry Wales Press, 1995) 105.

9   Barbara Prys-Williams, '"A consciousness in quest of its own truth": Some Aspects of R.S. Thomas's *The Echoes Return Slow* as Autobiography', *Welsh Writing in English: A Yearbook of Critical Essays*, Vol 2 (1996) 98-125.

10 The programme was part of 'The Poet's Voice' series and is cited hereafter as 'The Poet's Voice'. Transmission date: August 21st 1947 on B.B.C. Home Service.

11 'The Poet's Voice'. 'Hill Farmer' was published in *Wales* 29 (1948) 511, but never collected.

12 *CP*, 22.

13 *CP*, 22.

14 'The Poet's Voice'. [Emphasis added].

15 For an introduction to Clarke's work see John Goodby, 'From Irish Mode to Modernisation: the poetry of Austin Clarke', *Contemporary Irish Poetry*, ed. Matthew Campbell (Cambridge: CUP, 2003) 21-41.

16 Thomas MacDonagh, *Literature in Ireland: Studies Irish and Anglo-Irish* (Dublin: Talbot Press, 1916) 55. Of course, from its very inception this project rested on a contradiction: that, given the identification of language with national essence, and the lack of first language fluency in Irish amongst the intelligentsia, the 'Irish mode' was, in fact, a compromise.

17 Austin Clarke, *Collected Poems*, ed. Liam Miller (London: The Dolman Press in association with OUP, 1974) 587 n.

18 Clearly, this is by no means an exhaustive account of Irish prosody. For a detailed study of Irish verse forms see *Early Irish Verse*, ed. Ruth P. M. Lehmann (Austin: University of Texas, 1982).

19 *Collected Poems*, 126.

20 'R.S. Thomas in conversation with Molly Price-Owen', *David*

Jones Journal, R.S. Thomas Special Issue, Summer/Autumn (2001) 93-102, 99.

21 'The Poet's Voice'.

22 *The Dublin Magazine*, January-March 1948, 3. The final stanza of the poem appears to contain unconscious echoes of Yeats's 'He Wishes for the Cloths of Heaven' and Wordsworth's 'The Solitary Reaper'.

23 *Prose*, 29.

24 Sandra Anstey, 'Some Uncollected Poems and Variant Readings from the Early Work of R.S. Thomas', *The Page's Drift: R.S. Thomas at Eighty*, ed. M. Wynn Thomas (Bridgend: Seren, 1993) 22-35. A volume of R.S. Thomas's uncollected poetry, to be published by Bloodaxe, is currently being prepared by Professor Tony Brown and Dr Jason Walford Davies of the University of Wales, Bangor.

25 Five anthologies of Georgian poetry were published between 1912-1922. Among the poets represented were Rupert Brooke, W.H. Davies, Walter de la Mare, D.H. Lawrence, John Masefield and Robert Graves.

26 Taken from a tape of R.S. Thomas reading and discussing his own poems, 'Norwich Tapes Ltd: The Critical Forum', 1978. See also *Miraculous Simplicity*, 23.

27 R.S. Thomas, *The Stones of the Field* (Carmarthen: Druid Press, 1946) 9.

28 Tony Brown, *R.S. Thomas* (Cardiff: UWP, 2006) 17-19.

29 Kavanagh's first collection, *Ploughman and Other Poems* (1936), encouraged by his friend and mentor 'A.E.' (George Russell, 1867-1935), contains a number of mystical, neo-Georgian lyrics. In 'To a Blackbird' the sweet sound of the bird's song is set against a picturesque background of lakes and hills.

30 'The Parish and the Universe', *Collected Prose* (London: MacGibbon and Kee, 1964) 282.

31 "I made the Iliad from such / A local row. Gods make their own importance". Patrick Kavanagh, *Selected Poems*, ed. Antoinette Quinn (London: Penguin, 2000) 101. All future references to this volume.

32 *Selected Poems*, 14.

33 *Selected Poems*, 14. Lines like these are a reminder of the debt that Seamus Heaney's debut collection, 'Death of a Naturalist (1966), owes to Kavanagh, a debt which is freely acknowledged in essays like 'From Monaghan to the Grand Canal: The Poetry of Patrick Kavanagh' (1975). See Seamus

Heaney, *Preoccupations* (London: Faber, 1980) 115-130.
34 Patrick Kavanagh, 'Self Portrait', *Collected Pruse*, 13.
35 The *Standard*, 28th May 1943; see also *The Bell*, February 1951. For a fuller discussion of Kavanagh's critique of Synge, Gregory and Yeats see Antoinette Quinn's *Patrick Kavanagh, Born Again Romantic* (New York: Dublin and Syracuse, 1991) 166-170 and 196-8.
36 *Selected Poems*, xxiii.
37 In 1949 Kavanagh told Larry Morrow: "I'm the only man to have written in our time about rural Ireland from the inside." 'Meet Mr. Patrick Kavanagh', *The Bell*, 16, I (April 1949) 5-11.
38 'The Poet's Voice'.
39 'A Welsh View of the Scottish Renaissance', *Wales*, 30, November 1948, 603.
40 *CP*, 74.
41 *Selected Poems*, 24.
42 *CP*, 18.
43 *CP*, 57; 28.
44 *Selected Poems*, 19.
45 *Selected Poems*, 42.
46 *Selected Poems*, 34.
47 *Selected Poems*, 34.
48 Thomas's image directly recalls Kavanagh's portrait of Maguire "Turn[ing] over the weedy clods". *Selected Poems*, 20.
49 Anstey, 27-8.
50 *Ted Hughes and R.S. Thomas read and discuss selections of their own poems*, The Critical Forum (Sussex: Norwich Tapes, 1978).
51 *Life and Letters Today*, XXXVI: 67 (1943), 154.
52 M. Wynn Thomas, *Internal Difference: Twentieth-Century Writing in Wales* (Cardiff: University of Wales Press, 1992) 110.
53 Raymond Williams, *The English Novel from Dickens to Lawrence* (St Albans: Paladin, 1974) 82.
54 *Horizon* 5.25 (1942) 12-17. That Thomas did own the Cuala Press edition has been confirmed by the poet's son, Gwydion Thomas, in an email to Professor Tony Brown, October 2005.
55 *Horizon* 4.22 (1941) 232. A note relating to this discovery appeared in the March 2008 edition of *Notes and Queries*. See Samuel Perry, 'Patrick Kavanagh and *Horizon*: a source for R.S. Thomas'a use of "peasant"', *Notes and Queries* (Oxford: OUP, 2008).
56 In 1939, Kavanagh published three poems – 'Primrose',

'Memory of my Father' and 'Anna Quinn' – in the Autumn edition of *The Dublin Magazine*. R.S. Thomas contributed two poems – 'The Bat' and 'Cyclamen' – to the following July-September issue. The first complete edition of *The Great Hunger* was published by Cuala Press in April 1942. It was later printed as the concluding poem in *A Soul for Sale*. However, lines 9-32 of section II were omitted on grounds of obscenity.

57 Parallels can be drawn with the valorisation of the *gwerin* in Welsh literature and with the modes of thinking about Wales which we find in the writings of Saunders Lewis. Dafydd Glyn Jones notes the emphasis that Saunders Lewis places on the peasantry in his political writings in *Presenting Saunders Lewis* (Cardiff: UWP, 1973) 23-79.

58 Quoted by Quinn in *Selected Poems*, xix.

59 Patrick Maguire's name can be read as an ironic reference to the national saint of Ireland, marking him out as a representative figure, an Irish country Catholic Everyman.

60 *Selected Poems*, 40.

61 *CP*, 22.

62 *CP*, 167.

63 *Selected Poems*, 40-1.

64 Early on in his life, Yeats, sharing the antagonism felt by English writers of Pre-Raphaelite background – notably William Morris – to the urban and industrial harshness of contemporary English culture, sought a resistance to it in Irish peasant folk traditions and Ancient Celtic myth. In addition to *The Celtic Twilight*, Yeats edited an anthology entitled *Fairy and Folk Tales of the Irish Peasantry* (1888). It is notable too, that whereas Yeats claimed an eighteenth-century intellectual lineage that included "Goldsmith and the Dean, Berkeley and Burke", Kavanagh selected as his eighteenth century artistic ancestor Art McCooey, a farm-labourer poet from his native region.

65 *Selected Poems*, 41-2.

66 *Selected Poems*, 21.

67 *Patrick Kavanagh, Born-Again Romantic*, 157.

68 *Selected Poems*, 35. On R.S. Thomas's engagement with Wordsworth's version of pastoral see Sam Perry, 'The Pastoral Vision of R.S. Thomas', *Almanac - Welsh Writing in English: A Yearbook of Critical Essays*, 12 (2007-8).

69 *R.S. Thomas*, 27. Professor's Brown's study was written at the same time as this article.

70 *Wales*, IV: 6 (1944) 47.

71 *An Acre of Land* (1952) saw Thomas publish a poem with the

title, 'The Lonely Farmer', featuring yet another solitary male labourer who finds himself "betrayed by the heart's need" (*An Acre of Land*, Newtown: Montgomeryshire Printing Co, 1952) 34.

72 *Wales*, IV: 6 (1944) 47, my italics.

73 *Wales*, IV: 6 (1944) 47, my italics.

74 John Montague, *The Faber Book of Irish Verse* (London: Faber and Faber, 1974) 35.

75 John Montague, *The Figure in the Cave and Other Essays*, ed. Antoinette Quinn (Dublin: The Lilliput Press, 1989) 145.

76 Patrick Crotty, '"Lean Parishes": Patrick Kavanagh's *The Great Hunger* and R.S. Thomas's *The Minister*,' in *Dangerous Diversity: The Changing Faces of Wales*, ed. Katie Gramich and Andrew Hiscock, (Cardiff: University of Wales Press, 1993) 131-49.

77 Crotty, 133.

78 Crotty, 133-4.

79 Crotty, 133.

80 *Selected Poems*, 23.

81 This letter, which is dated 21st December 1955, is in the James Hanley papers at Temple University Library, Philadelphia, USA.

82 *CP*, 17.

83 *Selected Poems*, 31.

84 'The Fisherman', *W.B. Yeats: Collected Poems* (London: Macmillan, 1990) 166.

85 *Selected Poems*, 36.

86 *CP*, 19.

87 *Selected Poems*, 27.

88 *Selected Poems*, 20.

89 *CP*, 19.

90 *Selected Poems*, 35.

91 *CP*, 20.

92 Crotty, 132.

93 *Selected Poems*, 25.

94 *CP*, 20.

95 *CP*, 20.

96 *CP*, 20.

97 R.S. Thomas, *Collected Later Poems 1988-2000* (Tarset / Northumberland: Bloodaxe, 2004) 46.

98 *Autobiographies*, 103. Thomas is referring, of course, to *Cathleen ni Houlihan*.

'Magnifique, n'est-ce pas?':

Representations of Wales and the world in Islwyn Ffowc Elis's *Wythnos Yng Nghymru Fydd*

Craig Owen Jones
Bangor University

A great many authors with nationalist sympathies are accused of parochialism from time to time, but this criticism cannot be levelled at Islwyn Ffowc Elis. The pre-eminent authority on Elis' works, his biographer T. Robin Chapman, characterises him in two ways: as 'the committed writer for whom literature must serve a purpose outside itself', but also as 'the genre-bender, the man who has experimented with comedies of manners, family saga, science fiction, farce and downright good reads'.[1] Certainly, one can hardly speak of an author who has written novels with locales as diverse as an African plantation, the fictional planet Theros, and the depths of Eryri (Snowdonia) in terms of narrow-mindedness. At the same time, Elis also sought to promote the idea of Welsh nationalism as a cause with a specific world outlook, one that encouraged solidarity with other small nations and eschewed notions of militarism in favour of pacifist principles.

His fourth novel, *Wythnos Yng Nghymru Fydd* ('A Week In Future Wales', 1957), is a case in point – indeed, it represents the one occasion on which Elis tackled the nationalist issue head-on in novel form, with the declared intention of persuading as many readers as possible to look kindly on the nationalist dream of an independent Wales. The protagonist Ifan Powel's trips to two alternate visions of Wales in 2033 – one a Utopian independent nation-state, the other a materially- and culturally-impoverished province of England – provide insight into the internationalist streak that has been a hallmark of Welsh nationalism for decades. Awareness of the novel among the Cymry Cymraeg (Welsh-speaking Welsh people) has remained high over the years, and its renown is largely based on the famous scene in which Powel witnesses the death of the last speaker of Welsh in the dystopian Wales, a passage that has been recited from the stages of *eisteddfodau* on more than one occasion. The book was reprinted in the 1990s and again in 2007, and an abridgement for Welsh learners was published in 1993.[2] Given this, it seems odd to find that Elis looked very harshly on it in retrospect; indeed, he later contended that it was so deeply flawed as to be unworthy of the label 'literature'.[3] Though he saw no contradiction in combining the roles of novelist and polemicist (not at the time of the book's composition, at any rate), the flaws on which Elis predicated his comments nevertheless seem to arise from the conflict between the requirements of a good story and the requirements of an effective propaganda piece; they centre primarily around the awkwardness which ensued when the political aspects of the novel clashed with basic tenets of characterisation and plot function. Yet for all its faults, it remains an interesting novel, if only because of the light it casts on the aspirations of the nationalists in the 1950s, and the intriguing manner in which Elis conceptualises Welsh relations with the rest of the world.

It is fair to say that the novel stands as a somewhat anomalous addition to Elis's early output.[4] Born in Wrexham in 1924, he first came to prominence as an essayist, winning the Prose Medal at the National Eisteddfod in 1951 for *Cyn Oeri'r Gwaed* ('Before the Blood Cools'), his collection of often light-hearted essays on subjects ranging from the personality of traditional craftsmen to the psychological benefits of being a fly.[5] One of the essays is entitled 'Ar Lwybrau Amser' ('On the Paths of Time'), and it, together with another, 'Mynd i'r Lleuad' ('Going To The Moon'), reveals an early interest in science fiction. It is known that Elis was familiar with the works of Aldous Huxley as a teenager, and was particularly impressed by the dystopian novel, *Brave New World* (1930), set six hundred years in the future on an Earth where humans are grown in bottles and conditioned by hypnotic suggestion from an early age to enable them to carry out their predetermined role in society.

If there is one element of Huxley's lurid vision that influenced Elis during the writing of *Wythnos Yng Nghymru Fydd*, it is the challenge to the set order of things, represented in *Brave New World* by the appearance of the Savage, the man from the uncivilised wilderness who refuses to partake of the *soma* that inures his worldly companions against the essential meaninglessness of their existence; in so doing, the reader is invited to sympathise with him. The character of Ifan Powel bears this burden in Elis's novel. It is the indignation and revulsion that Powel feels on witnessing the dystopian Wales in the final pages of the novel that produce in him the desire for radical change; and while the multitude of guises Powel is progressively forced to assume – 'everyman', neophyte, ardent nationalist – ultimately compromise the integrity of his characterisation, there can be no doubt that the theme of the individual as an agent of change is a most important element of a novel whose *raison d'etre* is primarily didactic.

Even the most ardent follower of Elis's works must have been unprepared for the appearance of *Wythnos Yng Nghymru Fydd* in 1957 – it was, quite simply, unlike anything he had attempted before. His first and best-known work, *Cysgod y Cryman* ('Shadow of the Sickle'), appeared in 1953, and recounts the story of Harri Vaughan, the heir of a wealthy Powys farming family, and how his flirtation with Socialist principles jeopardises his comfortable position in life. Like the court of King Lear, Harri's family react with shock to his initial renunciation of his inheritance and societal position; but, unlike the king, a reversion to the *status quo* is eventually made possible.[6]

The sheer strength of the plot and the vividness with which the story is told ensured *Cysgod y Cryman*'s exceptional popularity, which remains to this day. His subsequent novels, *Ffenestri Tua'r Gwyll* ('Windows Towards The Dusk', 1955) and *Cysgod y Cryman*'s sequel, *Yn ôl i Leifior* ('Back To Lleifior', 1956), were less spectacularly successful but still best-selling in the Welsh context. *Wythnos Yng Nghymru Fydd* was, in comparison, a critical failure. Critical reception both at the time of its publication and since has been decidedly mixed; R.M. Jones wondered if it were not intended as a children's book, and W.J. Jones averred that the story was spoilt by the intrusion of politics, while Delyth George has pointed to 'naïfrwydd ei chymeriadau' (the naivety of its characters) as its main weakness.[7] What prompted Elis to turn his attentions to science fiction, and what did he hope to accomplish in the writing of *Wythnos Yng Nghymru Fydd*?

In attempting to answer these questions, it is important to acknowledge both Elis's political leanings, and the state of Welsh politics in the 1950s. In 1956, Elis turned his back on a career in the Calvinistic Methodist ministry to work as a freelance writer on a full-time basis – a remarkable leap of faith at a time when there was no Welsh-language television channel or radio station for which one could write to supplement one's income. Elis was a nationalist, a member of Plaid Cymru since his days at the University of Wales, Bangor, and his belief in the desirability of an independent Wales was apparent even in his early writings.[8] It was Plaid Cymru that originally published *Wythnos*, and it was dedicated to the party's president, and the man who would later become the party's first MP, Gwynfor Evans.

At this time Plaid Cymru's outlook was determinedly internationalist. Regular articles in the party's Welsh- and English-language news-sheets considered the political situations in other stateless nations – in 1952 and 1953 alone, *The Welsh Nation* published essays with such titles as 'The Story of Estonia', 'How the Faroe Islands Won Self-Government', 'Wales and European Federation', and 'The Green Saltire: The Basques' Year of Freedom', as well as shorter news stories on issues of self-determination and language maintenance in Friesland, Brittany, Cornwall, Scotland, and many other countries.[9] This open-minded attitude towards the question of Wales's position in the world arguably resulted in a modest increase in support for the party; indeed, the coup of a well-publicised visit by Gwynfor Evans to America in late 1958 to deliver a memorandum to the United Nations on the Welsh case for self-government afforded Plaid Cymru an unwonted degree of credibility on an international stage.[10]

At the polls, however, the outlook was less promising. Plaid's involvement in the cross-party 'Parliament for Wales' campaign of the 1950s brought scant rewards, and its share of the vote at the elections of 1951 and 1955 was meagre (although it is true that at neither election did the party contest every Welsh seat; it would not do so for some years). Unlike its counterpart in Scotland, the Scottish National Party, which returned an MP to Westminster as early as 1945, Plaid Cymru would not have a representative in the House of Commons until the mid-1960s.[11]

Finally and perhaps crucially, the novel was published at the height of the Tryweryn crisis. The decision of the Liverpool Corporation to drown the Tryweryn valley near Bala, in the face of virtually unanimous opposition from Wales's MPs, made clear to the Welsh population the inability of the country to protect its own interests.[12] Indignation over the way in which the Corporation rode roughshod over Welsh wishes was widespread and undoubtedly influenced the Zeitgeist in which Elis set about writing his provocative science fiction novel.

This, then, was the atmosphere in which Elis began to compose the novel. However, neither the advent of the 'Parliament for Wales' campaign nor the Tryweryn crisis were Elis's immediate motives for writing it. As T. Robin Chapman has noted in his biography *Rhywfaint o Anfarwoldeb*, Elis's intentions were twofold: firstly, to swell the coffers of Plaid Cymru, an aim that was achieved (the party made over three hundred pounds' profit from sales of the book), and secondly, to win over readers with no interest in politics to the idea of a 'free Wales'.[13] It is therefore arguably more appropriate to refer to *Wythnos Yng Nghymru Fydd* first and foremost as a propagandist piece, rather than as a work of science fiction. Indeed, the extent to which Elis managed to incorporate elements of nationalist policy, and especially Plaid Cymru's eagerness to consider Wales as a

discrete entity in relation to international affairs, is notice-
able from the very beginning.

It is something of an irony that the first representation of
this readiness to re-define Wales's place in the world
appears to be based on a misconception. Ifan Powel's gate-
way to the future is provided by Doctor Heinkel, a university professor from Germany, whose experiments on the
nature of 'Space-Time' allow him to propel Powel eighty
years into the future. It is interesting that Elis should have
chosen to make the instigator of Powel's journey a German
national. German technological prowess in many areas,
including aviation, atomic science, and rocketry – in which
they were world leaders – was unquestionable in the 1930s,
but efforts in virtually all fields were severely hindered by
the destruction of the German economy at the end of the
Second World War. Had Powel been a citizen of Wales in
1933, Doctor Heinkel's appearance would have made more
sense, but the fact that by 1953 a large proportion of Germany's foremost scientists were either dead, retired, or
working in America or the Soviet Union makes Doctor
Heinkel's presence in Wales anachronistic. The psychological rationale for creating the character of Doctor Heinkel,
however, outweighed considerations of plausibility along
these lines. It is true that, strictly speaking, the inclusion of
an American or English professor instead of a German one
would have been more believable; even the devising of a
time machine by a Welsh inventor in his garden shed could
perhaps have been made to sound plausible. None of these
solutions, however, would have contributed to the propaganda value of the book. One of the purposes of the novel
is to establish the validity of a conceptualisation of Wales as
an entity distinct from England, sufficiently well equipped
culturally and politically to interact with the rest of the
world, without the mediation of the English. Respect for
Wales, its sovereignty, and its customs would then follow;
and the appearance of Doctor Heinkel – a Continental visitor, learned, and sufficiently enamoured with and respectful
of Welsh culture to learn the indigenous language – so early

on in the book helps to prepare the reader mentally for what is to come.

Wythnos Yng Nghymru Fydd, in common with a number of science fiction texts from the 1950s, contains some predictions of technological changes in the future that have actually come to pass (its concept of receiving newspapers through the 'radio' can be construed as foretelling the advent of the Internet, its videophones are also already upon us, while its driverless cars can not be far away). Others appear more dubious: it will surely be some time before 'atomic lorries' roam our streets and crowds of Cardiffians watch magnetic football at Ninian Park (or, indeed, its soon-to-be-completed successor!). Yet descriptions of technological advancements are not where the interest of the book fundamentally lies, but rather, in the notion that radical social and political change is possible in the Welsh case. The Utopian Wales to which Powel is at first transported, together with Friesland, Bavaria, Scotland, Brittany, and (one presumes) several other stateless nations, is independent, and ruled over from Cardiff by a bicameral government. Everyone in Wales is functionally bilingual – the debates on the floor of the Senedd are extraordinary displays of code-switching – and religion is thriving thanks to an ecumenical revival. Policy regarding signage (and avoiding English loan words in spoken Welsh) is utterly different from that prevailing in the Wales of 1953, as Powel discovers during a stroll with his host, the university lecturer Llywarch, through the streets of Cardiff:

> Y peth cyntaf a'm trawodd oedd yr enwau Cymraeg uwchben y siopau: *Siôn Meirion, Dilledydd*; *Harri Tawe, Ffotograffydd*; *Bwrdd Trydan Cymru*; *Siop Siencyn*. Dywedodd Llywarch fod enwau'r siopau a'r strydoedd i gyd yn Gymraeg, ond bod y cyfarwyddiadau yng ngorsaf y rheilffordd a'r orsaf awyr yn Gymraeg a Saesneg, yn ogystal â'r cyfarwyddiadau i draffig ac ymwelwyr.
> 'Oes gan bawb syrnâm Cymraeg?' meddwn i.
> 'Cyfenw ydych chi'n feddwl? O na, fe gewch ambell

Jones a Williams a Davies o hyd. Ond mae'r mwyafrif mawr erbyn hyn yn cario enw sir neu ardal eu hynafiaid neu ryw enw Cymraeg arall...

(The first thing that struck me were the Welsh names over the shop fronts: *Siôn Meirion, Dilledydd(Draper)*; *Harri Tawe, Ffotograffydd (Photographer)*; *Bwrdd Trydan Cymru (Wales Electricity Board)*; *Siop Siencyn*. Llywarch said that all the street and shop names were in Welsh, but that the directions at the railway station and the airport were in Welsh and English, as well as the directions for traffic and visitors.

'Does everyone have a Welsh surname [syrnâm]?' I said.
'A *cyfenw*, you mean? Oh no, there are still a fair few Joneses and Williamses and Davieses. But by now the vast majority take the name of the county or district of their ancestors, or some other Welsh name...)[14]

A great deal of the novel's rhetorical force comes from this sort of sardonic comment on the habits of the readership at which Elis aims. It is a thick-skinned reader of *Wythnos Yng Nghymru Fydd* indeed who does not flinch upon, for example, seeing the character with whom they are invited to identify being castigated for using Cymricised English words instead of their proper Welsh equivalents, an exceedingly common (and often still frowned upon) trait among the Cymry Cymraeg of today. It was one of Elis's strengths as a writer that he could pinpoint those elements of a situation that he knew would sting his readership to the quick, and then, having elicited a reaction, hopefully bring about a dramatic change of opinion. A splendidly concise example of this strategy can be found in the short story 'Seren Unnos' ('One-Night Star'), from his collection of stories, *Marwydos* ('Embers', 1974).[15] In sparing language, the story chronicles the thoughts of a former musician whose singing partner becomes an international success (Elis' inspiration for the story is unclear, but on reading it one thinks instinctively of south Walian singer, Tom Jones). Much is made of the way in which the singer is complicit in the adoption of the stage name Marty Jones (as opposed to his given name of Gerallt Lewis) and attention is drawn to his assumption of an American accent. Published in the mid-1970s, at a time when Welsh-language pop music was becoming popular, the story addresses the debate, which still persists today, over whether or not Welsh pop performers should adopt a bilingual or monoglot English repertoire. Although this debate had been raging for some years in the pages of Welsh-language music magazines such as *Asbri* and *Sŵn*,[16] 'Seren Unnos' represents a highly complex, literary response to the coming of stardom to members of a Welsh-speaking community. The text appears to suggest that, in order to become a star, one must necessarily cast off one's original identity. Nevertheless, remaining true to oneself has its own rewards, as the reader learns at the conclusion, when it is revealed that the narrator married Glenda, the woman over whom he and 'Marty' had come to blows years earlier.

A similar strategy is used several times in *Wythnos Yng Nghymru Fydd* – with reference to everything from Welsh political institutions to clothing – with varying degrees of success. Sometimes the disparity between the Utopian Wales (with which the greater part of the book is concerned) and reality produces an effect which places an intolerable strain on readerly credulity, a case in point being the episode in which a public-spirited spectator at a Ninian Park football match defuses a row between a policeman and a fan who has unlawfully gained entry to the ground by volunteering to pay for his admission. But at other times the expedient of describing the more mundane aspects of the Utopian Welsh society – of imagining what was perfectly possible but simply not sanctioned in the Wales of the 1950s – has the desired effect. Elis's vision of the myriad English- and Welsh-language newspapers that constitute the Welsh press in 2033 seems somewhat optimistic, but must nevertheless have prompted the reader of the 1950s to consider what life would be like in a world with several Welsh dailies to choose from; similarly, the notion that Theatr Genedlaethol Cymru (The National Theatre of Wales) would have forged such a reputation by 2033 that the company would be invited to Munich to perform to Bavarian audiences would have brought home to 1950s audiences the possibility of links between the new nation-states of Europe and future Wales.

Nor are the links represented in the text merely cultural ones. Powel learns that Wales is now part of the Cymanwlad Brydeinig (British Commonwealth), and also of the Cynghrair Celtaidd (Celtic League), set up by the six Celtic countries to promote economic and cultural ties (the current organisation of the same name was established several years after the completion of the book). One may also infer from Powel's meeting with Telting, the Friesian ambassador, that Wales is similarly a part of at least some of the 'leagues and federations' to which the self-governing states of Friesland and Bavaria also belong. These ties, though given only the briefest of mentions, are essential to the viability of the edifice that Elis creates in his fictional world. In that world, although Wales maintains a relationship with England, it is seen to be looking beyond England to the wider world. Naturally enough, the point is later driven home when Powel visits the alternate, dystopian Wales – in this future, 'Britain' is now known as 'England', the term 'Wales' having been abolished as 'politically dangerous', and discussion of political and social links with other countries is very deliberately removed from the narrative.

Yet Wales's future relationship with England remains an issue even in the utopian vision. It is acknowledged that even in this Utopia, there will be some dissenters to the new order, be they Welsh citizens descended from English families, conservatives, or royalists, who wish to see Wales reunified with England. Elis therefore goes out of his way to emphasise the fact that British unionism in Wales continues, in the words of T. Robin Chapman, only in the guise of 'a paramilitary rump'.[17] A first hint of dissent against the new order comes during the visit of Powel and Llywarch to Ninian Park for a football match in chapter eight, when Powel is accosted during the half-time interval by a strange man 'with hardness in his eyes' who urges him to attend a political meeting to be held that night, with a view to Powel addressing the crowd:

> 'Gaf i ddweud,' meddai'r dyn, 'fy mod i'n falch o gyfar-fod â gŵr o'r hen ddyddiau dedwydd gynt? Y dyddiau llewyrchus pan oedd Cymru'n un â Lloegr a gwleidyddi-aeth yn gall.'
>
> 'Wel, fuaswn i ddim yn dweud eu bod nhw'n ddyddiau llewyrchus,' meddwn i. 'Mae Cymru – hynny welais ohoni – yn edrych yn fwy llewyrchus heddiw – '
>
> 'Gwrandewch.' Yr roedd y dyn yn annifyr o agos i'm hwyneb. 'Rwy'n gofyn ichi ddod i annerch cyfarfod mawr heno yn Neuadd Siarl y Trydydd. Fe fydd cerbyd yn eich disgwyl chi wrth dŷ Doctor Llywarch am saith.'
>
> 'Annerch cyfarfod! Ond... ond i beth?'
>
> 'I ddweud wrth y dyrfa hardd fydd yno mai dyddiau Pry-dain Unedig oedd oes aur Cymru, ac i roi darlun clod-forus o'ch cyfnod eich hun, ac i annog Cymru i fynd yn ôl i'w hen ffyrdd.'
>
> 'Ond,' meddwn i, 'dydw i 'rioed wedi annerch cyfarfod cyhoeddus yn 'y mywyd – '
>
> 'Dechreuwch heno. Fe dalwn ni'n hael ichi. Ac os na ddowch...'
>
> 'Wel?'
>
> 'Fe all fod yn edifar gennych.'

('May I say,' said the man, 'how glad I am to meet a man from the good old days? The prosperous days when Wales was one with England and politics was sensible.'

'Well, I wouldn't say that they were prosperous days,' I said. 'Wales – what I've seen of it – looks far more pros-perous today – '

'Listen.' The man was unpleasantly close to my face

'I'm asking you to come and address a big meeting tonight in Charles the Third Hall. A car will be waiting for you outside Doctor Llywarch's house at seven.'

'Address a meeting! But... but why?'

'To tell the great crowd that will be there that the time of the United Kingdom was the golden age of Wales, and to give an attractive account of your own period, and to encourage Wales to go back to the old ways.'

'But,' I said, 'I've never addressed a public meeting in
my life – '
'Start tonight. We'll pay you handsomely. And if you
don't come...'
'Well?'
'You could be sorry.'[18])

Llywarch, who is not witness to this exchange, returns
shortly, and explains that the strange man was 'one of the
scouts of the C. P. U.' – the Cynghrair Prydain Unedig, or
United Britain League.

The first part of the section dealing with Powel's visit to
Utopian Wales is especially entertaining when Powel is either
in direct contact with one or another of these advocates of
the reunification of the Home Countries, or else is discussing
their activities. The frequency and regularity with which
these passages appear may be explained in part by the fact
that they provide a welcome crease in the otherwise utterly
unruffled world of Llywarch, his daughter Mair, and the rest
of Wales. T. Robin Chapman puts it succinctly when he
writes that 'The most common criticism of *Wythnos Yng
Nghymru Fydd* is that the utopian section, which accounts
for a good three-quarters of the novel, is so worthy and dull.
Who would really want to live there?'[19] Discussion of the
political situation in Wales therefore provides a diversion
from Llywarch's blasé pontifications and Powel's soul-
searching over his unrequited love for Mair. Suspense is cleverly built up by the simple expedient of ensuring that Llywarch's first attempts at explaining the politics of the Utopian world are repeatedly postponed, by the resumption of
play at Ninian Park for example, or by the intervention of a
bored ambassador earlier in the novel during a discussion
about the *Senedd*:

'Ydi hi'n llwyddiant?' meddwn i.
'Yn llwyddiant?'
'Yr oedd y tri yn syllu arnaf yn syn.
'Hynny ydi,' meddwn i wedyn, gan deimlo fy mod wedi
rhoi fy nhroed ynddi braidd, 'ydi hi'n well ar Gymru dan
ei senedd ei hun nag oedd hi hebddi?'

'A oes modd iddi fod yn waeth ar wlad dan ei senedd ei
hun nag o dan senedd estron?' gofynnodd Telting.
Chwarddodd Baecker. Yr roedd yn amlwg wedi deall rhe-
diad y sgwrs.
'Gwyliwch i'r C. P. U. gael gafael arnoch chi, Herr
Powel,' meddai. 'Fe fyddan am eich cael chi'n ymgeisydd
seneddol.'
'C. P. U.?'
'Cynghrair Prydain Unedig,' eglurodd Llywarch.
'Nhw yw disgynyddion Torïaid eich dyddiau chi. Mae
ganddyn nhw aelodau yn seneddau Lloegr a'r Alban
hefyd.'
'Ydyn nhw'n gryfion?'
'Allan nhw byth gasglu digon o nerth i ffurfio llywo-
draeth.'
'Pwy sy'n ffurfio'r Llywodraeth ar hyn o bryd?'
'Y Cyd-weithredwyr, gyda chefnogaeth Meibion y Tir.
Wedyn, yn Wrthblaid, mae gennym ni Gynyddwyr, a
Marcsiaid Newydd, a – '
'Digon, digon!' ebe Baecker ar ein traws. 'Mae gwleidy-
ddiaeth yn sychach na dirwest.'

('Is it a success?' I said.
'A success?'
The three stared at me quizzically.
'That is,' I said presently, feeling that I had put my foot
in it somewhat, 'is it better for Wales with its own parlia-
ment than it was without it?'
'Is there any way that a nation could be worse off with
its own parliament than it would be under a foreign one?'
asked Telting.
Baecker laughed, having obviously got the gist of the
conversation.
'Watch out that the C. P. U. don't get hold of you, Herr
Powel,' he said. 'They'll make you a parliamentary can-
didate.'
'C. P. U.?'
'The United Britain League,' explained Llywarch.
'They are the equivalents [lit. 'descendants'] of the
Tories in your day. They have members in the parliaments
of England and Scotland as well.'
'Are they strong?'

'They could never gather enough strength to form a gov-
ernment.'
'Who forms the Government at present?'
'The Co-operatives, with the support of the Sons of the
Land. Then, in Opposition, we have the Progressives, the
New Marxists, and – '
'Enough, enough!' interrupted Baecker. 'Politics is drier
than temperance.'[20])

With the incomplete information provided by this sort of
interrupted exposition, the reader is invited to imagine
what sort of organisation the C. P. U. is, with its shadow
paramilitary wings, such as the Cymdeithas Filwrol Cymru
(Military Society of Wales), and the Crysau Porffor (Purple
Shirts), to whom much of the twenty-first chapter is devot-
ed. Piecing together fragments of information deftly scattered through the first fifteen chapters, the picture that (at
first) emerges of the C. P. U. is one of a fringe party well to
the political right. This is never explicitly stated, but in a
world in which the prevailing political wind blows from a
pacifist left (see below), the inference is clear. The resonance between the Crysau Porffor and the various fascist or
quasi-fascist organisations of the 1930s, for example, can
hardly be unintentional. Elis may well have had in mind
Oswald Mosley's Blackshirts, or perhaps even the Irish
Blueshirts, established just before the Irish general election
of 1932 and outlawed the following year, and with whom
W. B. Yeats briefly sympathised.[21] Incidents such as the
shooting of an outspoken critic of the Crysau Porffor, covered in a newspaper article which also notes that a sergeant
of the movement was being held by the police for ques-
tioning, do not encourage the reader to look kindly upon
what is evidently an immoderate unionist element in Welsh
society. Yet the C. P. U. is presented as being of less importance as an opposition party than either the Progressives or
even the New Marxists who sit in the *Senedd*, and are
reduced to tailing people who might provide useful public-
ity such as Powel in an attempt to win them over – the
scout at the football match makes a sinister reappearance

in the following chapter at a theatre attended by Powel.
Even the demonstrations of the volunteers of the Cymdeithas Filwrol Cymru, complete with rifles and fronted by a
marching band, evoke little interest in the inhabitants of
Cardiff, who, for the most part, ignore them:

> 'Byddin Cymru, mae'n debyg?' meddwn i.
> 'Nage,' meddai'n swta. 'Fe fyddai'n well gen i ichi fod
> heb weld y rhain. Dyma un o'r blotiau duon ar Gymru
> Rydd.'
> Gofynnais iddo egluro.
> 'Wel,' meddai, 'mae amryw o wledydd wedi dileu eu llu-
> oedd arfog erbyn hyn. Mae Cymru'n un ohonyn nhw. "Y
> Gwledydd pasiffistaidd" y gelwir ni. Y cyfan y wnawn ni
> yw cyfrannu mintai i'r heddlu cydwladol. Ond mae'r ysfa
> filwrol yn anodd iawn ei lladd. Ac rydych chi'n edrych
> nawr ar fintai o Gymdeithas Filwrol Cymru.

> ('The Army of Wales, I daresay?' I said.
> 'No,' replied [Llywarch] brusquely. 'I would have pre-
> ferred it you hadn't seen these. Here is one of the black
> marks on Free Wales.'
> I asked him to explain.
> 'Well,' he said, 'several countries have abolished their
> armed forces by now. Wales is one of them. "The pacifist
> countries" we are called. All we do now is contribute a
> company to the international police. But the military
> instinct is a very difficult one to kill. And you are now
> looking at a troop of the Military Society of Wales.'[22])

It transpires that by 2033 atomic weapons have been abolished. The mechanism by which this was made possible is
not explained, although, given the sensible nature of world
politics, one might usefully envisage an agreement such as
the one advocated by Jonathan Schell in *The Abolition*
(1984) being put into place, whereby the principles of
nuclear deterrence are kept in place, but the world's
nuclear arsenals are dismantled and the ability of countries
to rebuild weapons is carefully monitored. The main thrust
of Schell's thesis – namely, that it is possible to abolish

nuclear weapons without bringing into existence a world government[23] – had not been precisely articulated when Elis wrote the book. Nevertheless, he stumbles upon it as a solution to the problem of maintaining the integrity of a utopian world free of the fear of major armed conflicts while presenting utopian Wales as a completely independent and self-governing nation-state.

According to Schell, the two principal political doctrines in a nuclear-armed world formulated in the late 1940s – namely, deterrence and world government – were (and, in some quarters, continue to be) thought of as incompatible because the former, though preserving the principle of national sovereignty, relied on the existence of nuclear weapons to work, while the latter could successfully abolish nuclear weapons, but also required the abolition of national sovereignty. Elis, however, cannot hedge his bets in this regard. If the political aims of the novel are to be achieved, he requires both a pacifist (or at least largely pacifist) world and a free Wales, so he anticipates Schell's conclusions. We are thus led to infer that world peace – or something very close to it – has been attained in Elis's Utopia, though not apparently via the mechanism of world government. With nuclear weapons abolished, conflicts are kept in abeyance by some sort of conventionally-armed global watchdog. Such an arrangement would, of course, require the existence of a global authority with the ability to inspect facilities for weapons construction. The idea of establishing a policing body with the powers to examine the workings of a particular organisation in minute detail is advanced by Elis with regard to the Welsh government's inspection of the activities of Cymdeithas Filwrol Cymru, and Llywarch's comment on Wales' commitment to provide the 'international police' with a detachment of soldiers must refer to such a body. Llywarch's world is one in which violence does not pay.

However, it is difficult to reconcile this idea with the military pageantry and enthusiasm for military institutions of every sort that lingered on in many areas of British society after the Second World War. 'Human beings,' wrote George Orwell, 'don't only want comfort, safety, short working-hours, hygiene, birth-control and common sense; they also … want struggle and self-sacrifice, not to mention drums, flags and loyalty-parades.'[24] Elis knows this – "Mae'r ysfa filwrol yn anodd iawn ei lladd" ("The military instinct is a very difficult one to kill," p.34) – which is why he spends so much time dropping hints about the make-up of the C. P. U. The disposition of the Cymdeithas Filwrol Cymru in particular is explained in some detail. It is a voluntary society which the Welsh government does nothing to prohibit in the interests of free speech, but which is subjected to a mandatory annual inspection. It is very unpopular ('pur amhoblogaidd'), and relies on subscriptions and donations in order to exist:

> 'Ond mae'n rhaid bod ganddyn nhw ryw amcan,' meddwn i, wrth wylio'r fintai'n toddi rownd congl y stryd.
> 'Amddiffyn Cymru, meddan nhw. Ond y cwestiwn yw, rhag pwy? Y gwir yw mai adran ydyn nhw o Gynghrair Prydain Unedig – yr C. P. U. y clywsoch chi amdanyn nhw neithiwr. Mae 'na Gymdeithas Filwrol yn yr Alban hefyd. Mae Lloegr yn eu gwahardd nhw, fel y mae hi'n gwahardd llawer o gymdeithasau. Ond wrth reswm, mae gan Loegr ei lluoedd arfog swyddogol.'

> ('But they must have some purpose,' I said, while watching the company melt away round the street corner.
> 'Defending Wales, so they say. But the question is, from whom? The truth is that they are a section of the United Britain League – the C. P. U. you heard about last night. There is a Military Society in Scotland as well. England prohibits them, as it prohibits a lot of societies. But of course, England has its own official armed forces.'[25])

The Crysau Porffor come to the forefront from chapter sixteen onwards, as Powel is kidnapped and taken to Gwynedd. Organisational relationships between the Crysau Porffor and the Cymdeithas Filwrol are intentionally kept indistinct in order to further foster the impression of a shadowy underground group: Powel's captors seem to belong to the former while using the facilities of the latter. But Elis discredits them not only by having two of the members betrayed by their subordinates – by dint of which Powel escapes his kidnappers – but also by noting in passing that people of no political persuasion tend to join their ranks purely to join in their camping trips and processions. The group of Crysau Porffor volunteers Powel encounters in Beddgelert, far from wearing jackboots and proclaiming unswerving devotion to the Union Flag, are local lads who like dressing up in uniforms and improving their aim on firing ranges, and are also excellent four-part harmony singers, who 'keep off the politics for the most part'.[26] In short, by the twenty-first chapter, the sinister overtones of the organisation have all but disappeared.

This at least provides an answer of sorts to the question of the fate of the unionist lobby: reunification is never seriously addressed because no-one in Wales really wants it. It is far from being a fully satisfactory resolution to the problem of finding a tenable and self-consistent representation of the lingering unionist sentiment. After all, members of the C. P. U. are a palpable threat to national security in certain passages – having their own tracts of land and even aeroplanes – and akin to a group of incorrigible, headstrong scallywags in others (the section in which the local head constable addresses Powel's erstwhile captors reminds one of nothing so much as a headmaster telling off a pair of naughty schoolboys). Moreover, the protestations of the Beddgelert party to the effect that they would never willingly kill are not especially convincing.

One suspects that Elis sensed the inadequacy of this explanation, for the question of the utopian Wales's relations with England is never addressed again. Indeed, the extent to which Powel and his host manage to avoid discussion of England is surprising. Possibly this also was a very deliberate omission. Where England is referred to by Llywarch it is only for comparative purposes – its penal system, for example, is adjudged not to work as efficiently

as that of Wales, and there are hints here and there that the
country is under totalitarian rule: England prohibits the
formation of an English branch of the Military Society, "as
it prohibits a lot of societies".[27]

England only truly enters the narrative during Powel's
visit to the dystopian Wales. This country, if it can be
described as such – the very name 'Wales' has been banned,
in a manoeuvre that calls to mind Orwell's totalitarian government's methods of suppressing sedition by abolishing
the very words by which seditious thoughts might be con-
veyed in *Nineteen Eighty-Four* (1949) – is ruthlessly exploited for the benefit of England. Massive plantations cover the
country, uranium mines dot the landscape, riots and civil
unrest are common occurrences among the workforce (for
the purposes, it is made clear, of gaining better wages or
more food, rather than effecting political change), and vast
swathes of the coastline are covered with caravans for the
use of the hundreds of thousands of tourists who visit in the
summer. Political change was effected at local level by the
gradual displacement of Welsh members of local councils by
more industrious English incomers during the 1980s, but
this prosaic change does not mask the fact that the government of this 'England', with its 'political certificates' and
hidden microphones, is nothing short of totalitarian in spirit. Only two parties, the English Democrats and the State
Socialists, are allowed to sit in Parliament; becoming a member of any other political party is made difficult by means of
red tape. The differences between the two futures could
hardly be made clearer than in a comparison of Powel's
hosts – his host in dystopian Wales in Professor Rupert
Owen Richards, a native of Arfon who re-learnt Welsh after
losing it as a child when his family moved to England; and
whereas Llywarch entertains friends from the Continent and
harbours cosmopolitan views, Richards reveals that he
spent most of his life in England, his father having been
unable to find work in Wales. Everything in this world is sinister and dark – armed gangs roam the streets, tall fences
straddle the hillsides, and even the film poster Powel's eye

falls upon in Gwynedd advertises a film with the title *No Release From Hell*.[28]

Worse still for Powel, Welsh has died out almost completely, and speaking it in public is reason enough for people to look suspiciously on the pair. Richards accompanies him on a trip to find the remaining speakers. It is on this journey around Wales that Powel meets Mair – only in this reality, her name is Maria Lark, and she has no recollection of him – and he lingers in the back room of a filthy tavern just long enough to witness the death of the last native speaker of Welsh in what has become one of the most famous passages in Welsh-language literature, as previously mentioned. It is also on this trip that Elis seizes on an opportunity to further prick the conscience of the reader, by having Powel learn of the existence of several new lakes in Wales bearing the familiar names of centuries-old villages and prospering valleys, now submerged: Llyn Dyffryn Ceiriog, Llyn Dolanog, Llyn Ffestiniog, Llyn Nant Ffrancon, and Llyn Tryweryn. Clearly, in this future the English government has Wales under its thumb.

But this future is some way off after Powel's release from his kidnapping in the utopian Wales; and the chapter immediately preceding this kidnapping episode is of interest because it concentrates less on the political life of Wales compared to that in other nations, and more on the wider political question. What sort of role does Welsh culture play in the wider world in 2033, and how do people from other nations relate to it? Naturally, the cultural axis of the book is centred around Europe rather than the Americas. Even by the 1950s, the extent to which American cultural mores were invading British life was remarked upon; but discussion of American culture in the novel is glossed over, by dint of association with England, perhaps. Welsh culture is respected and cherished by other peoples. Indeed, young Welsh performers (like those of today) fuse contemporary styles with traditional Welsh musics; but in contrast to today's situation, this fusion attracts the attention of audiences across the globe, and is re-exported, so to speak. One of the most fascinating passages

in the book can be found in the fifteenth chapter, in which
Powel's experience of this 'Cerdd-dantata' – a strange mixture of *penillion* musical traditions, macaronic song, and
modern jazz, performed on this particular evening by the
world-famous Sim Sanders, depicted mopping his brow with
a handkerchief in the manner of Louis Armstrong – is
recounted:

> 'Mae'n anhygoel, on'd ydi?' ebe Llywarch. 'Mae'r galw
> am Gymry i ganu rhigymau fel yna – yn Gymraeg a Saes-
> neg, Cymraeg a Ffrangeg, Cymraeg a Sbaeneg – yn ddi-
> ben-draw. Mae Sim Sanders newydd ddod yn ôl o Amer-
> ica'n awr, wedi gwneud arian pur sylweddol, meddan
> nhw, yn canu "*Kerdantata*, the popular traditional
> rhythm of wild and wonderful Wales". Fe fyddai'r hen
> gantorion penillion yn troi yn eu beddau. Ond dyna fe,
> mae pethau fel'na'n anochel unwaith y mae cenedl yn
> mynd ar fap y byd.'

> ('It's incredible, isn't it?' said Llywarch. 'The demand for
> Welshmen to sing songs [lit. 'rhythms'] like that – in
> Welsh and English, Welsh and French, Welsh and Spanish
> – is endless. Sim Sanders has just recently come back
> from America, having made a very substantial amount of
> money, so they say, singing "*Kerdantata*, the popular tra-
> ditional rhythm of wild and wonderful Wales". The old
> penillion singers would be turning in their graves. But
> there it is, things like that are inevitable once a nation is
> put on the world map.'[29])

Elis was a keen advocate of the principle that Welsh musical
culture should move with the times. In this respect, it is
worth mentioning an article written by him for pop music
magazine *Asbri* over a decade after the publication of *Wythnos Yng Nghymru Fydd*, which reveals a great deal about his
attitude towards the cross-fertilisation of musical genres.[30]
In this little-known article, he refers to his own dalliances
with popular music in the 1940s, which then consisted of
writing ballads in a light style along with Meredydd Evans
and Gerallt Richards, and makes mention of the composi-

tions of Evans, Cledwyn Jones and Robin Williams, the famous 'Triawd y Coleg' (The College Trio), who wrote two songs every week for inclusion in a regular radio programme broadcast from Bangor in the 1940s, as well as praising the first 'swing' tunes set to Welsh words by artists such as Ifor Rees and Dafydd Ifans. Of especial relevance to the section of *Wythnos Yng Nghymru Fydd* dealing with Cerdd-dantata is the paragraph in which Elis notes how he and his fellow songwriters attempted to incorporate overseas influences into their songs – French *chanson*, German melody, 'fake-Hawaiian', and the various rhythms of Latin America: 'Ond tipyn o orchest oedd hyn i gyd, a dweud y gwir: ceisio profi i ni'n hunain y gallai'r Gymraeg ganu mewn unrhyw idiom gydwladol. A pham lai? Fe'i profwyd, beth bynnag.' (But to tell the truth, this was all a bit of an effort on our part: [we were] trying to prove to ourselves that one could sing in Welsh in any international idiom. And why not? So it proved, in any case.)[31]

This comment raises some tantalising questions. Is the Cerdd-dantata episode, and indeed the folk-dancing performance Powel witnesses earlier in the novel, intended as a demonstration of the ability of utopian Wales to preserve and foster native artistic traditions, or as a display of its ability to adapt to norms in the rest of the world? And if, as Elis discovered in his own endeavours, it was indeed possible to adapt Welsh to any musical idiom, did he then see that adaptation as a necessary step in order to gain wider acceptance? A definitive answer to the former question is hard to come by, but in the case of the latter, one might tentatively respond with a qualified no. Though the thrust of the sections dealing with Wales's relations with the world is away from cultural isolationism, to give the impression that Cerdd-dantata thrives to the detriment of unadulterated Welsh musical forms would subtract value from those forms, and ultimately from the notion that indigenous languages such as Welsh could endure in the face of the world's arterial languages. Elis therefore wisely shies away from discussing the present state of traditional forms such as *cerdd dant*, and has Llywarch express his personal dislike of Sim Sander's performance and Cerdd-dantata in general; his comment in the above quotation, demonstrating as it does knowledge of *penillion* singing, is arguably meant to indicate that traditional styles are still practised in their original forms for the benefits of musical purists such as Llywarch.

Yet the notion of trend-setting music fans of New York and Paris, while underscoring Wales' valued contribution to global culture in the utopian world, cannot in the end be sustained, because it ultimately relies on Cerdd-dantata's status as an exotic music. Elis implies as much when he has Llywarch recite the typical American description of it as coming from 'wild and wonderful Wales'; and the injection of exoticism into western musical tradition stems, all too often, from a passing fancy. On these grounds, then, Elis's utopian world view, though not recalling imagery of Aldous Huxley's 'paradise of fat little men'[32] exactly, is unconvincing. If Wales is anything to go by, it is an eminently reasonable society in which people always have enough food in their bellies, are tolerant to a fault, and, most importantly, have respect for each other's indigenous cultures. The trouble is that nations frequently *don't* respect one another's indigenous cultures: they appropriate the useful or attractive aspects of minority cultures, incontrovertibly changing that which is appropriated in the process for their own purposes. Elis, however, is straitjacketed by the need to present the future Wales as a nation unto itself, able to stand its ground with the rest of the world. As such, he must present the international arena in the same way that he presents the *Senedd*: everybody must have an equal voice, and no-one must be allowed to ride roughshod over the rights of another.

This sort of restriction is, of course, the bane of all authors who write with the furtherance of a 'cause' in mind. A similar problem arises with the characterisation of Powel. In the first part of the book, he treats much of what he sees in the utopian Wales with the mild. scepticism

appropriate to his status as a 1950s Welshman against
Home Rule or independence. But in the final part of the
book, when Powel visits the dystopian Wales, the indifference of the inhabitants of 'Western England' to the fate
of Welsh-speaking culture, calculated as it is to engender
feelings of remorse and indignation in the reader, requires
that Powel shares in these emotions. He is thus forced into
the impossible position of shrugging his shoulders about
Welsh culture and then, in short order, becoming a patriot
of the first rank. Elis does all he can to give Powel's conversion at least a veneer of authenticity by having Powel
clamber off the fence only during his kidnapping – that is,
at the one moment in the story when his life is imperilled,
and when he might therefore reasonably be expected to
reassert his old beliefs – when he is grilled by one of his
captors, Captain Steele, on the desirability or otherwise of
a free Wales. Making the change at this juncture also
strengthens the rhetorical force of the novel: Powel, though
previously firmly in favour of the *status quo*, sees the light
at precisely the moment when all seems lost, and is
redeemed because he was sufficiently emboldened to act at
the point when he was under the severest pressure – a powerful message of hope in 1957, a time of falling numbers
of Welsh speakers and dismay at the impending displacement of whole Welsh-speaking communities. Nevertheless,
Powel's conversion to nationalism is hurried, shoehorned
into the novel at an early stage as it had to be in order to
counter the arguments of Steele, and lacks sincerity on
account of its very expedience.

Strange as it may seem, this tension caused by the con-
flicting needs of characterisation and motive is the less crucial of the two important failings of the novel. The more
serious failing, because it pulls at the fabric of the utopian
world around which the first part of the book is based, is
the unresolved problem of demarcating Wales's cultural
sphere of influence. Elis makes valiant attempts to circum-
vent it, but these attempts are seldom overtly directed at
America or England; their cultures are ignored whenever it

is possible to do so. Whenever a foreign character or refer-
ent is required, other countries invariably supply it. The
flags of the embassies lining a Cardiff street glimpsed by
Powel as he passes by are those of Finland, Portugal,
Ghana, Venezuela, Nigeria, New Zealand and Austria
respectively – that is, relatively minor players on the international political stage of the 1950s. Even the expatriate
relative whose homecoming to Wales is discussed in the
public gallery of the *Senedd* is from Australia rather than
from America or Canada (or Patagonia, for that matter).
Indeed, practically the only time the existence of America
is acknowledged is when Powel overhears the conversation
of American tourists during the folk dancing performance
at a Cardiff restaurant, and even then Elis keeps one eye on
the Continent:

> 'I think it's perfectly charming, my dears.'
> 'Absolutely super.'
> 'I never imagined Wales could be so divinely different,
> did you?'
> Ac yn y blaen.
> Ar y dde inni yr oedd cwmni o Almaenwyr.
> 'Wunderschön, nicht wahr?'
> Ac o un o'r byrddau ar draws y llawr, daeth llais Ffrengig
> toreithog.
> 'Magnifique, n'est ce-pas? C'est magnifique!'

> ('I think it's perfectly charming, my dears.'
> 'Absolutely super.'
> 'I never imagined Wales could be so divinely different,
> did you?'
> And so on.
> To the right of us was a group of Germans.
> 'Wunderschön, nicht wahr?'
> And from one of the tables across the floor there came a
> full French voice.
> 'Magnifique, n'est ce-pas? C'est magnifique!'[33])

These representations of foreigners are remarkably in keeping with the other foreign personalities contained within

the book in that they are reasonable. They cannot be otherwise, because in order for the utopian, pacifist Wales to
endure, the nations of the world must also be reasonable,
and it is at this point that one sees the incongruity. From
the perspective of another, larger culture, minority cultures
and customs are frequently seen in reductive terms: as
'quaint' or 'exotic'. Yet Elis cannot afford to put such
words into the mouths of those foreigners that do appear
in *Wythnos Yng Nghymru Fydd*, for if he does, the principles of equality and respect on which his imagined world
society is based – and which also, one presumes, prevent
the nearest belligerent nation from landing troops at Porth-
cawl – become insupportable. Thus, Welsh dancing is
described as 'magnifique' and 'wunderschön'; it is not den-
igrated or patronized, but is simply 'different'. Doctor
Heinkel, and the ambassadors Baecker and Telting too, are
all eminently reasonable people. All three can speak Welsh
to some degree, and cultural differences between them and
Powel are confined to a brief speech by the former joking-
ly chastising Powel and his friend Tegid for being teetotal
back in 1953.[34]

Yet there is another unintended resonance in the above
passage. The tourists look for the 'divinely different', and
apparently find it in the folk dancing display; yet one's
reception of the passage is tempered by the knowledge that
in reality the process of exoticisation that is often implicit in
the act of making elements of indigenous cultures more suit-
able for mass consumption frequently lessens their value
within the culture whence they came. That those elements
of *Wythnos Yng Nghymru Fydd* Elis included in order to
emphasise Wales' cultural distinctiveness can be taken to
suggest the exact opposite in the globalised world of the
early twenty-first century is a supreme irony of the work.

References to the position of Wales in the world, then,
come from a variety of different viewpoints in the book.
Practically all are contained within the confines of Powel's
trip to utopian Wales, and one might plausibly argue that
they appear largely as a means to an end. After all, though

the existence of a utopian *world* is presupposed – how could the utopian Wales about which Elis wants to write possibly survive in the world of 2033 if the world's problems had not largely been solved? – it is not the subject of the book. It does not bear close examination, so it is kept at arm's length for most of the narrative, and the reader is left to infer that technological leaps forward, such as atomic power and the importation of sunshine from the tropics to the temperate and polar regions, have been accompanied by other advances that have raised the quality of life world-wide.

The way in which Wales interacts with the rest of the world is considered only when it seems necessary to do so, and on one level this seems a pity; but if one is to derive any enjoyment from the book one must accept this fact. After all, the most memorable passages of the novel are not the expository ones, but those that have an affective appeal, such as the one in the dystopian Wales in which Powel wheedles out of the last native speaker a final, half-remembered snatch of the mother tongue – the twenty-third Psalm – before she passes away. T. Robin Chapman compares the novel's tone to that of Plaid Cymru's essay series of the period in which party members gave their reasons why they joined, and makes the point that this sort of propaganda is reliant on the reader identifying with the author.[35] This gives a clue as to why this fascinating but flawed novel is probably second only to *Cysgod y Cryman* in the popular consciousness of Elis's works. For all its faults, it seems likely that it has done more to polarise popular sentiment among the Cymry Cymraeg in favour of their mother tongue than any other work of fiction ever written.

NOTES

1   T. Robin Chapman, *Writers of Wales: Islwyn Ffowc Elis* (Cardiff: University of Wales Press, 2000) p.2.

2   As part of the *Cam At Y Cewri* series of adaptations of famous Welsh-language novels for Welsh learners. See *Wythnos Yng Nghymru Fydd* by Islwyn Ffowc Elis (abridged by Basil Davies) (Llandysul: Gomer, 1993).

3   Quoted in *Writers of Wales: Islwyn Ffowc Elis*, p.46.

4   For an assessment of Elis's early years, see T. Robin Chapman,

Rhywfaint o Anfarwoldeb: Bywgraffiad Islwyn Ffowc Elis (Llandysul: Gomer, 2003), pp.21-46.

5   *Writers of Wales: Islwyn Ffowc Elis*, pp.18-22.

6   See *Cysgod y Cryman* by Islwyn Ffowc Elis (Llandysul: Gomer, 1990). An abridgement (Gomer, 1987) and an English translation by Meic Stephens (*Shadow of the Sickle*, Llandysul: Gomer, 1998) are also available.

7   For R.M. Jones and W.J. Jones, see *Writers of Wales: Islwyn Ffowc Elis*, p.48; for Delyth George's assessment, see *Llên y Llenor: Islwyn Ffowc Elis* (Caernarfon: Pantycelyn, 1990), p.27.

8   *Writers of Wales: Islwyn Ffowc Elis*, pp.7-8; *Rhywfaint o Anfarwoldeb: Bywgraffiad Islwyn Ffowc Elis*, pp.47-68.

9   See 'Estonia' by Dr Noelle Davies, *The Welsh Nation* Vol. XXII No. 7 (July 1953) p.8; 'Faroe Islands' by J.E. Jones, *The Welsh Nation* Vol. XXI No. 7 (July 1952) p.3; 'Wales', *The Welsh Nation* Vol. XXI No. 4 (April 1952) p.2; 'Basques' by Douglas Stuckey, *The Welsh Nation* Vol. XXII No. 7 (July 1953) p.5.

10 For the particulars of the visit, see Gwynfor Evans, *For The Sake of Wales* (Cardiff: Welsh Academic Press, 2001), pp.146-49.

11 For a brief summary of these events, see 'Welsh Politics: Cymru Fydd to Crowther' by Kenneth O. Morgan, in R. Brinley Jones (ed.), *Anatomy of Wales* (Gwerin, 1972), pp.117-44, especially pp.129-33.

12 See Gwyn Alf Williams, *When Was Wales?* (Harmondsworth: Penguin, 1985) p.291. For an account of the responses of contemporary Welsh artists to the Tryweryn crisis and its aftermath, and an assessment of the drowning of the valley on the Welsh psyche, see 'The Trauma of Tryweryn' in Iwan Bala, *Here + Now: Essays on Contemporary Art in Wales* (Bridgend: Seren, 2003) pp.38-46.

13 *Rhywfaint o Anfarwoldeb: Bywgraffiad Islwyn Ffowc Elis*, p.122.

14 *Wythnos Yng Nghymru Fydd* by Islwyn Ffowc Elis (Llandysul: Gomer, 1994; original edition, Plaid Cymru, 1957), p.31.

15 Islwyn Ffowc Elis, *Marwydos* (Llandysul: Gomer, 1974).

16 Hefin Wyn, *Be Bop a Lula'r Delyn Aur* (Talybont: Y Lolfa, 2002) covers this period of Welsh-language pop music history in detail, including the establishment of *Asbri*. For an English-language study of Welsh-language pop, see Sarah Hill,

Blerwytirhwng? (London: Ashgate, 2007).

17 *Writers of Wales: Islwyn Ffowc Elis*, p.44.

18 *Wythnos*, p.39.

19 *Writers of Wales: Islwyn Ffowc Elis*, pp.46-7.

20 *Wythnos*, pp.27-8.

21 R.F. Foster, *Modern Ireland: 1600-1972* (Harmondsworth: Penguin, 1988) pp.549-50.

22 *Wythnos*, p.34.

23 See 'Defining the Great Predicament', in *The Abolition* by Jonathan Schell (London: Picador, 1984) pp.1-90.

24 *The Collected Essays, Journalism and Letters of George Orwell, Volume 2: My Country Right or Left 1940-1943*, eds. Sonia Orwell and Ian Angus (Harmondsworth: Penguin, 1970) p.29.

25 *Wythnos*, pp.34-5.

26 *Wythnos*, p.117.

27 *Wythnos*, p.35.

28 *Wythnos*, p.222.

29 *Wythnos*, p.86.

30 "'Pop' 20 mlynedd yn ol" [sic] by Islwyn Ffowc Elis, *Asbri* No. 3 (Medi-Hydref, 1969) p.8.

31 *Ibid.*

32 George Orwell describes the dystopia of *Brave New World* as such in *The Road To Wigan Pier* (Harmondsworth: Penguin, 1962; original ed. London: Gollancz, 1937), p.169.

33 *Wythnos*, p.52.

34 *Wythnos*, p.27.a

35 *Writers of Wales: Islwyn Ffowc Elis*, p.48.

International Elements in Early *Poetry Wales*:

A Response to Malcolm Ballin

Matthew Jarvis
University of Wales, Lampeter

In his article 'Welsh Periodicals in English: *Second Aeon* and *Poetry Wales* (1965-1985)', Malcolm Ballin observes that, over the two decades with which he is concerned, '*Poetry Wales* [...] deliberately refrains from pursuing the cosmopolitanism that was the signature of *Second Aeon*'.[1] Thus, he notes that:

> The magazine does sometimes deal with international topics, but, in comparison with *Second Aeon*, the attention is relatively minor. There is one review of Portuguese poetry in 1971. However, no overseas poets appear in the comprehensive list of contributors published in the twenty-first birthday issue in 1971.[2]

Ballin goes on to note that, 'as the editorship of the magazine changed' between 1965 and 1985, 'examples of international awareness develop in later issues'.[3] But the implication of his remarks would seem to be that there is very little of international interest or origin in the early *Poetry Wales* – perhaps particularly over the years of Meic Stephens's and Gerald Morgan's editorships (which covered the period 1965-1973).

My concern in this brief response to Ballin's remarks is with precisely this early period of the magazine – in other words, with the years of its first two editors (1965-1973: issues 1.1 to 8.4).[4] I have no argument with Ballin's assessment of the general tenor of *Poetry Wales* over these years: its concentration was undeniably on the poetic life of Wales – which is entirely understandable, given that its underpinning ethos was the revitalisation of English-language poetry in Wales. However, it is simply inaccurate to assert that no overseas poets were included in what Ballin calls 'the comprehensive list of contributors' that was published in the winter 1971 issue of the magazine. Moreover, to note just one review of Portuguese poetry from this early period is fundamentally to misrepresent the scope of the international elements which *were* present at this time – and to miss entirely their deeper ideological function.

The list of poets in issue 7.3 (winter 1971) to which Ballin refers is titled 'A check-list of poets who have contributed to *Poetry Wales*, 1965-1971'; the names of Welsh-language poets in the check-list are rendered in italics, whilst all others are simply in roman type.[5] Ordered alphabetically, it does not take long to find the first – and most important – of the international contributors from this period: Joseph P. Clancy, the American poet and translator, whose work first received attention in only the second edition of the magazine, with Tony Conran's review of Clancy's important 1965 volume of translations, *Medieval Welsh Lyrics*.[6] Clancy's own poetry first appeared in *Poetry Wales* in issue 3.2 (summer 1967), which published three of his poems,[7] and identified him as 'Professor of English Literature at Marymount Manhattan College, New York City'.[8] Certainly, he was then 'In Aberystwyth on an American Philosophical Society grant for work on a companion volume to his *Medieval Welsh Lyrics*'.[9] But this situation was temporary, and although Clancy did eventually settle in Aberystwyth, he did not do so until 1990.[10] In short, there is no denying that Clancy should be classed as an overseas contributor to the early *Poetry Wales*: indeed, in a review published in *Poetry Wales* 6.1 (summer 1970), Clancy explicitly observes that 'I am American'.[11] Moreover, although his first three poems in *Poetry Wales* were described as *cywyddau*,[12] the poetic style of at least one ('In Absence') strikingly suggests the American confessional mode. Clancy was a regular contributor to *Poetry Wales* in the period with which I am concerned: in addition to those three first poems (in issue 3.2), his own work (or his translations from Welsh-language material) appeared in issues 3.3, 5.1, 5.2, 6.2, 7.2, 7.3, 8.1, and 8.4,[13] and he acted as a reviewer in issue 6.1;[14] his own books were reviewed in issues 1.2 and 6.2.[15] However, alongside Clancy, the check-list of poetic contributors to *Poetry Wales* in its earliest years also includes the Americans Joel Hedgpeth (a famous marine ecologist who also published poetry under the pseudonym Jerome Tichenor)[16] and the well-known poet Rolfe Humphries,[17] as well as the Canadian Philip Roberts.[18] Listed alongside these are John [*sic*: Jon] Dressel and Norman Schwenk – again, both Americans, but in these two cases, Americans who settled either for a long time or permanently in Wales (albeit, in Dressel's case, somewhat later than the list was compiled).[19] Finally, the prolific Italian writer Roberto Sanesi is also included – the solitary instance of the check-list noting an overseas poet whose work appeared in the magazine in translation.[20]

Of course, it must be acknowledged that seven poets do not constitute a particularly significant international constituency; moreover, they certainly make up only a very small fraction of the check-list itself, which runs to one hundred and thirty poetic contributors. But they are present, and their contribution to the early life of *Poetry Wales* must thus be acknowledged. However, part of the problem here is with the check-list itself which, with the exception of Roberto Sanesi, fails to acknowledge overseas poets who appeared in the magazine in translation; nor, of course, does it register the magazine's interest in reviewing poetry from outside the UK. And these, I would suggest, are two areas in which the magazine's early international engagements come into greater focus. The initial sign of such interests comes in the very first edition of the magazine, which includes Meic Stephens's piece 'Ker Ys', a poem that is – according to the note appended to it – 'Adapted from an old Breton song'.[21] This interest in material from Brittany is strong over the first three years of *Poetry Wales*, and is variously manifest in: a review of Patrick Creagh's 'imitations' of the nineteenth-century Finistère poet Tristan Corbière, published in the volume *A Picture of Tristan* (issue 2.2, summer 1966);[22] an article on 'Modern Breton Poetry' by Jean Piette (issue 3.1, spring 1967);[23] and an identically-titled selection of Breton work in translation in issue 3.3 (winter 1967).[24] Two of the translators of this latter material are familiar names from the early years of the magazine – Gerald Morgan and Harri Webb – whilst the third is Jean Piette, the author of the earlier article on Breton work, who is described as 'Breton by birth', 'Welsh by marriage and adoption', and 'lecturer in Breton at the University College of Wales, Aberystwyth'.[25] However, the poets featured in the Breton selection add significantly to the array of non-UK authors on display in the magazine's formative years: Maodez Glanndour, Erwan Gwegen, Roparz Hemon, Soaz Kervahe, Goulven Pennaod and Yann-Ber Piriou. This selection of Breton poetry is, without doubt, the most concentrated instance of overseas work in *Poetry Wales* under the editorships of either Meic Stephens or Gerald Morgan. But a small number of other translations also appeared in this period: of the Italian Roberto Sanesi in issue 4.3 and the Chilean Pablo Neruda in issue 7.1;[26] and of pieces from 'the Provencal of Frederic Mistral' and 'the Sardinian of Antioco Casula' (both translated by Harri Webb) in issue 5.1.[27] In other words, although Malcolm Ballin quotes from Duncan Glen's letter to *Poetry Wales* in 1971 which praised the magazine for 'its rejection of a facile and fashionable "Internationalism" which would have us all mid-Atlantic writers',[28] Glen's notion of internationalism here – which the phrase 'mid-Atlantic' construes in terms of engagement with America – really misses the point: the main thrust of the internationalism on display in the very earliest editions of *Poetry Wales* is substantially towards Europe's Celtic and regional cultures.

To this poetic material, one must add reviews of international work. As early as issue 1.2 (autumn 1965), Harri Webb reviewed P.L. Brent's edited volume *Young Commonwealth Poets*.[29] The issue following contained a review of the American Theodore Roethke's posthumous volume, *The Far Field*,[30] whilst issue 3.3 offered a 'Brief Notice' on a volume produced by the organisation Poésie Vivante, praising the book in question (which contained work by 'a British poet and a French presented both in original and translation, plus potted biography and critical essay') whilst simultaneously (and significantly, given my comments at the end of the previous paragraph) lamenting the fact that the organisation itself had not 'yet touched seriously on any of the Celtic countries'.[31] By the start of the 1970s, with Sam Adams becoming the magazine's reviews editor,[32] there was a string of reviews of work either by international authors on Welsh topics or of what the editorial for spring 1970 (issue 5.3) called 'books by major foreign poets'.[33] Thus, issue 5.3 reviewed work by the Greek poet George Seferis, as well as the translations of Dafydd ap Gwilym by a poetic contributor to an earlier issue, Rolfe Humphries (described in the review as 'an American poet of Welsh ancestry').[34] Issue 6.1 (summer 1970) is worth noting for an excoriating review *by* an international contributor (Joseph Clancy), again of translations from Welsh-language material. Clancy's target is Robert Gurney's *Bardic Heritage*, and his assessment concludes with a gloriously vitriolic passage, which surely deserves to see the light of day once more:

> To cap it all off, we are informed that *Bardic Heritage* is one of 'the first books to be honoured by an Arts Council translation grant.' Were I Welsh, I would be pelting my MP with petitions or composing curses in *cywyddau*. Since I am American, I can only hope that if this book cannot be dumped in the Atlantic, it never crosses it.[35]

Issue 6.3 (winter 1970) reviewed both a selection of work by the Chilean poet Pablo Neruda and *The Penguin Book of Irish Verse*.[36] Issue 6.4 (spring 1971) contained a long review of the volume *Notebook* by the American Robert Lowell.[37] Issue 7.1 (summer 1971) contained the review of the Portuguese poet Fernando Pessoa which Malcolm Ballin notes,[38] whilst even the special R.S. Thomas number (issue 7.4, spring 1972) turned an eye towards R.S.'s international reception by reviewing a recent German thesis on his work.[39] Finally, issue 8.1 (summer 1972) contained not only a review of an anthology of poetry from Mexico but also an assessment of the parallel-language anthology

French Poetry Today, edited by Simon Watson Taylor and Edward Lucie-Smith.[40] In short, when Sam Adams took over as editor of *Poetry Wales* in 1973 (beginning with issue 9.1), it is perhaps unsurprising that his first editorial noted, with some pride, the magazine's recent concern with reviewing a good amount of international work:

> Though our primary responsibility has been, and still is to the writer in Wales or from Wales and to the books he produces, reviews of important publications by writers of other countries have become a feature of the magazine recently. Few comparable journals could claim to have reviewed in depth the work of George Seferis, Fernando Pessoa, Robert Lowell and Pablo Neruda, and anthologies from Scotland, Ireland, France and Mexico all within the last year or so.[41]

Whether his latter contention is right (that 'comparable journals' did not reach this level of international engagement) is not my concern here. What is certainly striking, however, is the sense that, at this point in its life, *Poetry Wales* was – and had been for a number of issues at least – committed to the *idea* of international engagement. Indeed, the international reviews that Sam Adams notes in his first editorial can usefully be seen as a more expansive culmination of Meic Stephens's initial, more focused, interest in Breton poetry.

Against this, however, one must acknowledge that many of the magazine's international contributors were, in one way or another, Welsh-connected. For example, Jon Dressel, Rolfe Humphries and Philip Roberts are/were all of Welsh extraction,[42] whilst Roberto Sanesi was a translator of Vernon Watkins.[43] Moreover, the early concern with Breton poetry similarly suggests an international engagement which springs from an interest in poetry that emerges from a linguistic-cultural situation which, in some ways, parallels Welsh circumstances. In other words, it needs to be understood that elements of the internationalism within the early *Poetry Wales* are responses to the magazine's Welsh interests, rather than instances of internationalism for its own sake.

Indeed, even the concern with reviewing international work that has no apparent connection to Wales is subsumed into the magazine's central ethos when Meic Stephens and Gwilym Rees Hughes write, at the start of the 1970s, that:

> Our editorial policies will remain the same, of course, as they have been during the five years of the magazine's existence. First of all, we intend to go on publishing what we consider to be the best of the new poetry written by Welshmen in the English language. We will also carry articles on the work of individual poets and essays, reviews of all the numerous volumes of Anglo-Welsh poetry now being published, as well as occasional reviews of books by major foreign poets [...]. This magazine is committed to the fostering of Anglo-Welsh poetry, to its definition as part of a literature separate from the English and to its enrichment by critical assessment according to the highest possible standards which, we believe, are essential for its serious consideration both at home and abroad.[44]

In other words, the magazine's primary concern with promoting what is here called 'Anglo-Welsh poetry' included establishing such poetry as 'part of a literature separate from the English' – and the assessment of 'foreign poets' within the pages of *Poetry Wales* was part of that project.

International elements were, then, present within the earliest years of *Poetry Wales* to an extent that Malcolm Ballin simply does not acknowledge. However, when Ballin suggests that the magazine 'refrains from pursuing the cosmopolitanism that was the signature of *Second Aeon*',[45] he does have a point: *Poetry Wales*'s early international elements do not generally seem to represent cosmopolitanism for its own sake. Rather, they more importantly serve the magazine's central ethos of promoting and defining the English-language poetry of Wales, either by engaging with work that in some way parallels or offers a perspective on Welsh cultural conditions or by the more implicit suggestion that poetry emanating from Wales should be understood – like the 'foreign poets' to which it periodically attends – as crucially part of a non-English tradition.

NOTES

1   Malcolm Ballin, 'Welsh Periodicals in English: *Second Aeon* and *Poetry Wales* (1965-1985)', *Welsh Writing in English: A Yearbook of Critical Essays*, 11 (2006-2007), pp.147-87: p.163.
2   Ibid.
3   Ibid.
4   Meic Stephens edited issues 1.1 to 3.2 and 4.3 to 8.4; Gerald Morgan edited issues 3.3 to 4.2.
5   'A check-list of poets who have contributed to *Poetry Wales*, 1965-1971', *Poetry Wales*, 7.3 (winter 1971), p.6.
6   Anthony Conran, '[Review of Joseph P. Clancy, *Mediaeval* [*sic*] *Welsh Lyrics*]', *Poetry Wales*, 1.2 (autumn 1965), pp.25-26.
7   Joseph P. Clancy, 'Love's Language', 'In Absence', and 'The Graves', *Poetry Wales*, 3.2 (summer 1967), pp.18-22.
8   'Notes on New Contributions [*sic*]', *Poetry Wales*, 3.2 (summer 1967), p.63.
9   Ibid.
10 Meic Stephens, ed., *The New Companion to the Literature of Wales* (Cardiff: University of Wales Press, 1998), p.112.
11 Joseph P. Clancy, '[Review of Robert Gurney, *Bardic Heritage*]', *Poetry Wales*, 6.1 (summer 1970), pp.67-70: p.70.
12 'Notes on New Contributions [*sic*]', p.63.
13 Clancy's material in these issues is as follows: 'The Return' and 'The Sixth Brother', *Poetry Wales*, 3.3 (winter 1967), pp.15-16 (original poetry); 'Confession' and 'Anniversary', *Poetry Wales*, 5.1 (summer 1969), pp.13-15 (original poetry); 'Poem for Robert', *Poetry Wales*, 5.2 (winter 1969), pp.20-21 (original poetry); 'A Cywydd for Kate', *Poetry Wales*, 6.2 (autumn 1970), pp.17-18 (original poetry); 'Father's Day', *Poetry Wales*, 7.2 (autumn 1971), pp.31-32 (original poetry); 'A Cywydd for Christmas' and 'Homage to T. H. Parry-Williams', *Poetry Wales*, 7.3 (winter 1971), pp.57-64 (respectively, original poetry and translations from the Welsh of T. H. Parry-Williams); 'The Old Language', *Poetry Wales*, 8.1 (summer 1972), p.34 (translation from the Welsh of Waldo Williams); 'Eight Poems by Dafydd ap Gwilym', *Poetry Wales*, 8.4 (spring 1973), pp.65-76 (translations from the Welsh of Dafydd ap Gwilym).
14 See note 11 above.
15 See note 6 above, and Gwyn Williams, '[Review of Joseph P. Clancy, *The Earliest Welsh Poetry*]', *Poetry Wales*, 6.2 (autumn 1979), pp.63-67.

16 See Jeremy Pearce, 'Joel Hedgpeth, Marine Biologist and Advocate of Sea Life, Dies at 94', *New York Times*, 12 August 2006, <http://www.nytimes.com/2006/08/12/science/12hedgpeth.html>, accessed 1 July 2008.

17 For a brief assessment of Rolfe Humphries's career, see Ian Hamilton, ed., *The Oxford Companion to Twentieth-Century Poetry in English* (Oxford: Oxford University Press, 1996), p.245.

18 For the contributions of these poets, see: Joel Hedgpeth, 'Epitaph at Somersville', *Poetry Wales*, 4.3 (spring 1969), pp.24-25; Rolfe Humphries, 'For My Ancestors', *Poetry Wales*, 5.1 (summer 1969), pp.23-24; and Philip Roberts, 'Testing Song', *Poetry Wales*, 6.4 (spring 1971), pp.36-37.

19 For a summary of Jon Dressel's career to date, see Meic Stephens, ed., *Poetry 1900-2000* (Cardigan: Parthian, 2007), p.419. For the contributions of these poets in the period under consideration, see: Jon Dressel, 'To a Daughter Who Wasn't and a Son Who Was', *Poetry Wales*, 4.1 (summer 1968), unpaginated; Norman Schwenk, "To Yeats, Too Late', *Poetry Wales*, 4.1 (summer 1968), unpaginated.

20 For a brief assessment of Roberto Sanesi's career, see Richard Burns, 'Obituary: Roberto Sanesi', *The Independent*, 17 April 2001, <http://findarticles.com/p/articles/mi_qn4158/is_20010417/ai_n14382345>, accessed 1 July 2008.

21 Meic Stephens, 'Ker Ys', *Poetry Wales*, 1.1 (spring 1965), p.13.

22 Meic Stephens, '[Review of Patrick Creagh, *A Picture of Tristan*]', *Poetry Wales*, 2.2 (summer 1966), p.37. For a brief assessment of Tristan Corbière, see 'Corbière, Tristan', *Encyclopædia Britannica*, 2008, Encyclopædia Britannica Online, <http://search.eb.com/eb/article-9026245>, accessed 1 July 2008.

23 Jean Piette, 'Modern Breton Poetry', *Poetry Wales*, 3.1 (spring 1967), pp.3-10.

24 'Modern Breton Poetry', *Poetry Wales*, 3.3 (winter 1967), pp.25-32.

25 Ibid., p.32.

26 Roberto Sanesi, 'Elegy for Vernon Watkins', trans. Henry Martin, *Poetry Wales*, 4.3 (spring 1969), pp.38-39; Pablo Neruda, 'Walking Around', trans. Malcolm Parr, *Poetry Wales*, 7.1 (summer 1971), pp.52-54.

27 See, respectively, 'The Tree' and 'The Starry Bay', *Poetry Wales*, 5.1 (summer 1969), pp.41 and 42. Frédéric Mistral

'led the 19th-century revival of Occitan (Provençal) language and literature': see 'Mistral, Frédéric', *Encyclopædia Britannica*, 2008, Encyclopædia Britannica Online, <http://search.eb.com/eb/article-9053007>, accessed 1 July 2008. For Antioco Casula (1878-1957) – also known as Montanaru – see Manlio Brigaglia, ed., *La Sardegna*, Vol. 1 (Cagliari: Della Torre, 1984), pp.55 and 59-63.

28 Duncan Glen, 'From Duncan Glen', *Poetry Wales*, 7.3 (winter 1971), pp.27-31: p.30.

29 Harri Webb, '[Review of P.L. Brent, ed., *Young Commonwealth Poets*]', *Poetry Wales*, 1.2 (autumn 1965), pp.28-29.

30 Meic Stephens, '[Review of James Turner, *The Accident*; Theodore Roethke, *The Far Field*; George Mackay Brown, *The Year of the Whale*]', *Poetry Wales*, 2.1 (spring 1966), pp.39-40.

31 G.M. [Gerald Morgan], 'Brief Notice', *Poetry Wales*, 3.3 (winter 1967), p.55.

32 Sam Adams is first noted as the magazine's reviews editor in issue 5.3 (spring 1970), p.43.

33 Meic Stephens and Gwilym Rees Hughes, 'Editorial', *Poetry Wales*, 5.3 (spring 1970), pp.3-4: p.3.

34 Ken Snow, '[Review of George Seferis, *Collected Poems 1924-1955*, trans. Edmund Keeley and Philip Sherrard], *Poetry Wales*, 5.3 (spring 1970), pp.57-62; Glyn Jones, '[Review of Rolfe Humphries, *Nine Thorny Thickets*]', *Poetry Wales*, 5.3 (spring 1970), pp.62-65: p.62. For a brief commentary on the career of George Seferis, see 'Seferis, George', *Encyclopædia Britannica*, 2008, Encyclopædia Britannica Online, <http://search.eb.com/eb/article-9066585>, accessed 14 July 2008.

35 Clancy, '[Review of Gurney]', p.70.

36 Ken Snow, '[Review of Pablo Neruda, *Selected Poems*, ed. Nathaniel Tarn, trans. Anthony Kerrigan, W. S. Merwin, Alastair Reid and Nathaniel Tarn]', *Poetry Wales*, 6.3 (winter 1970), pp.52-56; Harri Webb, '[Review of Tom Scott, ed., *The Penguin Book of Scottish Verse*; Brendan Kennelly, ed., *The Penguin Book of Irish Verse*; Edward Lucie-Smith, ed., *British Poetry Since 1945*]', *Poetry Wales*, 6.3 (winter 1970), pp.66-69.

37 Ken Snow, '[Review of Robert Lowell, *Notebook*]', *Poetry Wales*, 6.4 (spring 1971), pp.66-70.

38 Ken Snow, '[Review of Fernando Pessoa, *Sixty Portuguese Poems*, trans. F.E.G. Quintanilha]', *Poetry Wales*, 7.1 (summer 1971), pp.68-72. For a brief introduction to the work of Fernando Pessoa, see 'Pessoa, Fernando', *Encyclopædia*

Britannica, 2008, Encyclopædia Britannica Online, <http://search.eb.com/eb/article-9059403>, accessed 14 July 2008.

39 Glyn Tegai Hughes, '[Review of Gisela Chan Man Fong, *Themen und Bilder in der Dichtung von Ronald Stuart Thomas*, Kiel University Dissertation, 1969]', *Poetry Wales*, 7.4 (spring 1972), pp.112-15.

40 Malcolm Parr, '[Review of Octavio Paz, ed., *New Poetry of Mexico*]', *Poetry Wales*, 8.1 (summer 1972), pp.83-86; Ken Snow, '[Review of Simon Watson Taylor and Edward Lucie-Smith, eds, *French Poetry Today*]', *Poetry Wales*, 8.1 (summer 1972), pp.86-88.

41 Sam Adams, 'Editorial', *Poetry Wales*, 9.1 (summer 1973), pp.3-4: pp.3-4.

42 See, variously, Stephens, *Poetry 1900-2000*, p.419; Jones, '[Review of Rolfe Humphries]', p.62; and 'Notes on New Contributors', *Poetry Wales*, 6.4 (spring 1971), p.42.

43 'Notes on New Contributors', *Poetry Wales*, 4.3 (spring 1969), p.44.

44 Stephens and Hughes, 'Editorial', pp.3-4.

45 Ballin, 'Welsh Periodicals in English', p.163.

Welsh Writing in English:
a bibliography of criticism 2007

compiled by Laura Wainwright
Cardiff University

This bibliography covers books, contributions to books, peodical articles, review-articles, reviews of listed critical writing and selected theses. Readers aware of relevant material published in 2007, which has been omitted, are kindly asked to forward details to the Editor, Katie Gramich, *Almanac – Welsh Writing in English*, School of English Communication and Philosophy, Cardiff University, CF10 3EU.

GENERAL CRITICISM

Aaron, Jane. *Nineteenth-Century Women's Writing in Wales: Nation, Gender and Identity*. Cardiff: University of Wales Press, 2007. ISBN 978-0-7083-2060-0.

Aaron, Jane. 'At Eternity's Window': Representing Church and Chapel in the Anglophone Literature of Wales. *Moment of Earth: Poems and Essays in Honour of Jeremy Hooker*. Aberystwyth: Celtic Studies Publications, 2007.

Adams, Sam. Letter from Wales. *PN Review* 33.3 (January / February 2007) 6-8. ISSN 01447076. (An account of contemporary Welsh literary culture, with a particular focus on the achievements of Raymond Garlick.)

Adams, Sam. Letter from Wales. *PN Review* 33.4 (March/ April 2007) 6-8. ISSN 01447076. (Focuses on Russell T. Davies, Roland Mathias and the publication, by Seren, of John Haynes's poetry collection, *Letter to Patience*.)

Brigley, Zoë. The One Thousand Column: Deterritorializing the Language. *Poetry Wales 42.4* (April 2007) 14-15. (On the linguistic possibilities of Welsh poetry in English.)

Curtis, Tony (editor). *Wales at War: Critical Essays on Literature and Art*. Bridgend. Seren, 2007. ISBN 97818541 1400. Contents: Introduction, by Tony Curtis, pp.7-11 – Haunted Landscapes: War in the Writings of Llewelyn Wyn Griffith, Robert Graves, Wilfred Owen and Edward Thomas, by Jeremy Hooker, pp.12-24 – David Jones: 'No End to these Wars, No End, No End / At All', by Duncan Campbell, pp.25-38 – From Mametz Wood to the Jaffa Gate: The Great War in Welsh Art, by Eric Rowan, pp.39-54 – Art in Wales during and from the Second World War, by Tony Curtis, pp.55-74 – 'Some Things You See in Detail, those You Need': Alun Lewis, Soldier and Poet, by Cary Archard, pp.75 -92 – Dylan Thomas and War, by James A. Davies, pp.93-106 – 'All Change!': Dannie Abse and the Twentieth-Century Wars, by Tony Curtis, pp.107-121 – Welsh Women Writers and War, by Katie Gramich, pp.122-141 – 'The Stones of the Field' and the Power of the Sword: R.S. Thomas as War Poet, by M. Wynn Thomas, pp.142-164 – Appendix: 'Soul-Conscripting War-Mechanic: Writers and Artists who Objected to War – Notes Towards Further Writing, by Tony Curtis, pp.165-175.

Davies, Hywel M. Wales in English Travel Writing 1791-8: The Welsh Critique of Theopilus Jones. *Welsh History Review* 23.3 (June 2007) 65-93. ISSN 0043-2431.

Donahaye, Jasmine. Is There Anybody Out There? *New Welsh Review* 77 (Autumn 2007) 49-55. ISSN 09542116. (On the challenges faced by the Library of Wales Series.)

Evans, Neil. The Atlantic in Black and White. *Planet: The Welsh Internationalist* 184 (August / September 2007) 22-28. ISSN 0048-4288. (Review-article on Daniel G. Williams, *Ethnicity and Cultural Authority: From Arnold to Du Bois* and *The Oxford Companion to Black British History*.)

Gramich, Katie (editor). *Almanac - A Yearbook of Welsh Writing in English: Critical Essays* Vol. 12 (2007-2008). ISBN 978-1-90576278-1.

Contents: Dialogues of Self and Soul: The Autobiographies of W.B. Yeats and R.S. Thomas, by Neal Alexander, pp.1-31 – 'A Poet At Last': William H. Davies and Edward Thomas, by Judy Kendall, pp.32-54 – 'The huge upright Europe-reflecting mirror': The European Dimension in the Early Short Stories and Poems of Glyn Jones, by Laura Wainwright, pp.55-88 – Glyn Jones and the Uncanny, by Tony Brown, pp.89-114 – 'I want to know what iss – behind all of them books...': Images of Education in Early Twentieth-Century Welsh Writing in English, by Alyce von Rothkirch, pp.115-139 – The Pastoral Vision of R.S. Thomas, by Sam Perry, pp.140-168 – From 'Black Water' to *Border Country*: Sourcing the Textual Odyssey of Raymond Williams, by Dai Smith, pp.169-191 – 'What a fine body of men they are!': Class, Gender and Sexuality in the Authorial Identity of Rhys Davies, by Huw Osborne, pp.192-227 – Welsh Writing in English: a bibliography of criticism 2006, by Laura Wainwright, pp.228-238.

Gramich, Katie. *Twentieth-Century Women's Writing in Wales: Land, Gender, Belonging*. Cardiff. University of Wales Press, 2007. ISBN 978-0-7083-2086-0.

Gray, Kathryn. At Home and Abroad. *New Welsh Review* 76 (Summer 2007) 27-36. ISSN 0954-2116. (On contemporary poetry published in Wales.)

Gregson, Ian. *The New Poetry of Wales*. Cardiff. University of Wales Press, 2007. ISBN 978-0-7083-1995-6. Contents: Introduction, pp.1-17 – Opposites of National Identification: Duncan Bush and Sheenagh Pugh, pp.18-33 – Baghdad Moon, the Pepsi Globe: Robert Minhinnick, pp.34-59 – Creative Discomforts of Bilingualism: Gwyneth Lewis, pp.60-74 – Oliver Reynolds and the National Subject, pp.75-87 – Stephen Knight's Cartoon Metamorphoses, pp.88-107 – Modes of Non-Realism: Paul Henry and Pacale Petit, pp.108-120 – Some Younger Poets, pp.121-138.

Lord, Peter. Biblical and Marxist Rhetoric in the Painting and Literature of the Depression. *Moment of Earth: Poems and Essays in Honour of Jeremy Hooker*. Christopher Meredith (editor). Aberystwyth. Celtic Studies Publications, 2007.

Peach, Linden. *Contemporary Irish and Welsh Women's Fiction: Gender, Desire and Power, Writing Wales in English series*. Cardiff: University of Wales Press, 2007. ISBN 978-0-7083-1998-7.

Rothkirch, Alyce von. 'I want to know what iss – behind all of them books...': Images of Education in Early Twentieth-Century Welsh Writing in English. *Almanac - A Yearbook of Welsh Writing in English: Critical Essays* Vol. 12 (2007-2008) 115-139.

Skoulding, Zoë. Border Lines. *Poetry Wales* 42.4 (April 2007) 40-41. (On poetry translation.)

Somerset, Adam. 'Who Needs a National Theatre?' *Planet: The Welsh Internationalist* 186 (December / January 2007-2008) 72-79. ISSN 0048-4288.

Taylor, Wendy. Charles Alexander Calvert and the Theatre Royal, Newport. *Theatre Notebook: A Journal of the History and Technique of the British Theatre*. 61.1 (2007) 35-39. ISSN 00405523.

Thomas, Gwyn. Poetry in Motion. *New Welsh Review* 75 (Spring 2007) 37-41. (Gwyn Thomas discusses the composition of 'screen poems', with particular reference to his own work, as well as that of R.S. Thomas and Dylan Thomas.)

Walford Davies, Damian, and Lynda Pratt (editors). *Wales and the Romantic Imagination*. Cardiff. University of Wales Press, 2007. ISBN 978-0-7083-2066-2.

Contents: Introduction: Devolving Romanticism, by Damian Walford Davies and Lynda Pratt, pp.1-12 – The Colony Writes Back: Brutus, Britanus and the Advantages of an Oriental Ancestry, by Michael J. Franklin, pp.13-42 – From the See of St David's to St Paul's Churchyard: Joseph Johnson's Cross-Border Connections, by Helen Braithwaite, pp.43-64 – 'A Subject of Conversation': Iolo Morganwg, Hannah More and Ann Yearsley, by Mary-Ann Constantine, pp.65-85 – Southey in Wales: Inscriptions, Monuments and Romantic Posterity, by Lynda Pratt, pp.86-103 – 'Redirecting the Attention of History': Antiquarian and Historical Fictions of Wales from the Romantic Period, by Andrew Davies, pp.104-121 – 'The Fostering Aid of a Sister Country': Wales in Irish Novels, 1796-1810, by Jim Shanahan, pp.122-140 – Walter Savage Landor and Wales in the 1790s, by David Chandler, pp.141-160 – 'That Deathless Wish of Climbing Higher': Robert Bloomfield on the Sugar Loaf, by John Goodridge, pp.161-179 – One Draught from Snowdon's Ever-Sacred Spring': Shelley's Welsh Sublime, by Cian Duffy, pp.180-198 – 'Sweet Sylvan Routes' and Grave Methodists: Wales in De *Quincey's Confessions of an English Opium Eater*, by Damian Walford Davies, pp.199-227 – 'Harp of the Mountain-Land': Felicia Hemans and the Cultural Geography of Romantic Wales, by Diego Saglia, pp.228-242 – 'Parallelograms and Circles': Robert Owen and the Satirists, by Jane Moore, pp.243-267.

Wallace, Diana. 'Mixed Marriages': Three Welsh Historical Novels in English by Women Writers. *Moment of Earth: Poems and Essays in Honour of Jeremy Hooker*. Christopher Meredith (editor). Aberystwyth: Celtic Studies Publications, 2007.

Wilkins, Owain. Reading the Nation. *Planet* 182 (April / May 2007) 18-24. ISSN 0048-4288. (On English-language Welsh drama.)

INDIVIDUAL AUTHORS

Dannie Abse

Curtis, Tony. 'All Change!': Dannie Abse and the Twentieth-Century Wars. *Wales at War: Critical Essays on Literature and Art*. Tony Curtis (editor). Bridgend: Seren, 2007.

Duncan Bush

Gregson, Ian. Opposites of National Identification: Duncan Bush and Sheenagh Pugh. *The New Poetry of Wales*. Cardiff: University of Wales Press, 2007.

John Cowper Powys

Dunn, John. Flight to Reality: The Wessex Novels of John Cowper Powys. *Powys Journal* 17 (2007) 87-101. ISSN 09627057.

Goodwin, Jonathan. Nationalism and Re-enchantment in John Cowper Powys's *A Glastonbury Romance. Powys Journal* 17 (2007) 41-60. ISSN 09627057.

Kusch, Celena E. Disorientating Modernism: National Boundaries and the Cosmopolis. *Journal of Modern Literature* 30.4 (Summer 2007) 39-60. ISSN 0022281X.

Krissdóttir, Morine. Descents of Memory: *The Life of John Cowper Powys*. New York and London: Overlook Duckworth, 2007. ISBN 9781585679171.
Review-article: Drabble, Margaret. Ichthyosaurus ego. *Times Literary Supplement* 5459 (November 16 2007).

Nash, Katherine Saunders. Narrative Progression and Receptivity: John Cowper Powys's *A Glastonbury Romance. Narrative* 15.1 (January 2007) 4-23. ISSN 10633685.
Rogers, Stephen. 'A Royal Personage in Disguise': A Meet-

ing between Ford and John Cowper Powys. *Ford Madox Ford's Literary Contacts*. Paul Skinner (editor). Amsterdam, Netherlands: Rodopi, 2007. ISSN 1569-4070.

Leonard Cox

Glomski, Jacqueline. *Patronage and Humanist Literature in the Age of the Jagiellons: Court and Career in the Writings of Rudolf Agricola Junior, Valentin Eck, and Leonard Cox*. Toronto: University of Toronto Press, 2007. ISBN 9780802093004.

Fflur Dafydd

Valencia, May B. Interview with Fflur Dafydd. *New Welsh Review* 78 (Winter 2007) 8-14. (Dafydd discusses the English translation of her Welsh-language novel, *Atyniad*.)

John Davies of Hereford

Vickers, Brian. *Shakespeare, 'A Lover's Complaint', and John Davies of Hereford*. Cambridge: Cambridge University Press, 2007. ISBN 978-0521859127.
Review-article: Love, Harold. Hallow the shallow. *Times Literary Supplement* 5440 (July 6 2007) 10-11.

Pennar Davies

Morgan, D. Densil. Spirit and Flesh in Twentieth-Century Welsh Poetry: A Comparison of the Work of D. Gwenallt Jones and Pennar Davies. *Christianity and Literature*. 56.3 (Spring 2007) 423-436. ISSN 01483331.

Peter Ho Davies

Bone, Alison. Wales in Wartime. *Bookseller* 5262 (January 5 2007) 16. ISSN 0006-7539. (An interview with Peter Ho Davies centred on his novel, *The Welsh Girl*.)

Rhys Davies

Osborne, Huw. 'What a fine body of men they are!': Class, Gender and Sexuality in the Authorial Identity of Rhys Davies. *Almanac - A Yearbook of Welsh Writing in English: Critical Essays* Vol. 12 (2007-2008) 192-227.

W.H. Davies

Kendall, Judy. 'A Poet At Last': William H. Davies and Edward Thomas. *Almanac - A Yearbook of Welsh Writing in English: Critical Essays* Vol. 12 (2007-2008) 32-54.

Saunders, Chris. Davies, Dawkins and the death of the author. *English Review* 18.1 (September 2007) 6-7. ISSN 0955-8950. (Discusses Davies's work in conjunction with that of Roland Barthes and the scientist Richard Dawkins.)

Dorothy Edwards

Brown, Tony. 'A personal isolated odd universe': Dorothy Edwards and her Short Fiction. *Moment of Earth: Poems and Essays in Honour of Jeremy Hooker*. Christopher Meredith (editor). Aberystwyth: Celtic Studies Publications, 2007.

Flay, Claire. Conquering Convention. *New Welsh Review* 77 (Autumn 2007) 60-66. ISSN 09542116.

Meredith, Christopher. Rhapsody's Lost Story. *Moment of Earth: Poems and Essays in Honour of Jeremy Hooker*. Christopher Meredith (editor). Aberystwyth: Celtic Studies Publications, 2007.

Jasper Fforde

Berninger, Mark and Katrin Thomas. A Parallelquel of a Classic Text and Reification of the Fictional – The Playful Parody of *Jane Eyre* in Jasper Fforde's *The Eyre Affair*. *A Breath of Fresh Eyre: Intertextual and Intermedial Revolv-*

ings of Jane Eyre. Margarete Rubik and Elke Mettinger-Schartmann (editors). Amsterdam: Rodopi, 2007. ISBN 9789042022126.

Rubik, Margarete. Invasions into Literary Tests, Re-Plotting and Transfictional Migration in Jasper Fforde's *The Eyre Affair*. *A Breath of Fresh Eyre: Intertextual and Intermedial Revolvings of Jane Eyre*. Margarete Rubik and Elke Mettinger-Schartmann (editors). Amsterdam: Rodopi, 2007. ISBN 9789042022126.

Wells, Juliette. An Eyre-less Affair? Jasper Fforde's Seeming Elision of Jane. *A Breath of Fresh Eyre: Intertextual and Intermedial Revolvings of Jane Eyre*. Margarete Rubik and Elke Mettinger-Schartmann (editors). Amsterdam: Rodopi, 2007. ISBN 9789042022126.

Dion Fortune

Graf Johnston, Susan. The Occult Novels of Dion Fortune. *Journal of Gender Studies*. 16.1 (March 2007) 47-56. ISSN 09589236.

Llewelyn Wyn Griffith

Hooker, Jeremy. Haunted Landscapes: War in the Writings of Llewelyn Wyn Griffith, Robert Graves, Wilfred Owen and Edward Thomas. *Wales at War: Critical Essays on Literature and Art*. Tony Curtis (editor). Bridgend: Seren, 2007.

Niall Griffiths

Williams, Jeni. Stories to Make the Grown-Ups Scream. *New Welsh Review* 78 (Winter 2007) 8-14. ISSN 0954 2116. (On depictions of childhood in literature and cinema, with particular reference to Eiluned Lewis's *Dew on the Grass* and Niall Griffiths's *Runt*.)

James Hanley

Barrett, Gerard. James Hanley and the Colours of War. *British Fiction after Modernism: The Novel at Mid-Century*. Marina Mackay and Lyndsey Stonebridge (editors). New York: Palgrave Macmillan, 2007. ISBN 9781403986429.

Felicia Hemans

Cronin, Richard. Felicia Hemans, Letitia Landon and 'Lady's Rule'. *Romantic Women Poets: Genre and Gender*. Lillia Maria Crisafulli and Cecilia Pietropoli (editors). Amsterdam. Rodopi, 2007. ISSN 9789042022478.

Diego, Saglia. 'A Deeper and Richer Music': The Poetics of Sound and Voice in Felicia Hemans' 1820s Poetry. *ELH: Journal of English Literary History* 74.2 (Summer 2007) 351-370. ISSN 00138304.

Kim, Benjamin. Personal Grief and Public Statement: Felicia Hemans' *The Siege of Valencia and Records of a Woman*. *Literature Compass* 4.6 (2007) 1650-1656. Reference number 2007: 217934.

Morrison, Lucy. Effusive Elegies or Catty Critic: Letitia Elizabeth Landon on Felicia Hemans. *Romanticism on the Net* 45 (2007). ISSN 14671255.

Paul Henry

Gregson, Ian. Modes of Non-Realism: Paul Henry and Pascale Petit. *The New Poetry of Wales*. Cardiff: University of Wales Press, 2007.

George Herbert

Bouchard, Gary M. The Roman Steps to the Temple: An Examination of the Influence of Robert Southwell, SJ, upon

George Herbert. *Logos: A Journal of Catholic Thought and Culture* 10.3 (Summer 2007) 131-150. ISSN 10916687.

Doumerc, Eric. Outline for a Commentary on George Herbert's 'Virtue'. *An Introduction to Poetry in English*. Eric Doumerc and Wendy Harding (editors). Toulouse: PU du Mirail, 2007). ISSN 07649169.

Dubie, Norman. George Herbert. *American Poetry Review* 36.2 (March /April 2007) 42. ISSN 03603709.

Mascetti, Yaakov. 'This Is the Famous Stone': George Herbert's Poetic Alchemy in 'The Elixir'. *Mystical Metal of Gold: Essays on Alchemy in Renaissance Culture*. Stanton J Linden (editor). New York: AMS, 2007. ISSN 0195-8011.

Song, Eric B. Anamorphosis and the Religious Subject of George Herbert's *Coloss* 3.3. *SEL: Studies in English Literature 1500-1900*. 47.1 (Summer 2007) 107-121. ISSN 00393657.

Strier, Richard. George Herbert and Ironic Ekphrasis. *Classical Philology* 102.1 (2007). Reference number 2007: 190337.

Wilcox, Allan; Wilcox, Helen. Matter and spirit conjoined: sacred places in the poetry of George Herbert, Henry Vaughan, R.S. Thomas and Rowan Williams. *Scintilla* 11 (2007) 133-151. Reference number 2007:197483.

Wilcox, Helen (editor). *The English Poems of George Herbert*. Cambridge: Cambridge University Press, 2007. ISBN 978052186821.

Jeremy Hooker

Cluysenaar, Anne. 'Embodied knowledge in a cutting touch': A Matrix in Jeremy Hooker's *The Cut of the Light*.

Moment of Earth: Poems and Essays in Honour of Jeremy Hooker. Christopher Meredith (editor). Aberystwyth: Celtic Studies Publications, 2007.

Kerridge, Richard. 'Leaves that we say are dead': Jeremy Hooker's Ecological Imagination. *Moment of Earth: Poems and Essays in Honour of Jeremy Hooker*. Christopher Meredith (editor). Aberystwyth: Celtic Studies Publications, 2007.

Meredith, Christopher (editor). *Moment of Earth: Poems and Essays in Honour of Jeremy Hooker*. Christopher Meredith (editor). Aberystwyth: Celtic Studies Publications, 2007. ISBN 978-1-891271-16-8.
Contents: Foreword, by Christopher Meredith, pp.xiii-xv – I. Earth and Words. Nettles, by Gillian Clarke, p.2 – Fantasia on a Theme from IKEA, by Philip Gross, pp.3-6 – Poem: for Jeremy, by Sam Adams, p.7 – 'Leaves that we say are dead': Jeremy Hooker's Ecological Imagination, by Richard Kerridge, pp.8-21 – Embodied knowledge in a cutting touch: A Matrix in Jeremy Hooker's *The Cut of the Light*, by Anne Cluysenaar, pp.22-40 – In the Footsteps of Roland Mathias, by Sam Adams, pp.41-55 – In Black and White: Weatherscapes in Joseph Conrad's *The Shadow-Line* and Per Olof Sundman's *Ingenjör Andrées luftfärd*, by John Barnie, pp.56-69 – Tench's Quotations: The Poem's You Take With You, by Gavin Edwards, pp.70-77 – II. Landscapes, Warscapes. Letter from West Wales, by Matthew Francis, pp.80-81 – After Kikushna-ni, by Norman Schwenk, p.82 – Various Restrictions, by David Lloyd, p.83 – 'Inwards where all the battle is': Alun Lewis's 'The Jungle', by John Pikoulis, pp.84-100 – Dancing in the Mud: Bunting's Documentary Tradition and the Anecdotage of Ford Madox Ford, by Colin Edwards, pp.101-113 – Prophetic Landscapes: Thomas Hardy and Richard Jefferies, by Roger Ebbatson, pp.114-134 – III. Welsh Women Writers. Change, by Anne Cluysenaar, p.136 – Question, by Wendy Mulford, pp.137-138 – Squirrels and Other Things, by Fiona Owen, p.139- 'A personal isolated

odd universe': Dorothy Edwards and her Short Fiction, by Tony Brown, pp.140-158 – *Rhapsody's* Lost Story, by Christopher Meredith, pp.159-170 – 'Mixed marriages': Three Welsh Historical Novels in English by Women Writers, by Diana Wallace, pp.171-184 – IV. Literature and Art. For Jeremy Hooker, by Seán Street, p.186 – Men of Iron, by Sheenagh Pugh, pp.187-188 – DJ visits Waterloo, by Tony Curtis, pp.189-191 – Biblical and Marxist Rhetoric in the Painting and Literature of the Depression, by Peter Lord, p.201-217 – That Golden Decade - David Jones, Ceri Richards, Merlyn Evans and Josef Herman: The Four Gold Medal Winners at the Welsh National Eisteddfod in the 1960s, by Tony Curtis, pp.218-233 – 'An inorganic life of things': Notes on Abstraction and Nature, by Jeff Wallace, pp.234-248 – V. Literature and Religion. The Shepherd, by Tony Conran, pp.250-251 – Northcourt, by Mimi Khalvati, pp.252-255 – Questions About Place, by David Lloyd, p.256 – 'At Eternity's Window': Representing Church and Chapel in the Anglophone Literature of Wales, by Jane Aaron, pp.257-272 – Spires of Grass: Emily Brontë's Fragment of Eternity, by Stevie Davies, pp.273-283 – R.S. Thomas, Denise Levertov and the Poetry of Contemplation, by M. Wynn Thomas, pp.284-301 – Bibliography of Jeremy Hooker, pp.303-308.

Richard Hughes

Barden, Corwin. Richard Hughes: Ford's Secret Sharer. *Ford Madox Ford's Literary Contacts*. Paul Skinner (editor). Amsterdam: Rodopi, 2007. ISSN 1569-4070.

Holmqvist, Ivo. Richard Hughes and the Critics Part I: British and American Reviews of *The Fox in the Attic. Phrasis: Studies in Language and Literature* 48.1 (2007) 29-48.

Holmqvist, Ivo. Richard Hughes and the Critics Part II: British and American Reviews of *The Wooden Shepherdess. Phrasis: Studies in Language and Literature* 48.1 (2007) 49-62.

Holmqvist, Ivo. Richard Hughes and the Critics Part III: Reviews in German. *Phrasis: Studies in Language and Literature* 48.1 (2007) 63-80.

Paul Jeff

Watt, Daniel. Transgressing the Witness at Three Sites of Knowledge. *Research in Drama Education*. 12.1 (February 2007) 79-91. ISSN 13569783.

B.S. Johnson

Tew, Phillip and Glyn White (editors). *Re-reading B.S. Johnson*. Basingstoke: Macmillan, 2007. ISBN 9780230524927.

David Jones

Andrews, Charles. War Trauma and Religious Cityscape in David Jones's *In Parenthesis*. *Journal of the Midwest Modern Language Association* 40.1 (2007) 87-96. ISSN 07425562.

Blissett, William. Footslogging. *David Jones Journal* 6.1/2 (2007) 35-43. ISSN 14641542. (On *In Parenthesis*.)

Britton, David. Poetic Inspiration and Metaphysical Knowledge. *David Jones Journal* 6.1/2 (2007) 146-161. ISSN 14645142.

Campbell, Duncan. David Jones: 'No End to these Wars, No End, No End / At All'. *Wales at War: Critical Essays on Literature and Art*. Tony Curtis (editor). Bridgend: Seren, 2007.

Dilworth, Thomas. From the Archives. *New Welsh Review* 75 (Spring 2007) 37-41. ISSN 0954-2116. (Introduction and afterword to a previously unpublished review by Jones of Richard Llewellyn's *How Green was My Valley*.)

Edwards, Kate. The Revolving Epoch: David Jones and Oswald Spengler. *Agenda* 43.1 (2007) 68-74. Reference number 2007:223604.

Gibson, Michael George. On British Poetry and Poems. *David Jones Journal* 6.1/2 (2007) 132-137. ISSN 14641542.

Hirst, Desirée. The two Davids: Jones and Rosenberg. *David Jones Journal* 6.1/2 (2007) 53-59. ISSN 1464152.

Hughes, Colin. Man on the field revisited. *David Jones Journal* 6.1/2 (2007) 17-34. ISSN 14641542.

Kynan-Wilson, William. Uniting the Strands. *David Jones Journal* 6.1/2 (2007) 970114. ISSN 14641542.

Medcalf, Stephen Eliot. David Jones and Auden. *The Oxford Handbook of English Literature and Theology*. Oxford: Oxford University Press, 2007. ISBN 9780199271978.

Price-Owen, Anne. David Jones and the Art of Hybridity. *Transactions of the Honourable Society of Cymmrodorion* 13 (2007) 176-192. Reference number 1007:217224.

Robichaud, Paul. *Making the Past Present: David Jones, the Middle Ages and Modernism*. Washington DC: Catholic University of America Press, 2007. ISBN 9780813214795.

Stevenson, Winifred. Time out: *In Parenthesis* and the legendary Otherworld. *David Jones Journal* 61.1/2 2007 44-52. ISSN 14641542.

D. Gwenallt Jones

Morgan, D. Densil. Spirit and Flesh in Twentieth-Century Welsh Poetry: A Comparison of the Work of D. Gwenallt

Jones and Pennar Davies. *Christianity and Literature*. 56.3 (Spring 2007) 423-436. ISSN 01483331.

Glyn Jones

Brown, Tony. Glyn Jones and the Uncanny. *Almanac - A Yearbook of Welsh Writing in English: Critical Essays* Vol. 12 (2007-2008) 89-114.

Wainwright, Laura. 'The huge upright Europe-reflecting mirror': The European Dimension in the Early Short Stories and Poems of Glyn Jones. *Almanac - A Yearbook of Welsh Writing in English: Critical Essays* Vol. 12 (2007-2008) 55-88.

W.S. Jones

Stephens, Meic. W. S. Jones. *Independent* (November 20 2007) 34-35. (Obituary.)

Stephen Knight

Gregson, Ian. Stephen Knight's Cartoon Metamorphoses. *The New Poetry of Wales*. Cardiff: University of Wales Press, 2007.

Alun Lewis

Archard, Cary. Alun Lewis, *A Cyprus Walk – Letters to 'Frieda'*, with a memoir by Freda Aykroyd. *Poetry Wales* 43.1 (Summer 2007) 57-59. ISSN 03322202. Review-article.)

Archard, Cary. 'Some Things You See in Detail, those You Need': Alun Lewis, Soldier and Poet. *Wales at War: Critical Essays on Literature and Art*. Tony Curtis (editor). Bridgend: Seren, 2007.

Pikoulis, John. 'Inwards where all the battle is': Alun Lewis's 'The Jungle'. *Moment of Earth: Poems and Essays in Honour of Jeremy Hooker*. Christopher Meredith (editor). Aberystwyth. Celtic Studies Publications, 2007.

Eiluned Lewis

Williams, Jeni. Stories to Make the Grown-Ups Scream. *New Welsh Review* 78 (Winter 2007) 8-14. ISSN 09542116. (On depictions of childhood in literature and cinema, with particular reference to Eiluned Lewis's *Dew on the Grass* and Niall Griffiths's *Runt*.)

Gwyneth Lewis

Gregson, Ian. Creative Discomforts of Bilingualism: Gwyneth Lewis. *The New Poetry of Wales*. Cardiff. University of Wales Press, 2007.

The Mabinogion and related materials

Breeze, Andrew. Some Critics of the Four Branches of the Mabinogi. *Constructing Nations, Reconstructing Myth: Essays in Honour of T.A. Shippey*. Andrew Waun, Graham Johnson and John Walter (editors). Turnhout: Brepolis, 2007. ISBN 9782503523934.

Green, Thomas. Tom Thumb and Jack the Giant-Killer': Two Arthurian fairytales? *Folklore* 118.2 (August 2007) 123-140. ISSN 0015587X.

Hunter, Jerry. Llywelyn's Breath, Arthur's Nightmare: The Medievalism within Welsh Modernism. *Cambrian Medieval Celtic Studies* 53-54 (Summer 2007) 113-132. ISSN 13530089.

Nickel, Helmut. About the Knight with Two Swords and the Maiden under a Tree. *Arthuriana* 17.4 (2007) 29-42. ISSN 10786279.

O' Brien, Derek. *The Mabinogion*, trs Sioned Davies. *The Independent* (4 March 2007). (Review-article.)

McKenna, Catherine. Performing Penance and Poetic Performance in the Medieval Welsh Court. *Speculum: A Journal of Medieval Studies* 82.1 (January 2007) 70-96. ISSN 00387134.

Sayers, William. La Joie de la Cort (Erec et Enide), Mabon, and Early Irish Síd (Peace; Otherworld). *Arthuriana* 17.2 (Summer 2007) 10-25. ISSN 10786279.

Sims-Williams, Patrick. Shape Swaps. *Times Literary Supplement* 5440 (July 6 2007) 10-11. (Review-article on Sioned Davies's translation of *The Mabinogion*.)

Owen Martell

Martell, Owen. A Writer's Writer. *New Welsh Review* 77 (Autumn 2007) 94-96. ISSN 09542116. (Martell discusses the influence of Dostoyevsky and T. H. Parry-Williams on his Welsh-language novels *Cadw dy ffydd, brawd* and *Dyn yr Eiliad*, which have been translated into English under the titles, *Keep Your Faith*, + *Brother* and *The Other Man*.)

Roland Mathias

Adams, Sam. In the footsteps of Roland Mathias. *Moment of Earth: Poems and Essays in Honour of Jeremy Hooker*. Christopher Meredith (editor). Aberystwyth: Celtic Studies Publications, 2007.

Adams, Sam. Roland Mathias: One of Wales's finest English-language poets of the 20th century. *The Guardian* (17 October 2007). (Obituary.)

Minhinnick, Robert. Roland Mathias, 1915-2007. *Planet: The Welsh Internationalist* 186 (December / January 2007-2008) 90-91. ISSN 0048-4288. (Obituary.)

Stephens, Meic. Roland Mathias: Poet and Literary Critic. *The Independent* (17 August 2007). (Obituary.)

Thomas, M. Wynn. Roland Mathias 1915-2007. *New Welsh Review* 78 (Winter 2007) 64-67. (Obituary.)

Robert Minhinnick

Gregson, Ian. Baghdad Moon, the Pepsi Globe: Robert Minhinnick. *The New Poetry of Wales*. Cardiff: University of Wales Press, 2007. ISBN 978-0-7083-1995-6.

Iolo Morganwg

Constantine, Mary-Ann. 'A Subject of Conversation': Iolo Morganwg, Hannah More and Ann Yearsley. *Wales and the Romantic Imagination*. Damian Walford Davies and Lynda Pratt (editors). Cardiff: University of Wales Press, 2007. 65-85.

Daniel Owen

Rhys, Robert. *Daniel Owen: Writers of Wales*. Cardiff. University of Wales Press, 2007. ISBN 0-7083-1795-2. (Includes a discussion of Owen's influence on the development of the Welsh novel in English.)

Pascale Petit

Gregson, Ian. Modes of Non-Realism: Paul Henry and Pascale Petit. *The New Poetry of Wales*. Cardiff: University of Wales Press, 2007.

Katherine Philips

Hutson, Lorna. The Body of the Friend and the Woman Writer: Katherine Philips's Absence from Alan Bray's *The Friend* (2003). *Women's Writing* 14.2 (2007) 196-214. Reference number 2007:196816.

Misantoni, Luisiana. Katherine Fowler Philips: the Matchless Orinda. Una poetessa inglese del Seicento. *Studi sul canone*. Mirella Billi (editor). Viterbo: Sette Città, 2007. ISBN 9788878530850.

Stanton, Kamille Stone. Painting Sentinels: Erotics, Politics and Redemption in the Friendship Poetry of Katherine Philips. *Comitatus: A Journal of Medieval and Renaissance Studies* 38 (2007) 155-172. ISSN 00696412.

Sheenagh Pugh

Gregson, Ian. Opposites of National Identification: Duncan Bush and Sheenagh Pugh. *The New Poetry of Wales*. Cardiff: University of Wales Press, 2007.

Oliver Reynolds

Gregson, Ian. Oliver Reynolds and the National Subject. *The New Poetry of Wales*. Cardiff: University of Wales Press, 2007.

Kitty Sewell

Foster, Jordan. The Most Remote Place on Earth. *Publishers Weekly* 254.49 (December 10 2007) 32. ISSN 00000019. (On Sewell's novel, *Ice Trap*.)

Owen Sheers

Rickett, Joel. Interview: Owen Sheers says Second World War plans for a British resistance provided inspiration for his debut novel. *The Independent* (10 June 2007).

Mercer Simpson

Stephens, Meic. Mercer Simpson: Poet of the East Anglian Landscape. *The Independent* (22 June 2007). (Obituary.)

Howard Spring

Magrs, Paul. The Nooks and Crannies of Her Being: Howard Spring's *Shabby Tiger* and Northern Camp. *British Fiction after Modernism: The Novel at Mid-Century*. Marina Mackay and Lindsey Stonebridge (editors). New York: Palgrave Macmillan, 2007. ISBN 9781403986429.

Dylan Thomas

Davies, James A. Dylan Thomas and War. *Wales at War: Critical Essays on Literature and Art*. Tony Curtis (editor). Bridgend: Seren, 2007.

Frost, Robert. The Hunchback in the Park. *English Review* 18.2 (November 2007) 9-11. ISSN 0955-8950.

Wigginton, Chistopher. *Modernism from the Margins: The 1930s Poetry of Louis MacNeice and Dylan Thomas*. *Writing Wales in English series*. Cardiff: University of Wales Press, 2007. ISBN 978-0-7083-1927-7.

Edward Thomas

Hooker, Jeremy. Haunted Landscapes: War in the Writings of Llewelyn Wyn Griffith, Robert Graves, Wilfred Owen and Edward Thomas. *Wales at War: Critical Essays on Literature and Art*. Tony Curtis (editor). Bridgend: Seren, 2007.

Kendall, Judy. 'A Poet At Last': William H. Davies and Edward Thomas. *Almanac - A Yearbook of Welsh Writing in English: Critical Essays* Vol. 12 (2007-2008) 32-54.

R.S. Thomas

Alexander, Neal. Dialogues of Self and Soul: The Autobi-ographies of W.B. Yeats and R.S. Thomas. *Almanac - A Yearbook of Welsh Writing in English: Critical Essays* Vol. 12 (2007-2008) 1-31.

Jarman, Mark. Praying and Bird Watching: The Life of R.S. Thomas. *Hudson Review* 60.1 (Spring 2007) 169-176. ISSN 0018702X. (Review-article on Byron Rogers, *The Man Who Went Into the West: The Life of R.S. Thomas.*)

Perry, Sam. 'Hoping for the Reciprocal Touch': Intimations of the Manus Dei in the Poetry of R.S. Thomas. *Literature and Theology: An International Journal of Religion, Theory, and Culture* 21.2 (June 2007) 178-197. ISSN 02691205.

Perry, Sam. The Pastoral Vision of R.S. Thomas. *Almanac - A Yearbook of Welsh Writing in English: Critical Essays* Vol. 12 (2007-2008) 140-168.

Thomas, M. Wynn. R.S. Thomas, Denise Levertov and the Poetry of Contemplation. *Moment of Earth: Poems and Essays in Honour of Jeremy Hooker*. Christopher Meredith (editor). Aberystwyth: Celtic Studies Publications, 2007.

Thomas, M. Wynn.'The Stones of the Field' and the Power of the Sword: R.S. Thomas as War Poet. *Wales at War: Critical Essays on Literature and Art*. Tony Curtis (editor). Bridgend: Seren, 2007.

Wilcox, Allan and Helen Wilcox. Matter and Spirit Conjoined: Sacred Places in the Poetry of George Herbert, Henry Vaughan, R.S. Thomas and Rowan Williams. *Scintilla* 11 (2007) 133-151. Reference number 2007:197483.

Rachel Tresize

Jelbert, Steve. Valley Girl. *Independent* (June 3 2007) 32-33. (Review-article on *Dial M for Merthyr*.)

Henry Vaughan

Dickson, Donald R. Henry Vaughan as Country Doctor. *Explorations in Renaissance Culture* 33.2 (2007) 171-195. ISSN 00982474.

Dickson, Donald R. Henry Vaughan's Medical Annotations. *Huntingdon Library Quarterly* 70.3 (2007) 427-452. ISSN 00187895.

Nelso, Holly Faith. Historical Consciousness and the Politics of Translation in the Psalms of Henry Vaughan. *Studies in Philology* 104.4 (Fall 2007) 501-525.

Rudrum, Alan. 'These Fragments I have Shored against My Ruins': Henry Vaughan, Alchemical Philosophy, and the Great Rebellion. *Mystical Metal of Gold: Essays on Alchemy and Renaissance Culture*. Stanton J Linden (editor). New York: AMS, 2007. ISSN 0195-8011.

Thomas, M. Wynn. 'Fidelities where beams together run': Vernon Watkins and Henry Vaughan. *Scintilla* 11 (2007) 169-184. Reference number 2007:197484.

Wilcox, Allan and Helen Wilcox. Matter and Spirit Conjoined: Sacred Places in the Poetry of George Herbert, Henry Vaughan, R.S. Thomas and Rowan Williams. *Scintilla* 11 (2007) 133-151. Reference number 2007:197483.

Sarah Waters

Carroll, Rachel. Becoming My Own Ghost: Spinsterhood, Heterosexuality and Sarah Waters's *Affinity*. *Genders* 45 (2007). (Electronic journal article).

Hoggard, Liz. Sarah Waters: Tales of a Reluctant Celebrity. *The Independent* (8 April 2007).

Jeremiah, Emily. 'The 'I' Inside 'Her' ': Queer Narration in Sarah Waters's *Tipping the Velvet* and Wesley Stace's *Misfortune*. *Women: A Cultural Review* 18.2 (Summer 2007) 131-144. ISSN 09574042.

Stevenson, Sheryl. Waters's *Affinity*. *Explicator* 65.2 (Winter 2007) 124-127. ISSN 00144940.

Vernon Watkins

Barnie, John. Vernon Watkins, *New Selected Poems*, edited by Richard Ramsbotham *Poetry Wales* 42.3 (January 2007) 63-64. ISSN 03322202. (Review-article.)

Thomas, M. Wynn. 'Fidelities where beams together run': Vernon Watkins and Henry Vaughan. *Scintilla* 11 (2007) 169-184. Reference number 2007:197484.

Raymond Williams

Franco, Jean. Residuales y emergentes: Carlos Monsiváis y Raymond Williams. *El arte de la ironía: Carlos Monsiváis ante la crítica*. Mexico City: Universidad Nacional Autónoma de México, 2007. ISBN 9703242057. (Compares Williams with the Mexican political and cultural commentator, Carlos Monsiváis.)

Rustin, Michael. *The Long Revolution* Revisited. *Soundings: A Journal of Politics and Culture* 35 (Spring 2007) 16-30. ISSN 13626620.

Smith, Dai. 'Black Water' to *Border Country*: Sourcing the Textual Odyssey of Raymond Williams. *Almanac - A Yearbook of Welsh Writing in English: Critical Essays* Vol. 12 (2007-2008) 169-191.

Rowan Williams

Wilcox, Allan and Helen Wilcox. Matter and Spirit Conjoined: Sacred Places in the Poetry of George Herbert, Henry Vaughan, R.S. Thomas and Rowan Williams. *Scintilla* 11 (2007) 133-151. Reference number 2007:197483.

OMISSIONS FROM 2006 BIBLIOGRAPHY

GENERAL CRITICISM

Adams, Sam. Letter from Wales. *PN Review* 32.4 (March /April 2006) 6-8. ISSN 01447076. (On Welsh cultural anniversaries in 2005.)

INDIVIDUAL AUTHORS

John Cowper Powys

Drabble, Margaret. The English Degenerate. *The Guardian* (12 August 2006.)

Gervais, David. Dostoyevsky and the English novel: Dickens, John Cowper Powys and D.H. Lawrence. *Cambridge Quarterly* 35.1 (2006) 49-71. ISSN 0008199X.

Marie-Leverrou, Florence. John Cowper Powys dans le contexte moderniste: le Hors-texte au coeur du texte. *Etudes Britanniques Contemporaines: Revue de la Société d'Etudes Anglaises Contemporaines* 30 (June 2006) 4-53. ISSN 11684917.

Evan Evans

Prescott, Sarah. 'Gray's Pale Spectre': Evan Evans, Thomas Gray and the Rise of Welsh Bardic Nationalism. *Modern Philology: Critical and Historical Studies in Literature, Medieval Through Contemporary* 104.1 (August 2006) 72-95. ISSN 00268232.

James Hanley

Pridmore, Joseph. 'Vindicating the honour of Lancashire': Textual Variation between Editions of James Hanley's *Boy*.

Textual Variations: The Impact of Textual Issues on Literary Studies. Rebecca Styler and Joseph Pridmore (editors). Leicester: Department of English, University of Leicester, 2006. ISBN 0953231941.

Felicia Hemans

Cass, Jeffrey. 'The Race of the Cid': Blood, Darkness and the Captivity Narrative in Felicia Heman's *The Siege of Valencia*. *European Romantic Review* 17.3 (July 2006) 315-326. ISSN 10509583.

Forbes Aileen. Besieged Vision: *The Siege of Valencia* and Felicia Hemans's Theatre of Sacrifice. *Keats-Shelley Journal* 55 (2006) 158-178. Reference number 2006:10423.

Osman, Sharifah. 'Mightier than Death, Untamable by Fate': Felicia Hemans's Byronic Heroines and the Sorority of the Domestic Affections. *Romanticism on the Net* 43 (August 2006). ISSN 14771255.

George Herbert

Achinstein, Sharon. Reading George Herbert in the Restoration. *English Literary Renaissance* 36.3 (2006) 430-465. ISSN 00138312.

Barnes, A. W. Editing George Herbert's Ejaculations. *Textual Cultures: Texts, Contexts, Interpretation* 1.2 (Autumn 2006) 90-113. ISSN 1592936.

Gaston, Paul L. George Herbert, the 'Hymn Menders', and the Anglican Hymn Tradition. *John Donne Journal: Studies in the Age of Donne* 25 (2006) 315-332. ISSN 078389655.

Mattison, Andrew. 'Keep your Measure': Herrick, Herbert, and the Resistance To Music. *Criticism: A Quarterly for Literature and the Arts* (Summer 2006) 323-346. ISSN 00111589.

David Jones

Dentinger, H. W. Welsh Enough: The Reception of David Jones in Wales. PhD thesis, University of Wales [Aberystwyth], 2006. 56-15692.

Price-Owen, Anne. From Medieval Manuscripts to Postmodern Hypertexts in the Art of David Jones. *Writing and Seeing: Essays on Word and Image*. Rui Carvalho Homem and Maria de Fátima Lambert (editors). Amsterdam: Rodopi, 2006. ISBN 9789042016889.

Gwyneth Lewis

Lewis, Gwyneth. Caught Between Two Cultures. *The Guardian* (18 November 2006).

The Mabinogion and related materials

Pael, O.J. Geoffrey of Monmouth and the Development of the Merlin Legend. *Cambrian Medieval Celtic Studies* 51 (Summer 2006) 37-65. ISSN 13530089.

Miles-Watson, J. Mapping Medieval Welsh Myth: A Neo-Structuralist Analysis of the *Mabinogion*. PhD thesis, University of Aberdeen, 2006. 56-15708. BL: DXN108568.

Iolo Morganwg

Constantine, Mary-Ann. Songs and Stones: Iolo Morganwg (1747-1826), Mason and Bard. *Eighteenth Century* 47.2/3 (Sumer 2006) 233-251. ISSN 01935380.

Kate Roberts

Jones, Harri Pritchard. Kate Roberts. *British and Irish Short-Fiction Writers*, 1945-2000. Cheryl Malcolm and

David Macolm (editors). Detroit: Thomson Gales, 2006. ISSN 10968547.

Bernice Rubens

Brauner, David. Below at Your Elbow, Roth Breathing down Your Neck: Gender and Ethnicity in Novels by Bernice Rubens and Linda Grant. *'In the Open': Jewish Women Writers and British Culture*. Claire M. Tylee (editor). Newark: University of Delaware Press, 2006. ISBN 9780874139334.

Iain Sinclair

Gilbert, Ruth. The Frummer in the Attic: Rachel Lichtenstein and Iain Sinclair's *Rodinsky's Room* and Jewish Memory. *International Fiction Review* 33.1-2 (2006) 27-37. ISSN 03154149.

Hampson, Robert G. Spatial Stories: Conrad and Iain Sinclair. *Conradian* 31.1 (Spring 2006) 52-111.

Dylan Thomas

Sung, Lee Ye. A Study on Dylan Thomas's Challenging Death. *Unitas: A Quarterly for the Arts and Sciences* 79.1 (March 2006). ISSN 00417149.

Ed Thomas

Rabey, David Ian. Ed Thomas: Jazz Pictures in the Gaps of Language. *Companion to Modern British and Irish Drama, 1800-2005*. Mary Luckhurst (editor). Malden, MA: Blackwell, 2006. ISBN 9781405122283.

R.S. Thomas

Adams, Sam. Letter from Wales. *PN Review* 32.4 (November / December 2006) 6-7. ISSN 01447076.

Lily Tobias

Donahaye, Jasmine. 'The Link of Common Aspirations': Wales in the Work of Lily Tobias. *'In the Open': Jewish Women Writers and British Culture*. Claire M. Tylee (editor). Newark: University of Delaware Press, 2006). ISBN 9780874139334.

Sarah Waters

Armitt, Lucie and Sarah Gamble. The Haunted Geometries of Sarah Waters's *Afinity*. *Textual Practice* 20.1 (March 2006) 141-170. ISSN 0950236X.

Caroll, Rachel. Rethinking Generational History: Queer Histories of Sexuality in Neo-Victorian Feminist Fiction. *Studies in the Literary Imagination* 39.2 (Fall 2006) 135-147. ISSN 00393819.

Costantini, Mariaconcetta. 'Faux-Victorian Melodrama' in the New Millenium: The Case of Sarah Waters. *Critical Survey* 18.1 (2006) 17-39. ISSN 00111570.

Letissier, Georges. Le Texte Victorien à l'âge postmoderne: Jouvence ou senescence? *Fingersmith* de Sarah Waters et le mélodrame victorien. *Cashiers Victoriens et Edouardiens: Revue du Centre d'Etudes et de Recherches Victoriennes et Edourdinnes de l'Université Paul Valéry, Montpellier* 63 (2006) 277-293. ISSN 02205610.

Wormald, Mark. Prior Knowledge: Sarah Waters and the Victorians. *British Fiction Today*. Philip Tew and Rod Mengham (editors). London: Continuum, 2006. ISBN 9780826 487322.

Vernon Watkins

Thomas, M. Wynn. Vernon Watkins and the Nostalgia of Literature. *PN Review* 33.2 (November/December 2006) 50-54. ISSN 01447076.

NOTES ON CONTRIBUTORS

Malcolm Ballin is a Research Associate at Cardiff University. His book, *Irish Periodical Culture: 1937-1972, Genres in Ireland, Wales and Scotland* was published by Palgrave Macmillan in 2008. He is currently working on a book about periodicals and the public sphere in Wales.

Damian Walford Davies is Reader in English in the Department of English and Creative Writing at Aberystwyth University. He has published widely on Romanticism and on the two literatures of Wales, and is the General Editor of the forthcoming Oxford Literary History of Wales.

Robert Gossedge is a lecturer in English Literature at Cardiff University. He has published on the Arthurian legend and has research interests in British and American medievalism from the eighteenth century to the present, myth and modernism, Celticism and Britishness, and Welsh writing in English.

Matthew Jarvis is the Anthony Dyson Fellow in Poetry in the Department of English at the University of Wales, Lampeter. His volume *Welsh Environments in Contemporary Poetry* was published by the University of Wales Press in 2008. His current project, *An Introduction to Welsh Poetry in English, 1965-2005*, will also be published by the University of Wales Press.

Craig Owen Jones received his PhD in Music from Bangor University, where he is a lecturer at the School of Music. He specialises in popular music, and his research interests include Welsh-language hip-hop and the Welsh-language music press. He is a regular contributor to *Planet: The Welsh Internationalist*.

Tomos Owen is a PhD student at the School of English, Communication and Philosophy, Cardiff University. He works on London-Welsh literary culture at the turn of the twentieth century and has published an essay on Amy Dillwyn's The Rebecca Rioter in a volume entitled Riots in Literature eds. David Bell and Gerald Porter (Cambridge Scholars Publishing, 2008).

Sam Perry teaches English Literature at the University of Leicester. He has published articles on R.S. Thomas, Edward Thomas and Philip Larkin and is currently writing an essay that situates Larkin's poetry within the context of the Surrealist movement. His forthcoming book R.S. Thomas and the English Literary Tradition will be published by the University of Wales Press.

Lucy Thomas has recently completed her PhD thesis on the work of Hilda Vaughan at Cardiff University.

Laura Wainwright is currently working on her PhD thesis on Welsh Modernism at Cardiff University. She has written on the European dimension in the early work of Glyn Jones (Almanac, Vol. 12); on comedy in Jean Rhys (Journal of International Women's Studies, forthcoming); and on memory in Dannie Abse's poetry, in a sourcebook on Abse (Seren, forthcoming).

Acknowledgements

almanac – welsh writing in english: a yearbook of critical essays is published with the financial support of the Welsh Books Council; the editor also gratefully acknowledges the support of the Association for Welsh Writing in English. We are as ever indebted to those scholars who have found time in busy schedules to act as readers of papers submitted for publication; their advice and guidance are indispensable.

Information for Contributors

Correspondence and contributions for publication should be addressed to the editor: Dr Katie Gramich, School of English, Communication and Philosophy, Cardiff University, Humanities Building, Colum Drive, Cardiff, CF10 3EU (email: GramichK @cf.ac.uk). The *almanac* publishes essays on literary topics, not on purely Welsh historical matters. While its primary concern is the study of Welsh writing in English, papers on Welsh-language authors, written in English, will be considered; the Yearbook will also consider papers which relate the two literatures of Wales or discuss the literatures of Wales in international, comparative contexts. Papers should not normally exceed 8,000 words in length.

Manuscripts (two copies) should be typed on one side of the page, double spaced, and produced according to the current MHRA Style Guide. Include a computer disk with the hard copies, and note the word-processing programme used. All contributions will be refereed. While a decision will be made as expeditiously as possible, allow three months for a decision. Contributors of published papers receive two complimentary copies of the issue in which their paper appears. The *almanac* web page, which includes information on past issues, is at:

www.cardiff.ac.uk/encap/periodic/welshwrit.html